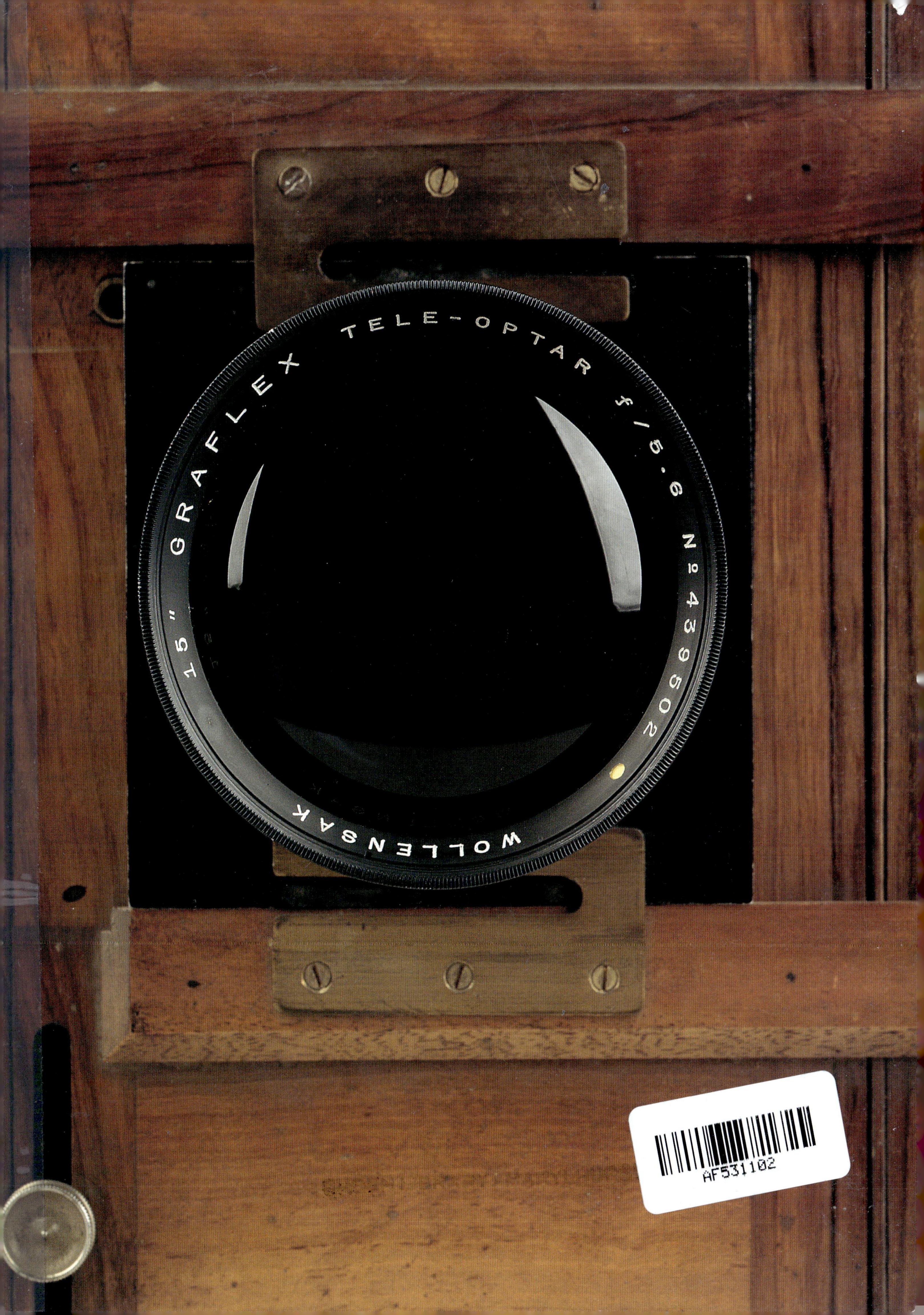
GRAFLEX TELE-OPTAR f/5.6 № 4395502
WOLLENSAK
15"
AF531102

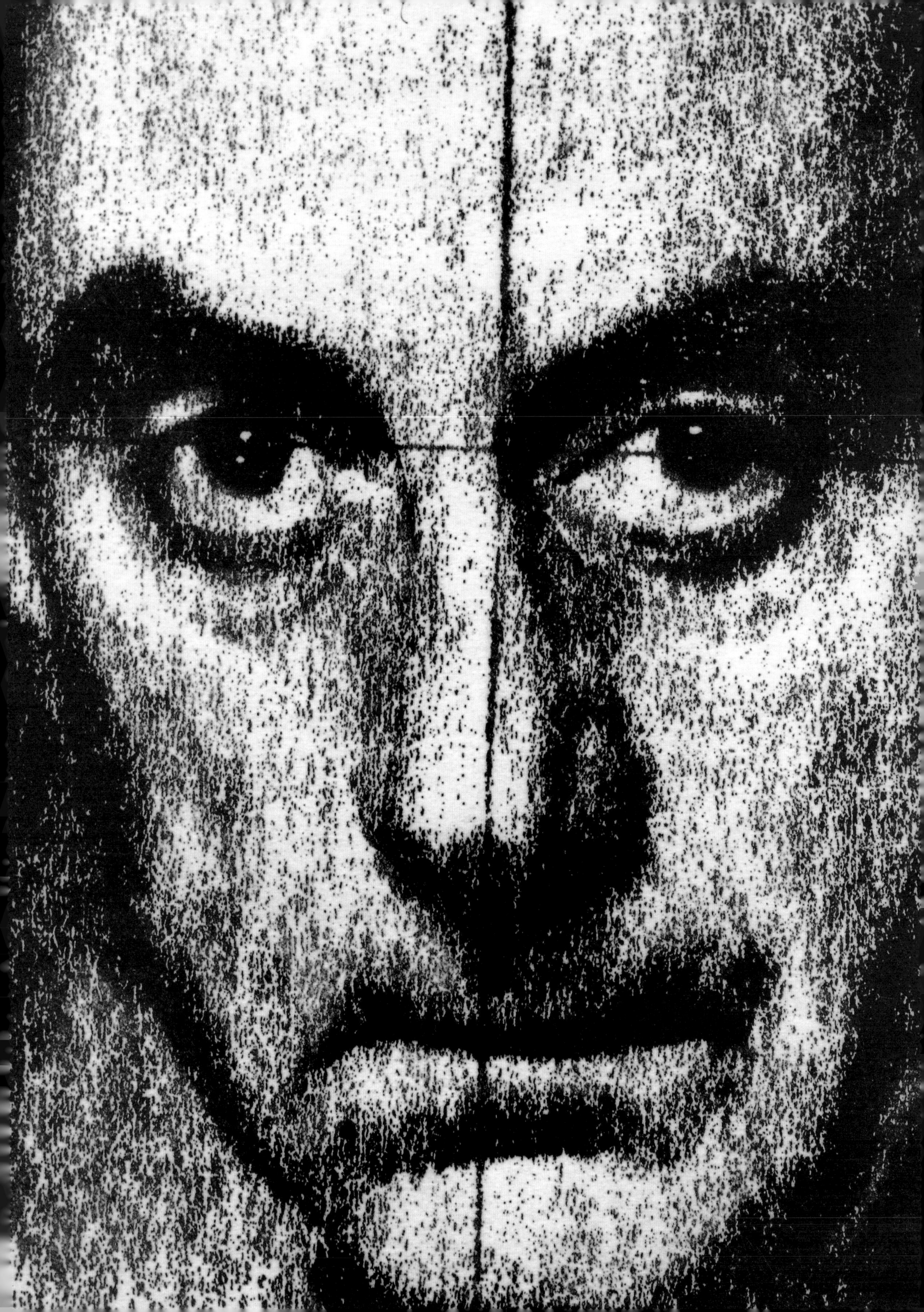

TRACK 16 GALLERY / ROBERT BERMAN GALLERY

MAN RAY

Paris~LA

SMART ART PRESS 1996

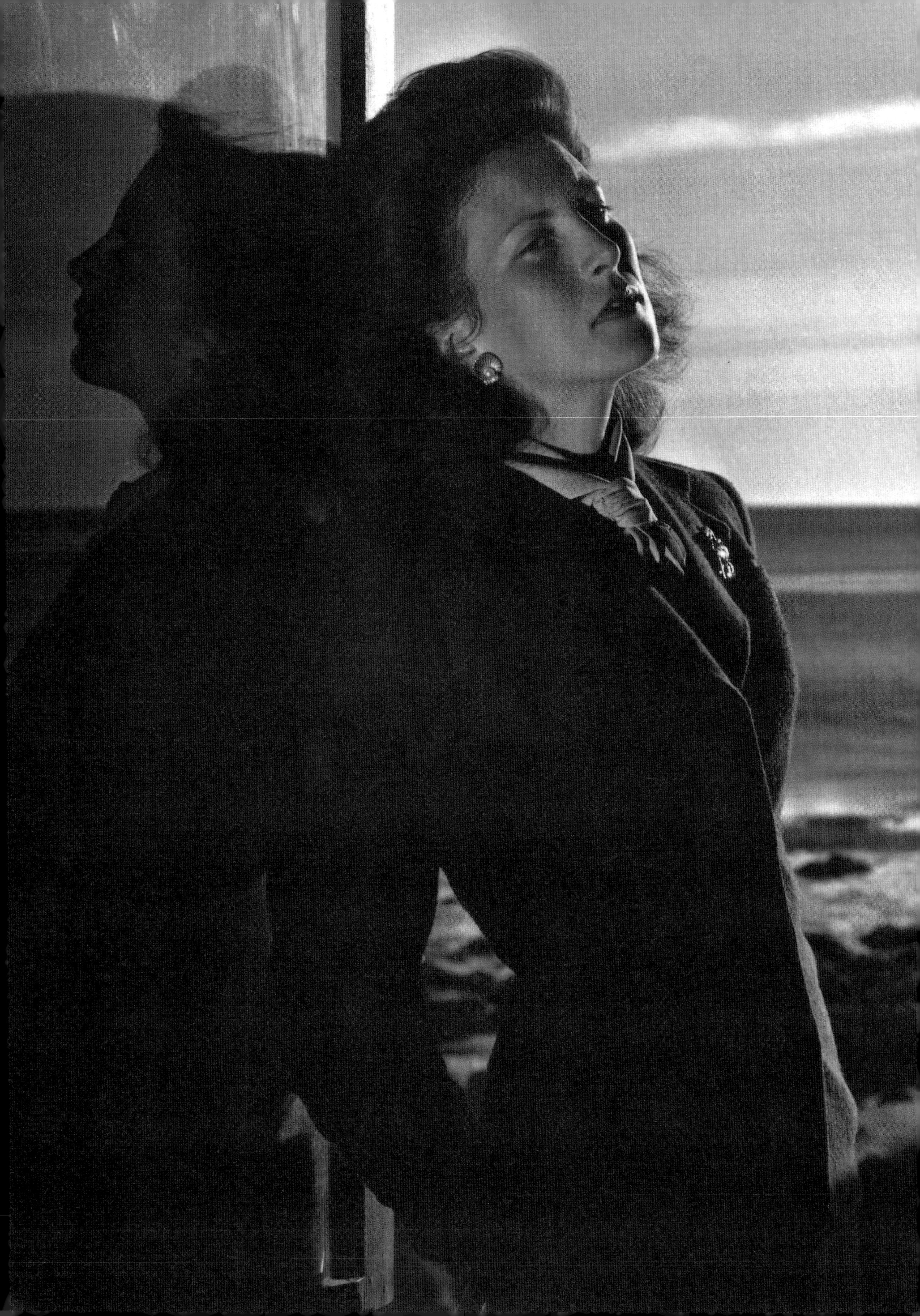

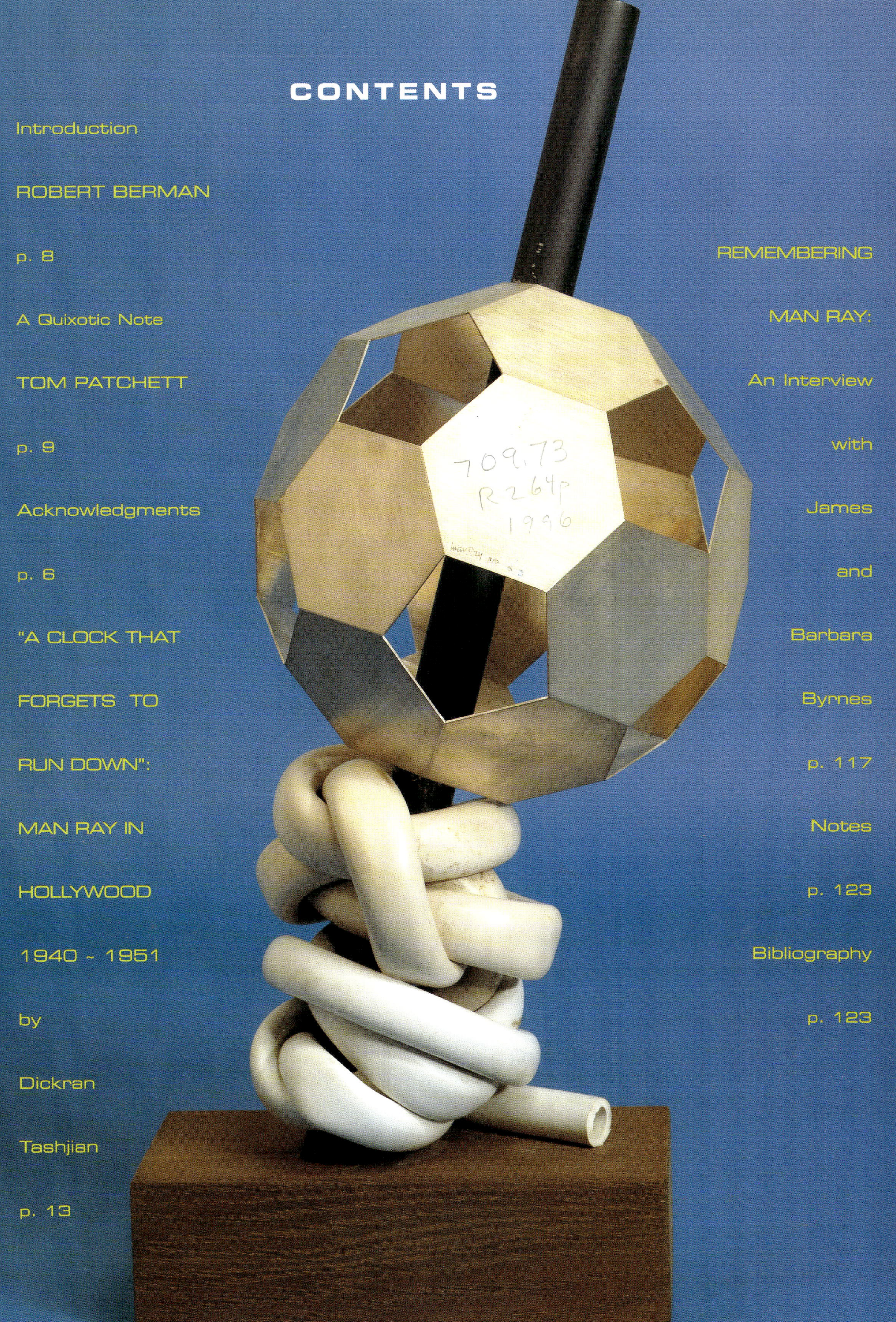

CONTENTS

ACKNOWLEDGMENTS

A host of knowledgeable and dedicated individuals in the United States and Europe have brought their expertise and passion to Man Ray: Paris>>LA. Without their support and assistance this publication and exhibition would not have been possible. Our first thanks must go to the estate of Juliet and Man Ray: The Man Ray Trust.

In the U.S., the cooperation and collaboration of Man Ray expert Timothy Baum has been invaluable. In Europe, special thanks to: Andrew Strauss, Director of Sotheby's, Paris; Marion Meyer of Galerie Meyer Bugel, Paris; Lucien Treillard, Secretaire de l'Association Man Ray; and Paris galerist Marcel Fleiss.

We are particularly pleased that art historian Dickran Tashjian accepted our invitation to write for this publication. He has provided us with the first in-depth examinationof Man Ray in Los Angeles. James and Barbara Byrnes also offered great insight into Man Ray's California years. The support of art historian Francis Naumann has been extremely beneficial.

Our project coordinator and editor of this publication, Pilar Perez, cannot be given enough credit for pulling together this most extensive exhibition and catalogue. Douglas Martin's design lends cohesion and meaning to the hundreds of Man Ray works produced during the span of these years. The enthusiasm of Susan Martin, managing director of Smart Art Press, has generated great anticipation. We would also like to acknowledge Laurie Steelink, registrar of Track 16 Gallery, for her help in organizing the numerous objects in the exhibition.

We are also pleased to recognize: the Browner family; Maitre Jean-Claude Binoche; Yves Bugel; Claudia Borges da Fonseca; Naomi Savage; Pierre-Yves Butzbach; the Mayor Gallery, London; The Mill House, Berkshire, England; Oliver Barker of Sotheby's, London; Steven Lieber; David Fahey; José Luis Rueda; Alfonso de la Torre; and Lee Kaplan.

Lest we not forget the tireless staff at Track 16 Gallery and Robert Berman Gallery: thanks to Fortino Delgadillo, Brad Hopper, Scott Hopper, Ransom Mayfield, Sean Meredith, Jody Zellen, Gabriella Trench, Michael Long, and Danica Derpic.

Robert Berman and Tom Patchett

First and foremost, I want to thank Naomi Sawelson-Gorse, a scholar's scholar, who shared without hesitation her store of knowledge about Man Ray in Hollywood; Tom Patchett and Robert Berman, whose mania for Man Ray took over the project, and who, with James and Barbara Byrnes, gave me quintessential California from Mulholland Drive to Musso and Frank's on Hollywood Boulevard; Pilar Perez, whose steadiness kept this project in the carpool lane; Douglas Martin, a designer with a sharp eye that Man Ray would have appreciated; Susan Martin and the staffs of Track 16 and the Robert Berman Galleries—always cooperative and helpful; the staffs of great libraries across the Southland: Interlibrary Loan at the University of California, Irvine; Special Collections at the University of California, Los Angeles; Special Collections, The John Paul Getty Center for the History of Art and the Humanities, Los Angeles; Kate Ware and Weston Naef of the Department of Photographs, The John Paul Getty Museum, Los Angeles; my new colleagues in the Department of Art History, Irvine, who have deluded themselves in thinking that I'm an art historian; Betty and Sam Eisenstein, who risked blindness at the microfilm viewer at the Pasadena Public Library; Richard Press, book dealer in the heat of Sacramento, and Leonard Kaplan, who also came to California in the 1940s; Ann Tashjian, who sometimes came along for the ride, but most often has taken the wheel. Finally, this one's for Gloria.

Dickran Tashjian, Laguna Beach, June 1996

cov
(detail) ***Juliet****, Hollywood,* c. 19

end piece front and ba
Man Ray Chess set*,* c. 19

p
Half plate tailboa
folding plate camer
French, 1920s *Fruitwood boo*
plated metal fittings, with lat
15in. Graflex f/5.6 Tele-Optar le

p.
(detail) ***Self-Portrait****,* 19
Screenpri

p.
Untitled*, Los Angeles,* 194
Gelatin-silver pri

p.
Non-Euclidian Object*,* 1932–19
Object of metal elements ar
plastic tubing mounte
on a wooden bas

(opposite) p.
Permanent Attraction*,* 19
Three large wood
chess pieces and boa

p.
(detail) ***Man Ray***
cactus garde
Pasadena, 19
Gelatin-silver pri

p.
Unconcerned But N
Indifferent*,* c. 19
Pen and pencil on pap

p. 1
(detail) ***What Is Insanit***
A Clock That Forge
to Run Down*,* 19
Gelatin-silver pri
Collection of T
J. Paul Getty Museu
Malibu, Califorr

MAN RAY: PARIS ~ L
September 21, 1996 ~ January 31, 19

Track 16 Gallery ar
Robert Berman Galle
Bergamot Stati
2525 Michigan Avenu
Building
Santa Monica, CA 904

Track 16 Galle
310. 264. 4678 t
310. 264. 4682 f

Robert Berman Galle
310. 315. 9506 t
310. 315. 9508 f

Editor: Pilar Pere
Design+Direction: Douglas Mart

Photography: Patrick Hous
Bill Short, and Diversified Pho
Copyeditor: Sherri Schottlaend

Printed and bound
Jomagar, S/L, Madrid, Spa

Photomechanicals
Lucam S.A., Mad

Published by Smart Art Pre
2525 Michigan Aven
Building
Santa Monica, CA 904
310. 264. 46

FIRST EDITIC

Distributed by D.A
636 Broadway New Yo
New York 10C
800. 338. BOC

Library of Congre
Cataloging-in-Publication Numb
96-0690

International Standa
Book Numb
0-9646426-8

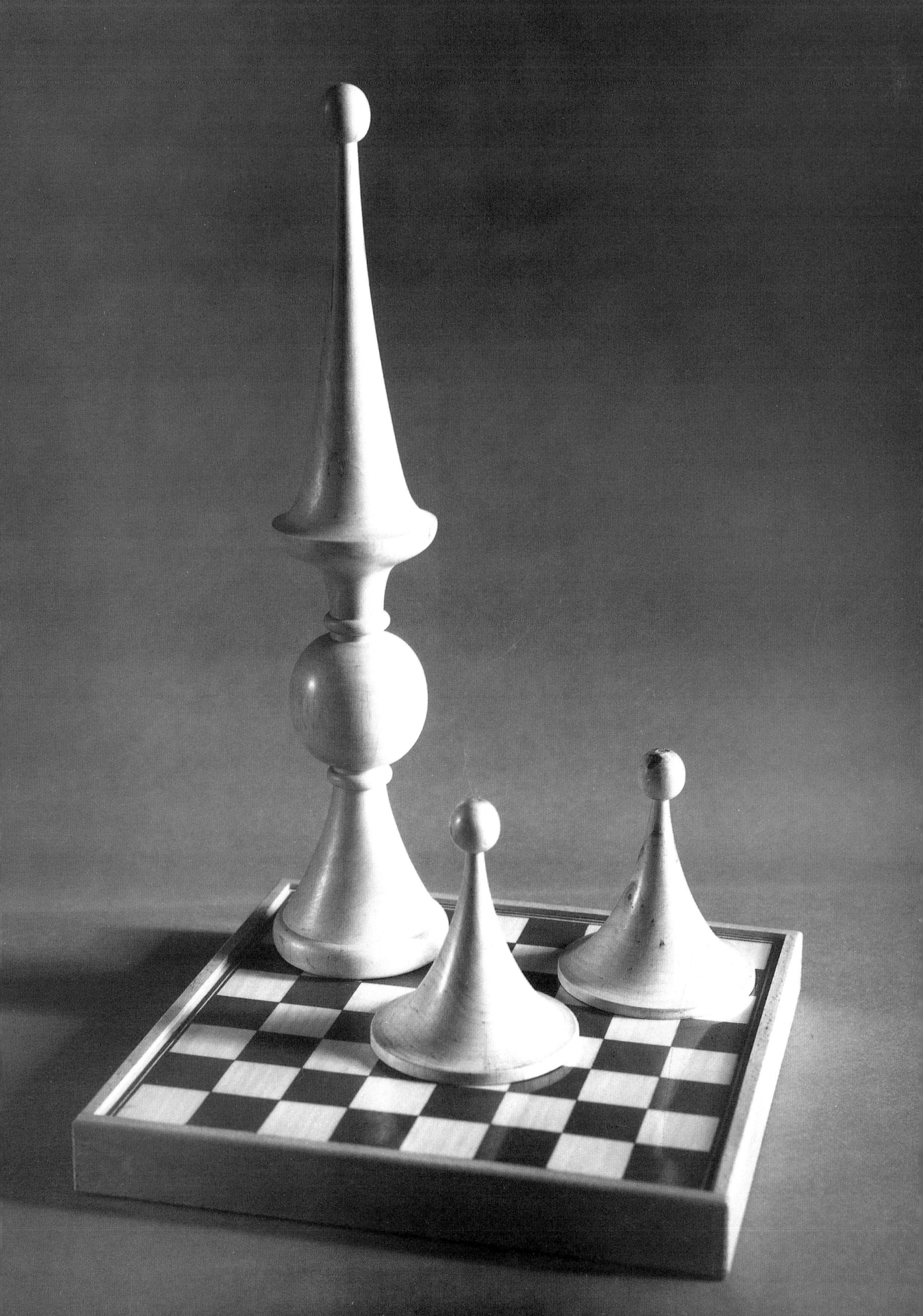

As a private art dealer living in Paris in the mid-1970s, I was confronted almost daily with the genius of Man Ray, who enjoyed a strong reputation in Europe and whose inventiveness in a variety of media made him unique among American artists. When I returned to the United States in 1976, shortly after Man Ray's death, I was surprised at how little known he was in this country–except as a photographer. It has been my hope since then to be able to one day present an exhibition that highlighted his talent as a filmmaker, painter, and maker of objects, as well as an incomparable photographer.

A window of opportunity opened to do just that after the passing of Juliet Browner in 1992. Man Ray and Juliet not only retained some of his best art work, but also left behind a trove of correspondence, casual photographs, and ephemera that provides us with a deeper understanding of Man Ray's mind and his need to make art in his own way. Thanks to the Man Ray Estate and supplemented with work provided by collectors, dealers, and institutions across two continents, much of this material is exhibited here for the first time.

Although there have been numerous books on Man Ray's life and art, few have devoted much attention to the productive decade he spent in Los Angeles. Los Angeles provided Man Ray sanctuary from the war and allowed him to create an exceptional body of work that was exhibited on both coasts. Here he formed a creative community with other friends cast adrift by the war–Marcel Duchamp, Max Ernst, Dorothea Tanning, Henry Miller, Igor Stravinsky, and dealer/artist William Copley. And, of course, he met Juliet Browner, the true object of his affection and inspiration for his continued productivity.

This exhibition would not have been possible without the interest and support of Tom Patchett, my quixotic partner in this project. In the spirit of Man Ray's yard sale before he left his Vine Street studio for Paris in 1951, Track 16 Gallery and Robert Berman Gallery have joined forces to present this significant survey, undoubtedly the most comprehensive to focus upon Man Ray's middle years. Finally, twenty years after his death: to be continued and noticed, *Man Ray: Paris>>LA.*

ROBERT BERMAN

A Quixotic Note

Six or seven years ago, I stood among the many who thought MAN RAY was a new make of sunglasses. I've since rationalized such ignorance by thinking (a) a person can learn a hell of a lot in seven years plus (b) I've had the thrill of discovering Man Ray's work as his original patrons and collectors did, with constant and escalating amazement. Getting to know Man Ray after the fact is sort of like saving the center of the cinnamon roll for last.

I'd like to thank my friend Robert Berman and his passion for Man Ray for much of that education, and for talking me into devoting my time, my energy, my gallery, and my children's inheritance to this monumental exhibition.

TOM PATCHETT
Track16 Gallery/Smart Art Press

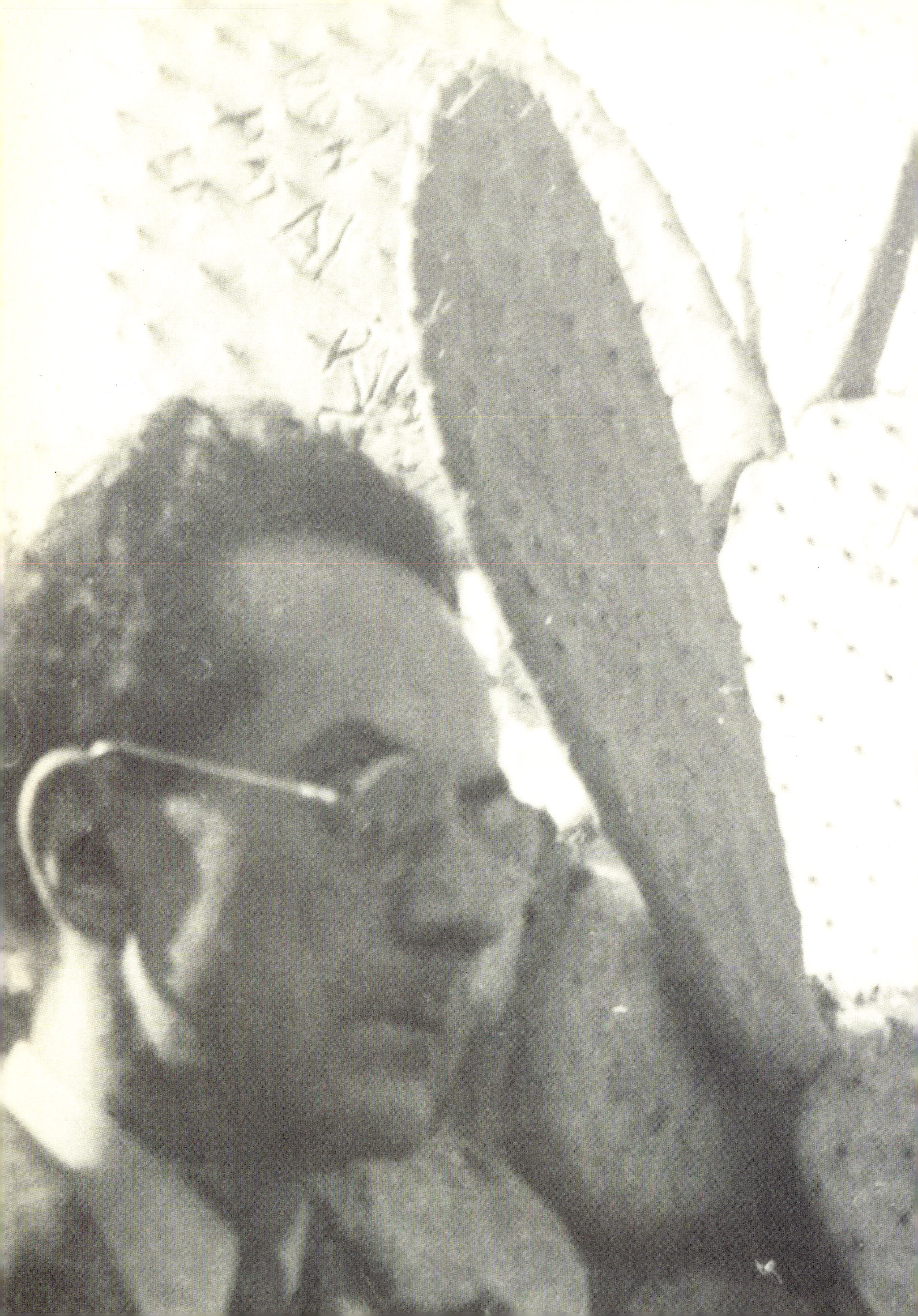

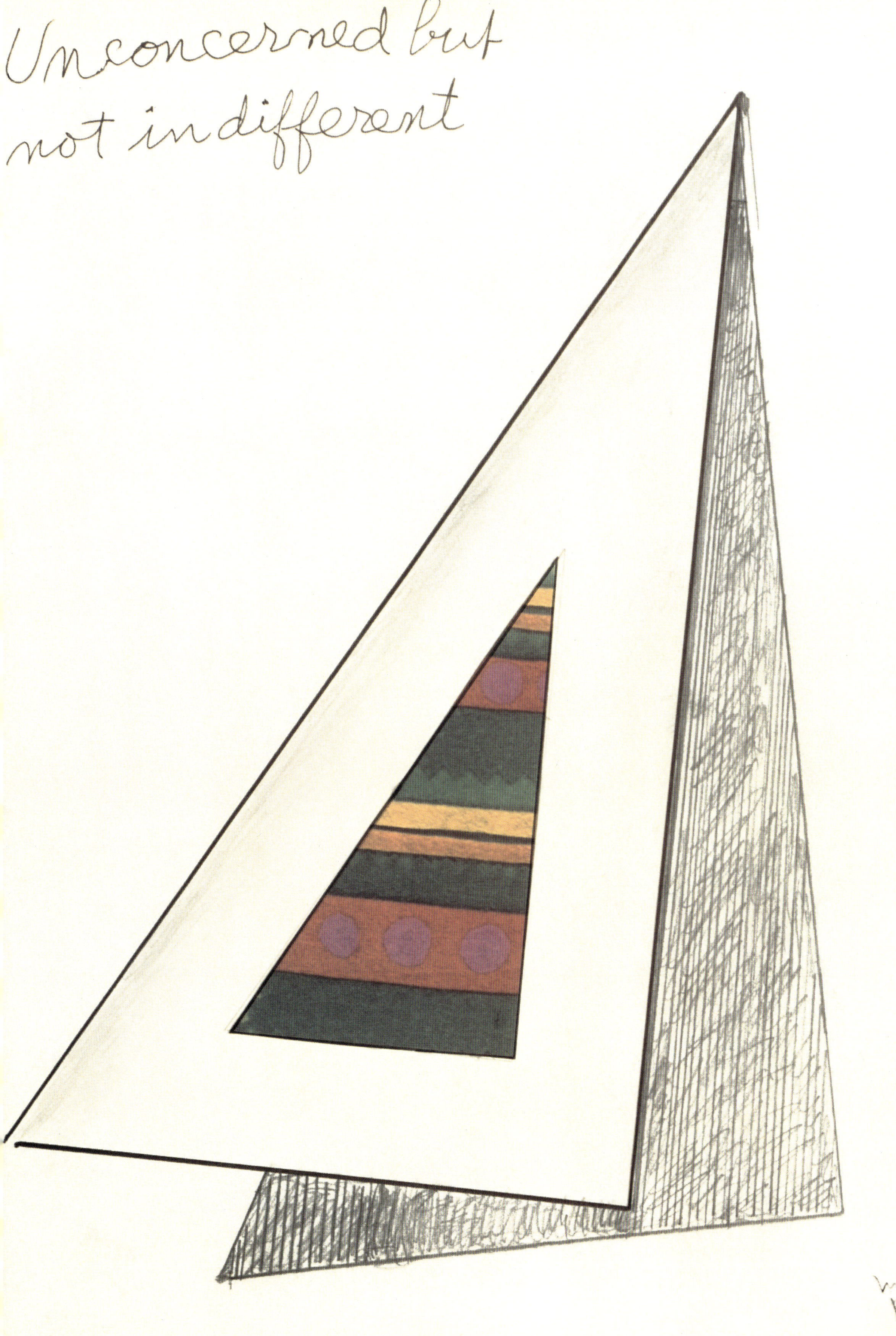
Unconcerned but
not indifferent
man
Ray

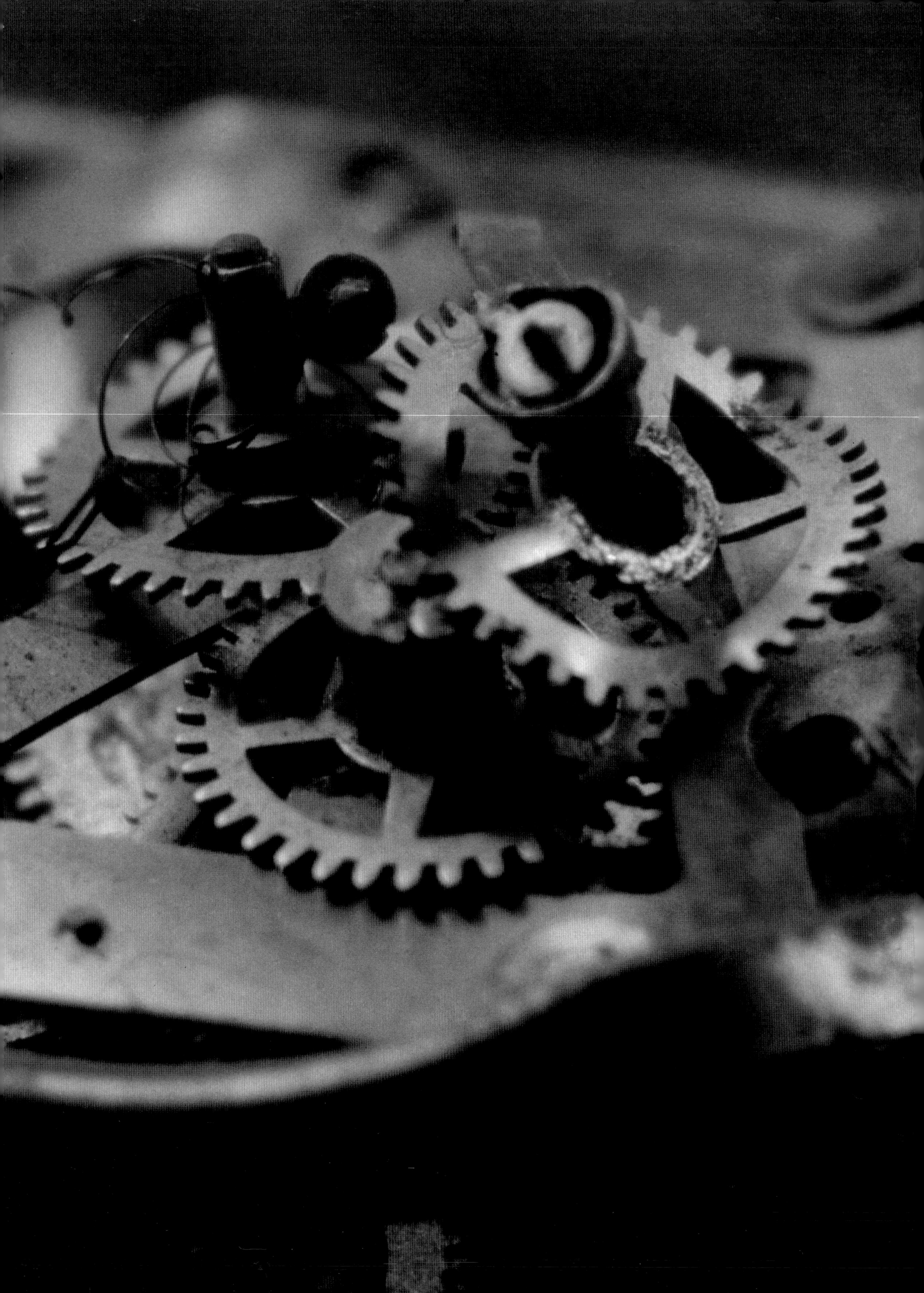

A CLOCK THAT FORGETS TO RUN DOWN:

MAN RAY IN HOLLYWOOD

1940~1951

Dickran Tashjian

"Going into exile is 'the journey of no return.' Anyone who sets out on it dreaming of coming home is lost."

Karl Zuckmayer, German émigré playwright, exiled in Hollywood during the Second World War.[1]

When Man Ray disembarked from the *Excambion* in Hoboken on August 16, 1940, he knew exactly where he was and he didn't like it. Any feeling of relief at having left France, which had been overrun by Nazi Germany, had dissipated in the difficult crossing; his discomfort was compounded by the theft of his camera equipment. Now came insult on injury: Salvador Dalí, a one-time Surrealist compatriot, was hogging the limelight as reporters and photographers sought out the latest celebrities washed ashore by the onslaught of war. Fortunately, his sister Elsie Siegler and his young niece Naomi were at the pier to welcome him to their home in Jersey City. More than Man Ray realized at the time, Elsie would be a reassuring presence to help ease his dislocations over the coming decade.[2]

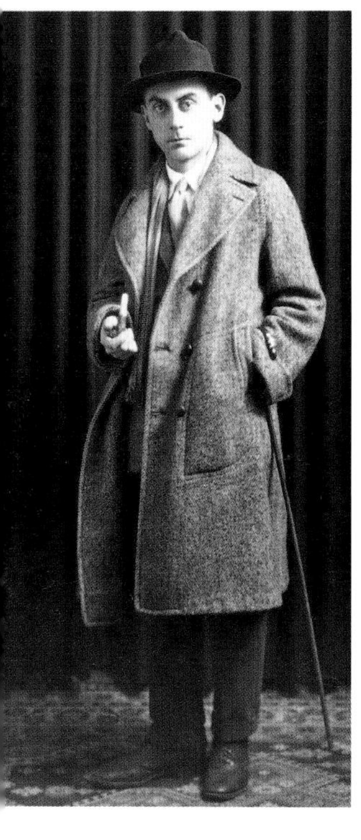

Self-portrait with Pipe, 1921
Gelatin-silver print on carte postale *paper*

The United States had not been home to Man Ray for almost two decades. He had eagerly left New York in 1921—tellingly, on the fourteenth of July—to seek a French independence from the tyrannies of American middle-class life. Only Elsie had remained as a tie to his family back in Brooklyn, a distant reminder of his bourgeois origins.

Once settled in Paris, Man Ray worked hard as a freelance photographer in the world of fashion, where he became something of a celebrity with the camera, a reputation he found difficult to shed when he eventually decided to concentrate on painting. Economic security provided the artistic freedom that Man Ray wanted to maintain, especially among the anarchistic Dadaists, who were happily at war among themselves and with the Parisian bourgeoisie.

Introduced by Marcel Duchamp, and so immediately acclaimed as a New York Dadaist, Man Ray moved freely among the kaleidoscopic factions of the avant-garde. He was trusted by all parties, most crucially by André Breton, a former medical student turned poet who gained dominance in the avant-garde skirmishes of the day by declaring himself the leader of Surrealism in 1924. In looking back on those tumultuous times, the American art dealer Julien Levy rightly noted that the peripatetic Man Ray held many of the Surrealists together during the 1930s.[3]

To remain autonomous Man Ray became something of a cultural chameleon. He cultivated his exotic status as an American at a time

Untitled, *Paris,* n.d. *Gelatin-silver print*

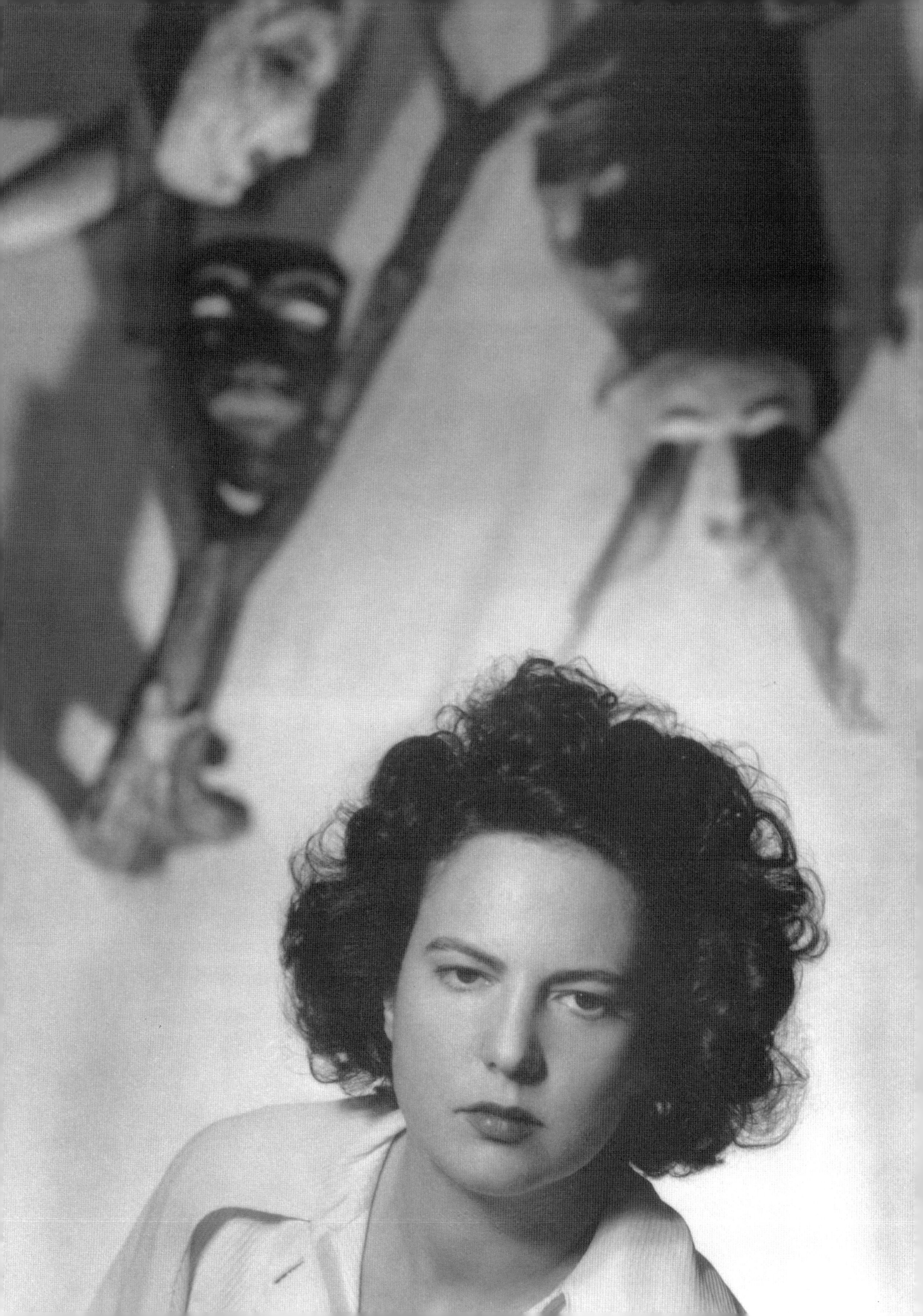

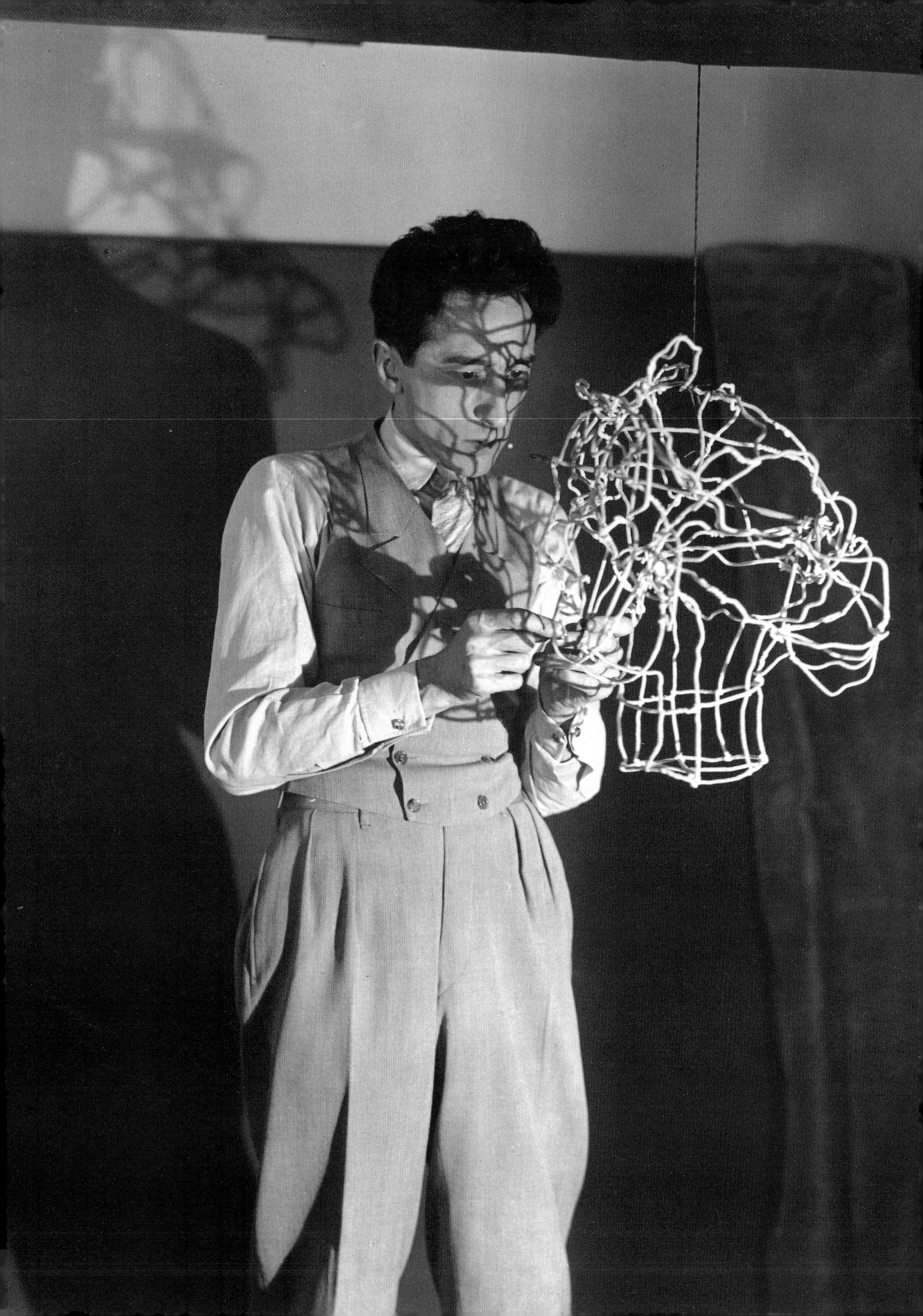

when Europeans were infatuated with life across the Atlantic. Ironically, however, as the decades passed, Man Ray became increasingly pegged as a European by American critics. His reluctance to leave Paris long after the Nazi invasion of Poland in September 1939 might seem to confirm the impression that France had become his adopted country. But in truth, he was a man caught in the middle, an American Jew living in a European country about to be turned inside out by invading forces. Consequently, he did not hesitate to declare his U.S. citizenship when it became necessary to cross European borders to escape to America.[4]

Unprepared for the fast endgame played by the Nazi Blitzkrieg around inept French defenses, Man Ray was frustrated in his first attempt to escape Paris by car. Getting only to the west coast of France, he and his lover Adrienne Fidelin (Ady) were forced to return through the chaos of refugees, traffic jams, prisoners of war, and military checkpoints to Nazi-occupied Paris. Four weeks later, he took a train to Biarritz, where, with the American composer Virgil Thomson, he managed to take another train to Lisbon, which had become "a madhouse" of refugees. There he anxiously waited to book passage on the *Excambion* for the United States.[5] Returning to America, however, was not quite the same as returning home. The ironic contradictions that Man Ray playfully exercised in his art suddenly became deadly serious in his life.

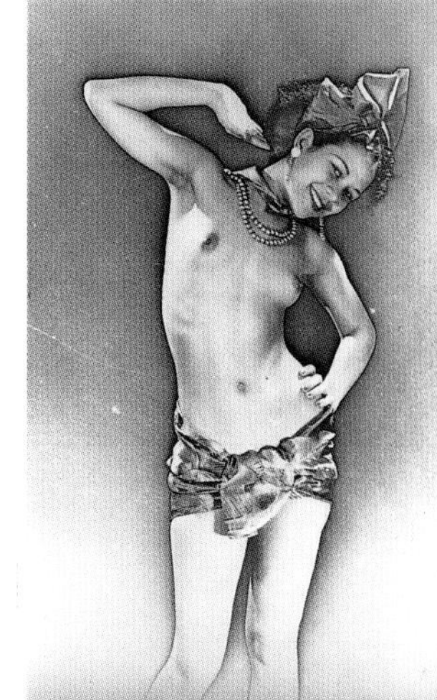

Adrienne Fidelin, c. 1937
Gelatin-silver print

During his stay with Elsie, there seemed blessed little to bridge the chasm created by the war. Man Ray's poignant letters Ady, who had chosen to stay behind in Paris, remained unanswered, returned a year later because of disruptions in the French postal service. Dispirited and depressed, Man Ray wrote to Ady that he lacked the courage to settle in New York and face the world;[6] a resumption of the middle-class life he had renounced some nineteen years before was out of the question. He came up with Tahiti as a destination—perhaps with tongue in cheek, but it was plausible, nonetheless. It was certainly remote from the European war (and seemingly safe, since the attack on Pearl Harbor was still over the horizon). Tahiti offered Man Ray a voyage in the wake of Gauguin, and unlike Jersey City, it was an island paradise worth setting against the civilized, most likely doomed, Paris.

Jean Cocteau with self-portrait wire sculpture, c. 1926 *Gelatin-silver print*

A family friend offered another opportunity. Harry Kantor, variously described as a "quasi-bohemian" and "traveling necktie salesman," proposed that Man Ray accompany him on a business trip by car to Los Angeles.[7] Southern California was not quite Tahiti, but the region boasted its own palm trees and the glamour of Hollywood. Voluntarily taking off for California would be a new adventure for Man Ray. At the very least, the trip would provide a much-needed vacation, but it also held out the possibility of a new beginning.

Man Ray had become adept at starting anew. In 1911 a young Emanuel Radnitsky decided to shed his immigrant identity and take a new name: "Man Ray" had a perfect ring to it, elegant in its concision and suggestive of all that was modern. Determined to be an artist in New York, Man Ray resisted the protests of his parents. His forceful, at times harsh rejection of their way of life indicated his strongly felt need to be a self-made man against the strictures of ethnic clannishness. In 1921 he reversed the American immigrant experience by going abroad to find a community of like-minded artists in Paris.

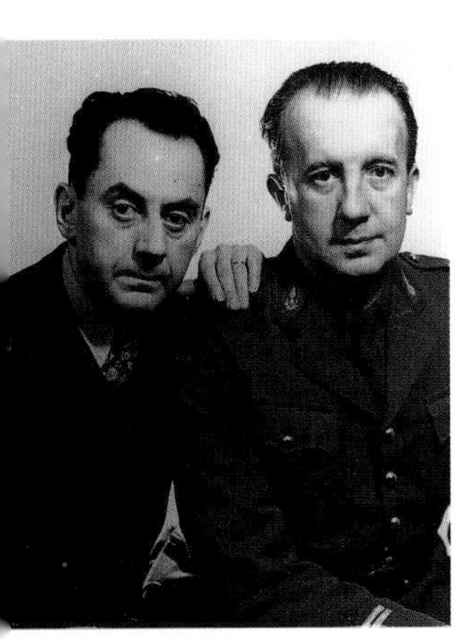

Self-portrait with Paul Eluard, 1939
Gelatin-silver print

But in June 1940, the City of Light was darkened by Nazi occupation, and Man Ray was fifty years old. Reluctant to give up what still seemed a peaceful way of life, confessing to Elsie that he was "getting a bit tired of continual effort," he thought he might "stick out the war" in Europe. Once uprooted, could he manage to fashion a new life yet again? The subsequent strain—if not the fatigue—would stay with him long after his trip across the continent as he tried to stake out a life for himself along the San Andreas fault. Nevertheless, his survival skills would take over in Hollywood; as he would somberly write to Elsie, "I am pretty used to the idea of starting all over again after each crisis."[8]

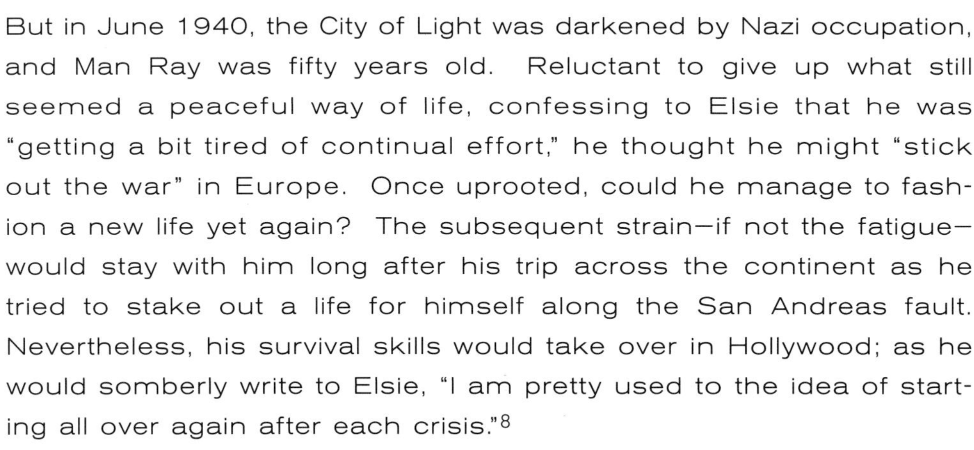

Man Ray's remaining energies were immediately expended in establishing himself as an artist in Southern California, a social and cultural terrain that exerted its own constraints and pressures, which were compounded by the difficult and uncertain circumstances of a nation at war. Without the congenial presence of his Surrealist friends, also scattered by the war but slowly regrouping in New York, Man Ray became an *isolato* in Hollywood, an entrepreneur seeking ways to reconnect to a traumatized American society.

Helen Tamiris, n.d. *Gelatin-silver print*

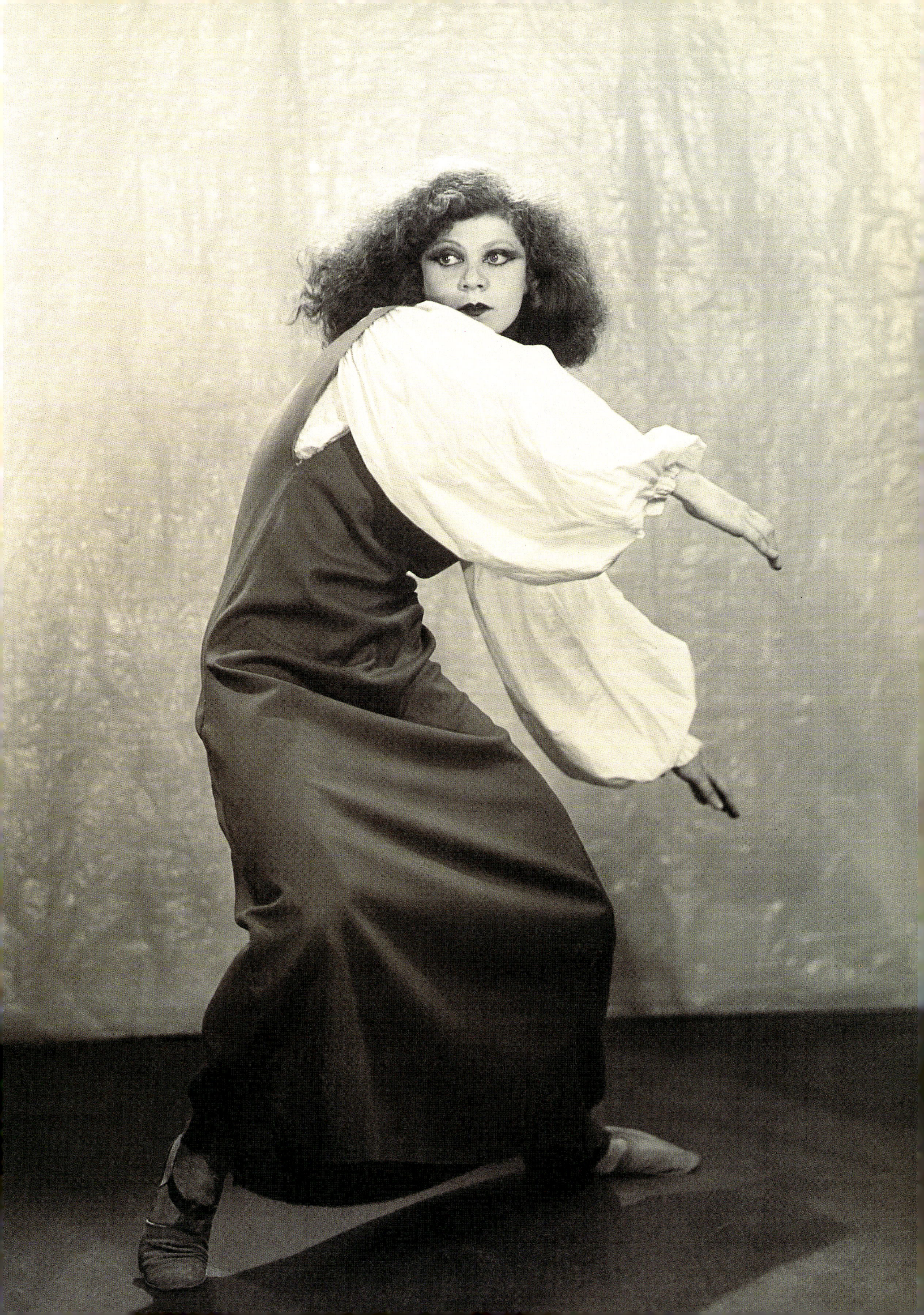

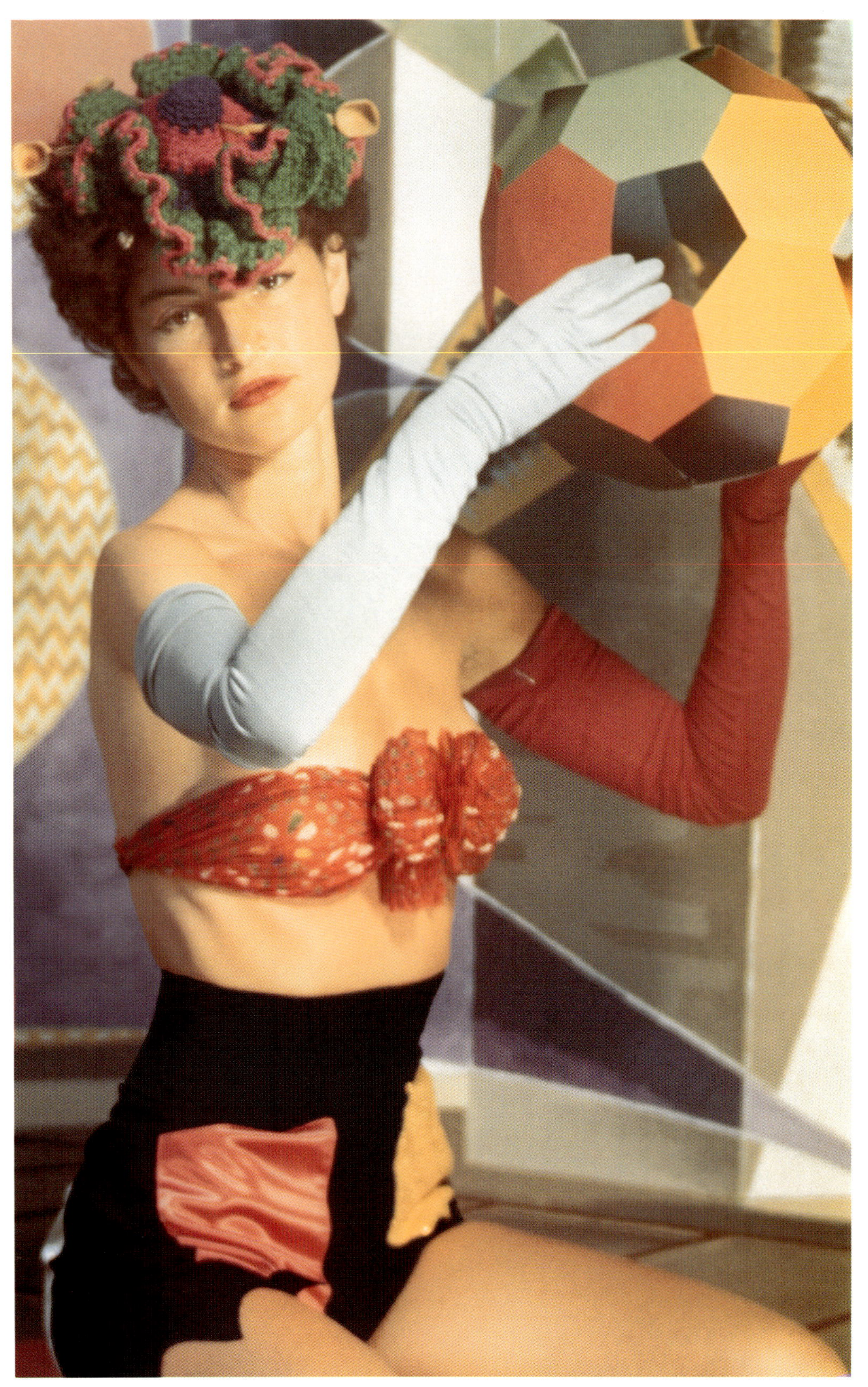

That Man Ray worked extraordinarily hard during his decade in Hollywood has been occasionally acknowledged, although the Mediterranean climate of Southern California has doubtless contributed to the illusion that he was on extended holiday. Though he increasingly looked forward to a resumption of his modernist days in Paris, his time in Hollywood was extremely productive. A mature artist, he engaged in protean activities, with prodigious effort in all media at hand, including photography, despite his disavowal of commercial assignments. With an economy of means that only an accomplished artisan could command, Man Ray intensified the interconnections among his paintings, photographs, drawings, and objects—superimposing and varying themes, motifs, and media in a self-referential body of achievement that became his California legacy.[9]

And so on September 24, 1940, Harry Kantor and Man Ray drove to Chicago and then headed south to New Orleans, where they turned west on Route 66 to Los Angeles, arriving the first week in October. Driving into Los Angeles at night, and on to Hollywood (whose low-slung buildings reminded him of a "frontier town"), Man Ray understandably still had war-torn France on his mind: when he saw searchlights, they were not sweeping the Parisian sky for enemy planes as he briefly imagined, but instead heralding a movie premiere or the opening of a new supermarket. In a few days, Man Ray's prospects improved markedly. Through a mutual friend he met Juliet Browner, "with faun-like features and slanted eyes."[10] She would remain his muse for the rest of his life. From the start Man Ray celebrated her likeness in all the media at his hand, from drawings and photographs to paintings.

An aspiring dancer in the ambience of Martha Graham, an artist's model and intimate of the handsome Willem de Kooning—having led a bohemian life in Greenwich Village during the late 1920s and the Depression years, Juliet Browner knew of Man Ray before she met him on a blind date in Hollywood. She was thirty, vivacious, and agreeable—compliant, actually, like a "feather" in Man Ray's arms. She must have reminded him somewhat of Ady, also an easygoing dancer.

Certainly Juliet was no strong-willed Lee Miller, Man Ray's darkroom protégé in the late 1920s. An independent spirit, Miller became a photographer in her own right and left a devastated Man Ray behind.

***Juliet**, Hollywood,* c. 1945 *Three-color carbon transfer print*

He needed someone of Juliet's sunny disposition to counterbalance his own intensities, bleak moods, and depressions when they took over. In active collaboration with Man Ray, "her body became the natural instrument it seemed designed to be."[11]

Man Ray invited Juliet to move in with him at the Chateau des Fleurs, an apartment hotel on Franklin Avenue in Hollywood. They soon required larger accommodations so that he could have studio space. Feeling "cramped," Man Ray found quarters in the "original heart of Hollywood" at the St. George, a nearby residential hotel (now called the "Villa Elaine") at 1245 Vine Street. "I couldn't have imagined anything more perfect," he later recalled. The interior courtyard revealed a California garden, at the end of which he saw a "beautiful apartment," with a "high-ceilinged studio, den, dining room, kitchen, and loggia with bedroom and bath, completely furnished."[12]

In Paris and New York before that, Man Ray's work quarters required darkroom facilities as well as space to paint and make objects. His studio also doubled as a living area. By the 1930s, when he was making a prosperous living as a fashion photographer, there was little pressure to sell his paintings and objects, only to display them in exhibitions sponsored by the Surrealists and their avant-garde allies. As a consequence, his work often remained in the studio as an integral part of his domestic arrangements. Paintings, objects, drawings, photographs—all reverberated against one another with an intimate presence in his studio household. The Vine Street apartment once again filled the bill.

Although the all-night Hollywood Market was conveniently located across the street, the sprawl of Los Angeles necessitated an automobile. By mid-January of 1941, Man Ray had purchased a car on the installment plan. "It's a beauty," he wrote to Elsie, "a Graham-Page '41 model, blue and streamlined like a submarine." The diminutive Man Ray clearly asserted his masculinity in his new purchase; he boasted to Elsie that the Graham suited his temperament. With its "super-charged motor," and if he felt "desperate enough," he could speed through the Southern California landscape like a native. He was about to become the *Hollywood Supercharger*, or so he self-mockingly fantasized.[13]

***Untitled** (Juliet)*, 1942 *Pen and india ink on paper*

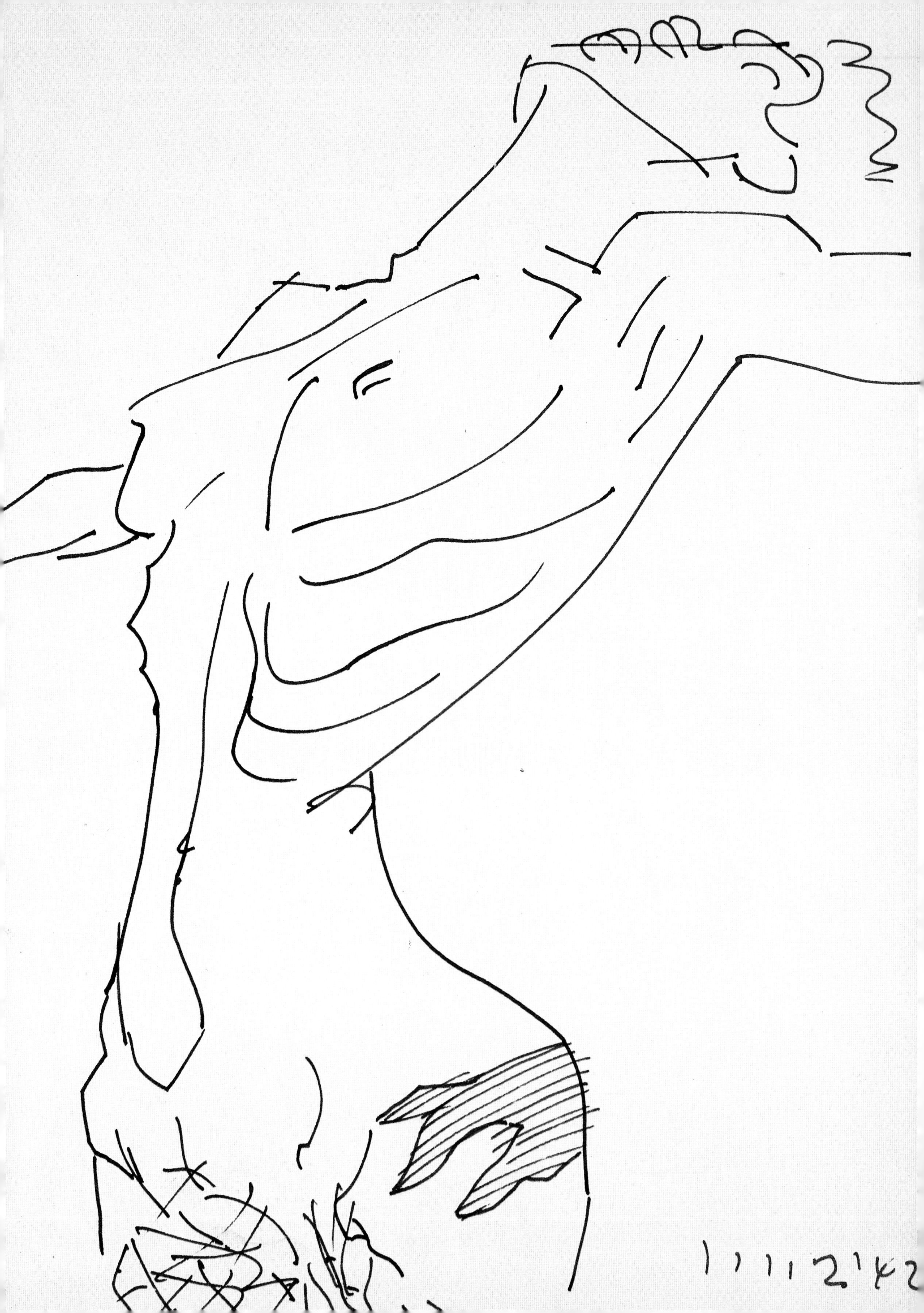

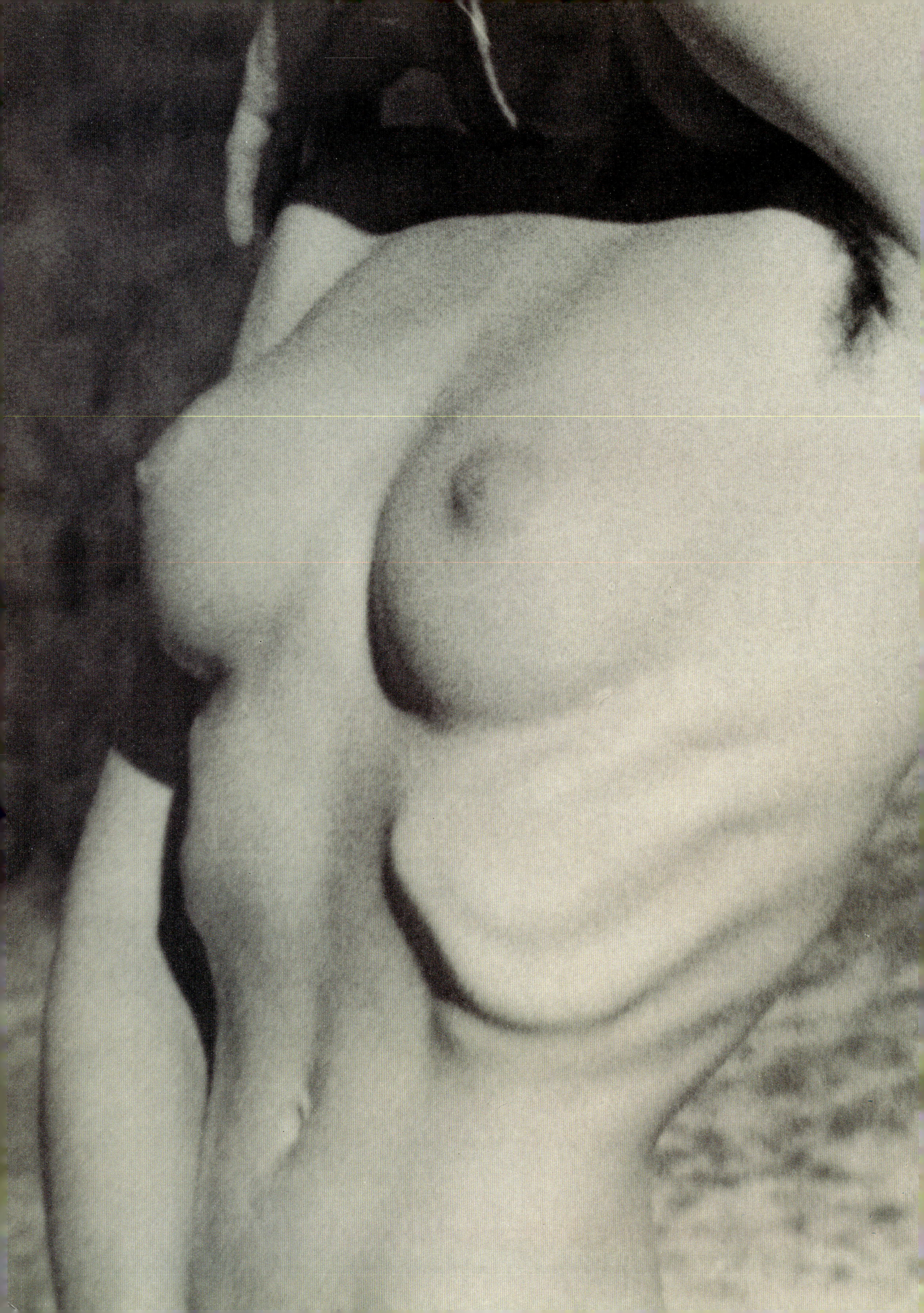

Fast cars and women and the ambience of Hollywood suggested a sybaritic life. At the very least, the Graham-Page was calculated to impress Juliet. The California dream seemed to promise an extended vacation as a way of life: with the Graham-Page, Man Ray and Juliet gained the mobility to tour California, north to Santa Barbara and beyond to San Francisco, south to San Diego and Tijuana. (Despite war rationing, Man Ray had access to gasoline because he was classified as a professional photographer.)[14] Always a dapper dresser in Paris, Man Ray discarded jackets and ties for casual clothing. Outside his door he enjoyed a climate redolent of the Côte d'Azur: New York (and Paris) winters simply became a bad memory.

Even earthquakes were a novelty at first. On the first occasion, soon after moving to Vine Street, Man Ray reassured Elsie that "it's a rather agreeable sensation, like a gently rocking boat." Yet on January 11, 1950, a year before he returned to Paris, he reported another earthquake to Elsie. "One of these days," he direly predicted, "everything will come down, I'm sure; if my luck holds I'll be out of here before this comes!"[15] The climate also proved problematic, for it dissipated the urge to work. Man Ray's reactions provide a seismic reading of his ambivalent feelings toward life in Southern California.

Early in his stay, Man Ray complained to Elsie that "California is a beautiful prison." He added, however, an important qualification: "I like being here, but I cannot forget my previous life" in Paris. His sense of confinement had as much to do with the war as the constraints exerted by the peculiar social and cultural terrain of Los Angeles. After Pearl Harbor on December 7, 1941, the war came close to home, as the entire west coast was subject to hysteria and anxiety over the possibility of Japanese attack and invasion. From its disruptive beginnings in Europe, the war cast a long shadow. Man Ray, who tried unsuccessfully to find defense-related work in Los Angeles, often felt "low and tired."[16]

Above all, he felt helpless to stem the onslaught of events. That he had been forced out of Paris was bad enough, but there was also the matter of his property and belongings left behind, entrusted to the care of Ady and other friends. He was especially worried about his art work: at least two cases of paintings in Paris, and other material stored in his small house in Saint-Germain-en-Laye. Finally, on

***Untitled** (Juliet)*, 1942 *Gelatin-silver print*

April 27, 1941, he received reassuring news from Duchamp in Marseille that Ady was safe and his house intact. She had wisely sold his old Peugeot before it completely broke down, or worse, was requisitioned by the Nazis. Yet by summer 1944, Man Ray still believed that a lifetime of paintings, photographs, and objects had been lost. No dollar amount could be assigned to this loss: how could he recuperate? And with what energy? His references to an "easy going California life" masked a severe, perhaps impossible challenge.[17]

During his early years in Hollywood, Man Ray lived frugally on savings from his fashion photography. He generated almost no new income from the sales of his paintings and objects. And even though he was still in demand among the fashion houses and trade magazines upon his return to the United States, he refused to return to commercial photography, even if it meant proceeding under a severe financial handicap. His last studio sessions had taken place in Paris for *Harper's Bazaar* at the beginning of the war. These photographs appeared in three issues of the magazine, from October 1940 to November 1942, and signalled the end of a brilliant career as fashion photographer.[18]

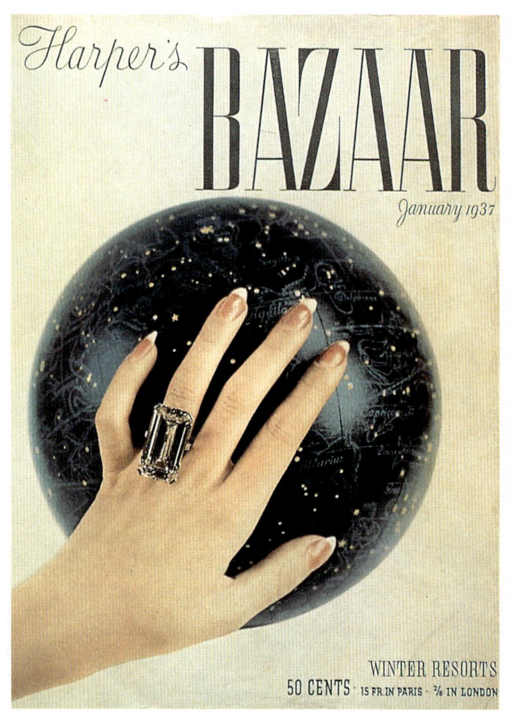

left:
Harper's Bazaar *cover, January, 1937*

opposite:
Purple Mask*,* 1948
Oil on canvas

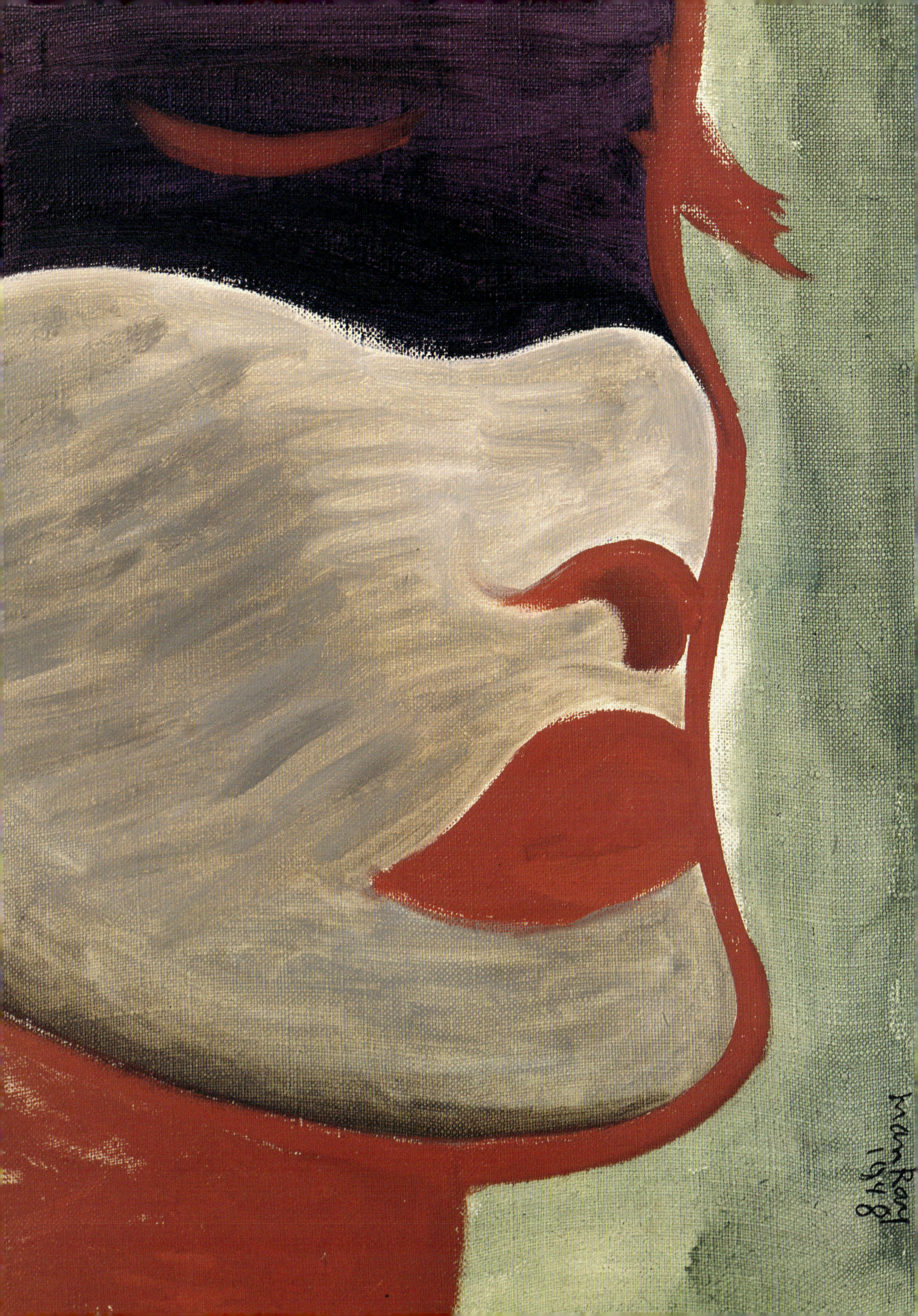
Man Ray
1948

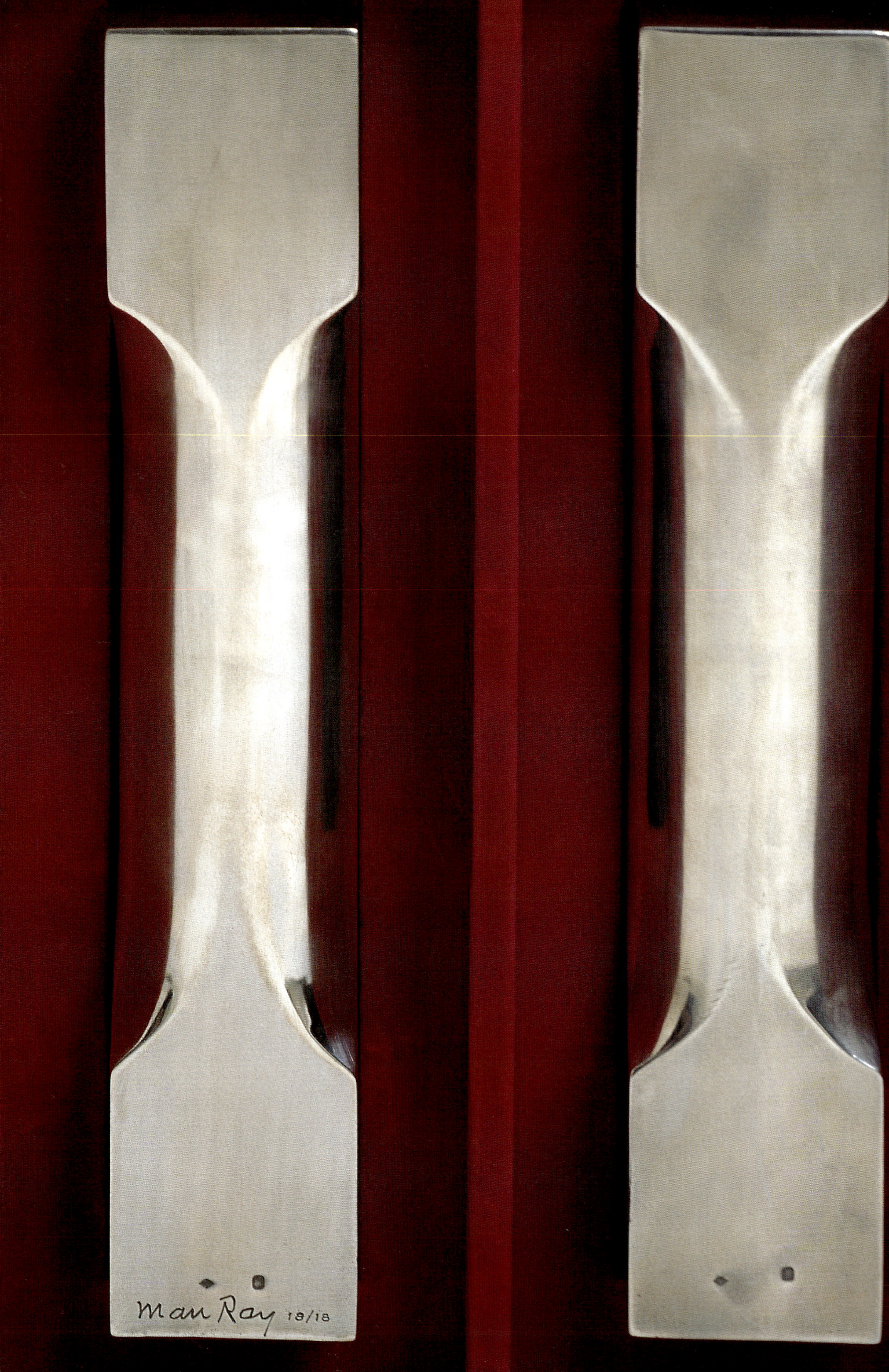
Man Ray 18/18

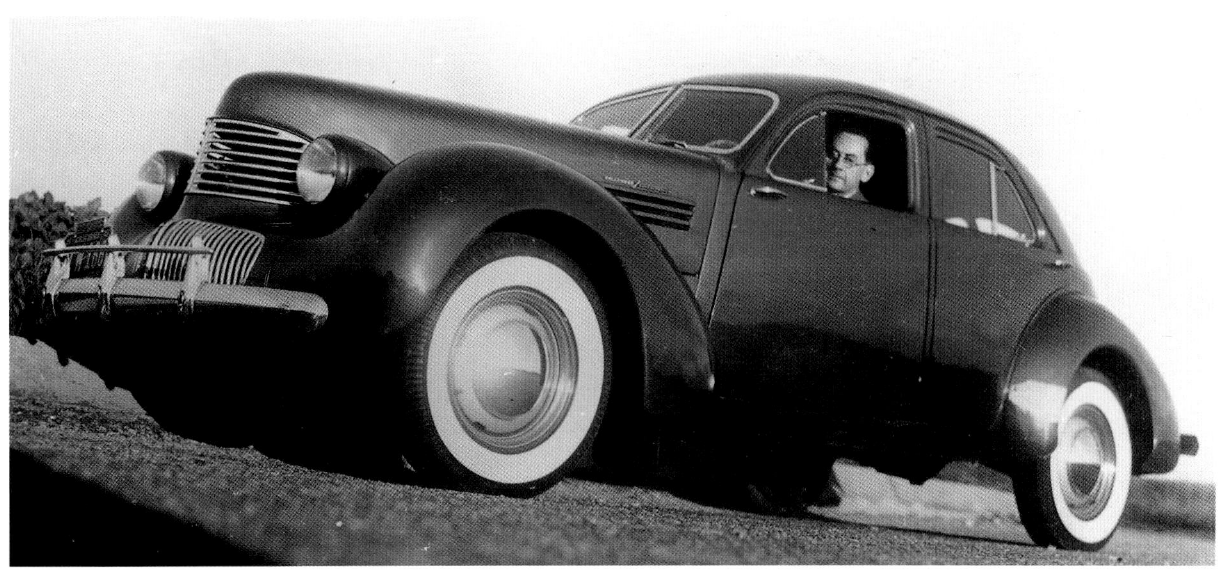

His Graham-Page could overcome the distances but not the cultural sprawl attenuating the art world in Los Angeles . . . .

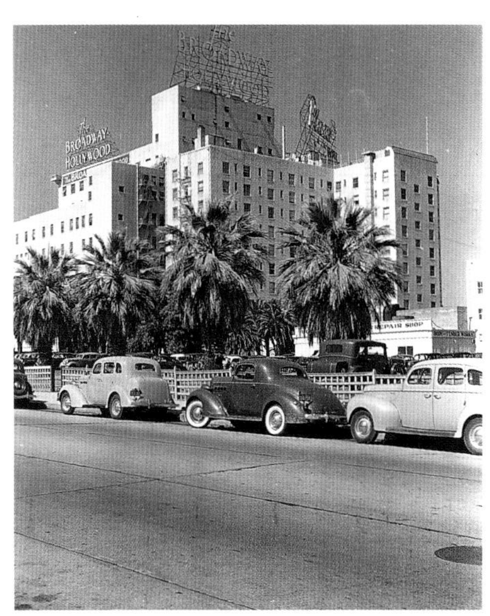

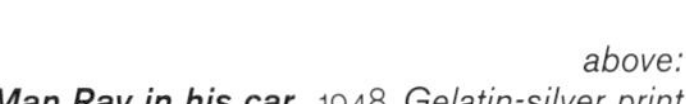

above:
***Man Ray in his car**, 1948 Gelatin-silver print*

right:
***The Broadway Building**, Los Angeles, 1940s Gelatin-silver print*

opposite:
***Square Dumb Bells**, 1966*
Silver dumbbells in a wooden box

Man Ray's seemingly perverse decision meant that he had to earn a living as a painter and maker of objects—with all the attendant tensions and anxieties that came from such a precarious vocation. As a stranger in Southern California, he urgently needed to make contacts for exhibitions. Visual exposure became paramount in an unfamiliar cultural landscape. California was not New York—emphatically not New York—much to Man Ray's initial relief, but unlike Manhattan, Los Angeles spread far and wide. Arthur Millier, art critic for the *Los Angeles Times*, described the city as "a sprawling, traffic-bedeviled, mushrooming, formless metropolis." As Man Ray noted, "it's always at least ten miles to anyone or any place. . . ." His Graham-Page could overcome the distances but not the cultural sprawl attenuating the art world in Los Angeles. In 1942 Man Ray wrote to Elsie that he was "very busy trying to make some connections for the future. It's very hard. . . ."[19] Something like a "Hollywood Supercharger," indeed, was in order.

"Hollywood," of course, was a municipal metaphor for the film industry, which dominated Southern California and the formation of a local art world. In the complex industry of filmmaking, the studios absorbed—some might say devoured—writers, photographers, musicians, composers, and visual artists. This Hollywood was marginally linked to the regional network of galleries, only a handful of which exhibited modern art. When a national magazine like *Art Digest* did a large spread on Southern California, it could not resist featuring movie actors and directors as glamorous collectors; their visual interests and enthusiasms, however, did not venture far beyond Post-Impressionism.[20]

The major museum in the area was the Los Angeles County Museum of History, Science, and Art, its name suggesting its priorities. The County Museum was located in Exposition Park, away from the commercial galleries that dotted Hollywood and Beverly Hills. While the art world of Southern California was not especially promising, neither was it quite as dismal as Man Ray's young friend William Copley would later insinuate in dismissing the County Museum as a "mausoleum . . . which harbored some misacquisitions of William Randolph Hearst and a few stuffed animals."[21]

Under these circumstances, Man Ray desperately needed to make social connections. He later admitted that Tahiti or a desert island probably would not have been such a good idea after all. Despite what he described to Elsie as his "hermit periods" of depression, he conceded that he preferred the social opportunities of a large city like Los Angeles where he could at least choose his company without involuntary isolation. And meet people he did, renewing old friendships and acquaintances: among the earliest were Walter and Louise Arensberg, patrons of Duchamp since his arrival in New York in 1915. With Duchamp's assistance they had assembled a major collection of modern art. They moved to Los Angeles in 1921 after Louise became tired of their hectic salon life in Manhattan; the crazy days of New York Dada gave way to the serenity of life at 7065 Hillside Avenue in Hollywood. Through the Arensbergs, Man Ray began to make connections in the California art world.[22]

From February 25 to March 24, 1941, some five months after his arrival, Man Ray had his first one-man exhibition in California, at the Frank Perls Gallery, at 8634 Sunset Boulevard in Hollywood. Perls was one of the few Los Angeles dealers interested in showing modern art. In notes for the exhibition catalogue, the libertarian Man Ray trenchantly declared "an irresistible desire to violate" established laws, and offered "his most recent [work] in a spirit of provocation."[23] A forthright announcement of his long-held views seemed the best way to make his presence known.

For a brief moment Man Ray's strategy seemed to work. On March 1, 1941, *Art Digest* announced to its readers that Man Ray, whom Picasso had dubbed "*enfant terrible* of Montparnasse," had returned to the United States and was living in Hollywood, a survivor of "Paris' bombardment and surrender." And Arthur Millier's short piece in the *Los Angeles Times* began promisingly enough—"Surrealist Man Ray Puts on Exhibition in Hollywood"—only to dismiss the work in the end. Millier proceeded to survey the range of work on display, from early Cubist-inspired paintings to the "queer image-world of surrealism," from Rayographs to "mystifying" drawings. The critic's adjectives, however, did not signal approval, let alone any attempt to understand the artist's efforts. Refusing to rise to Man Ray's provocations, he decided that "America [and California] . . . is on a different track" from the European movements to which the artist had belonged. Millier relegated Man Ray from avant-garde to rearguard: to "a period . . . remote in feeling and in time."[24]

the following pages in order:

p. 32
Presse-Papier a Priape
(Priapus Paperweight), 1968
Bronze

p. 33
Another Spring, c. 1960
Metal spring, wooden cigar box, nails, and marble egg

p. 34
Fer Rouge (Red Hot Iron), 1966
Red painted flatiron presented in a leather-covered box

p.35
Self-Portrait, 1971 *Bronze*

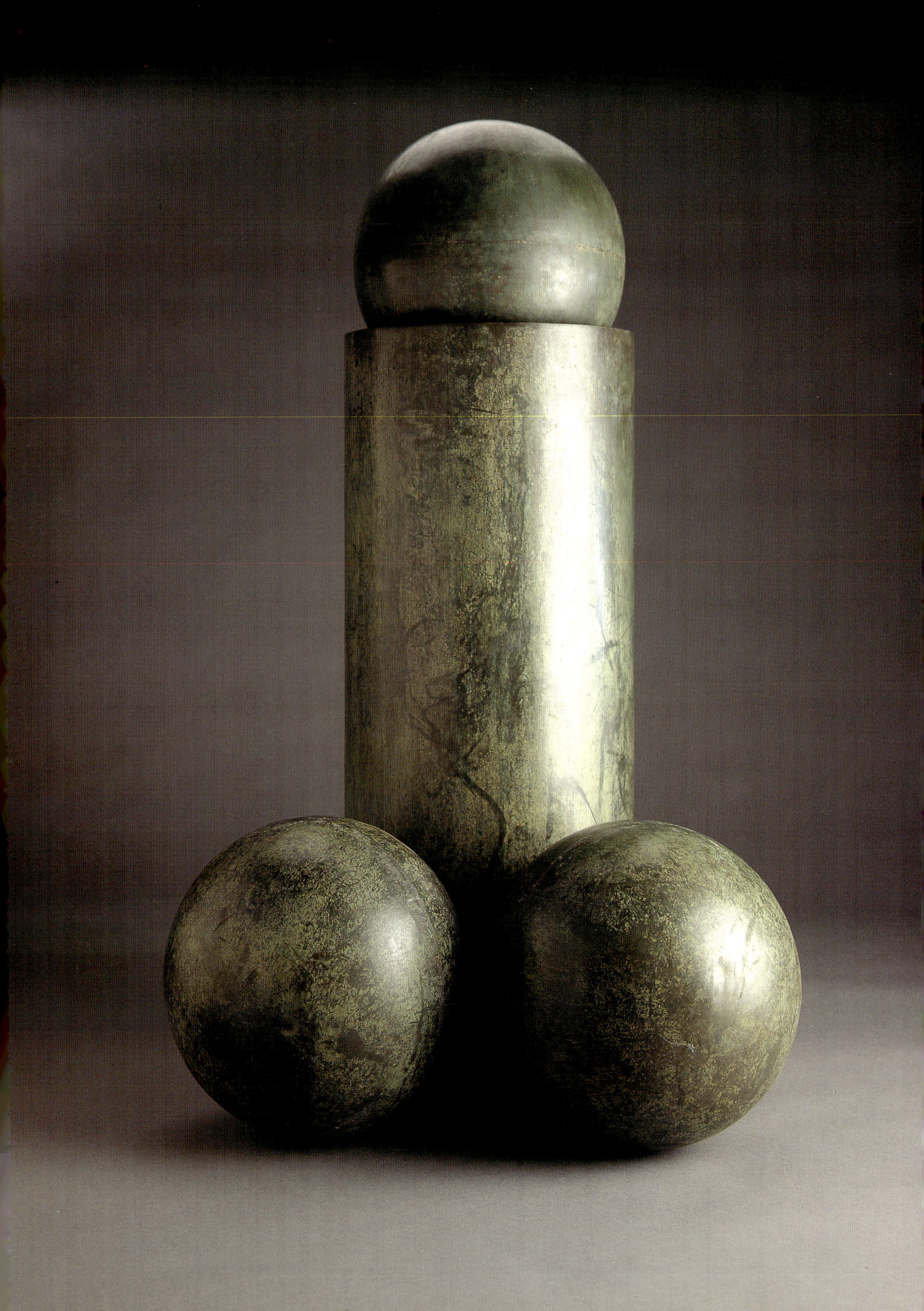

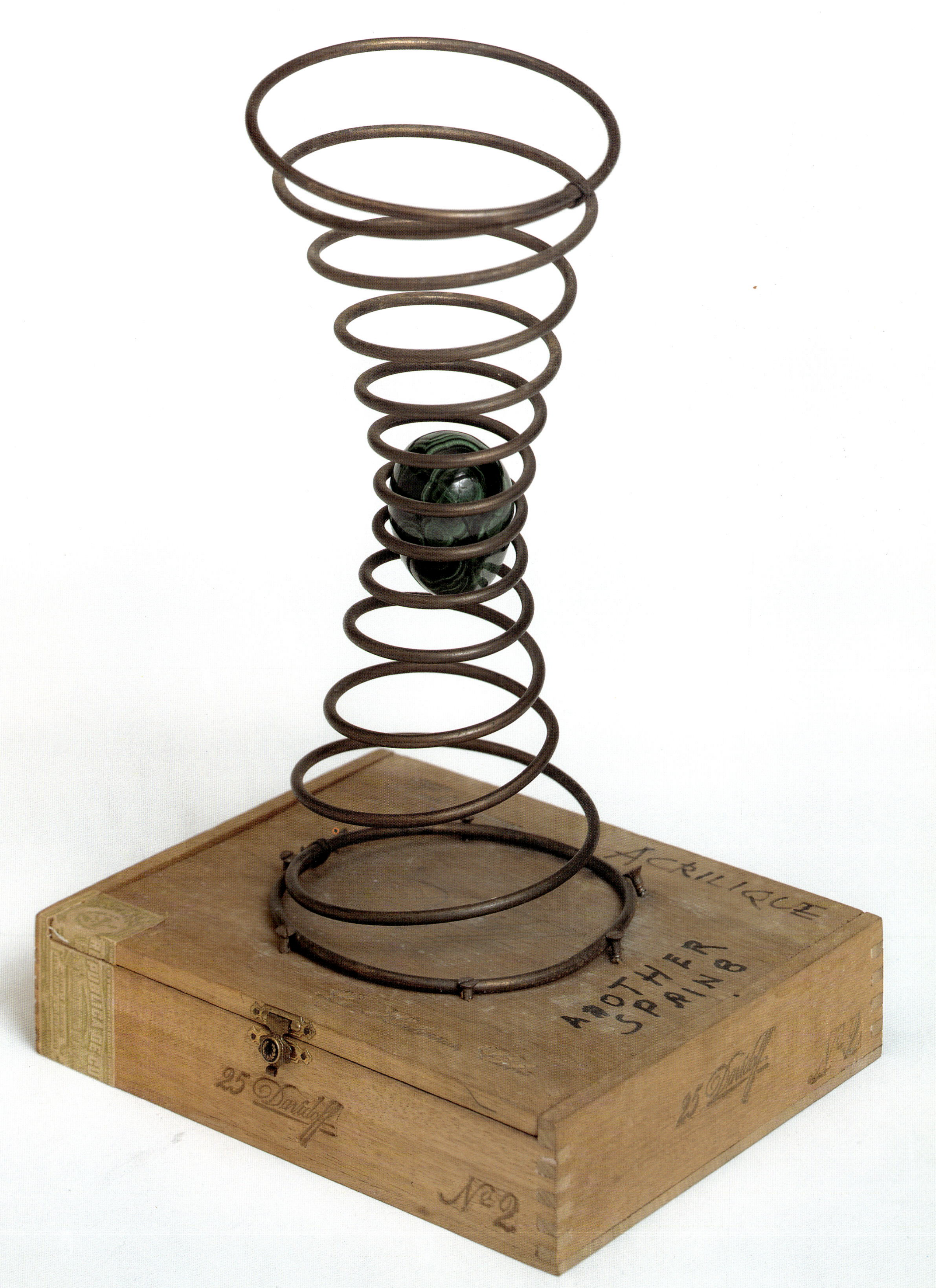
ACRILIQUE
ANOTHER SPRING
25 Davidoff
Nº2

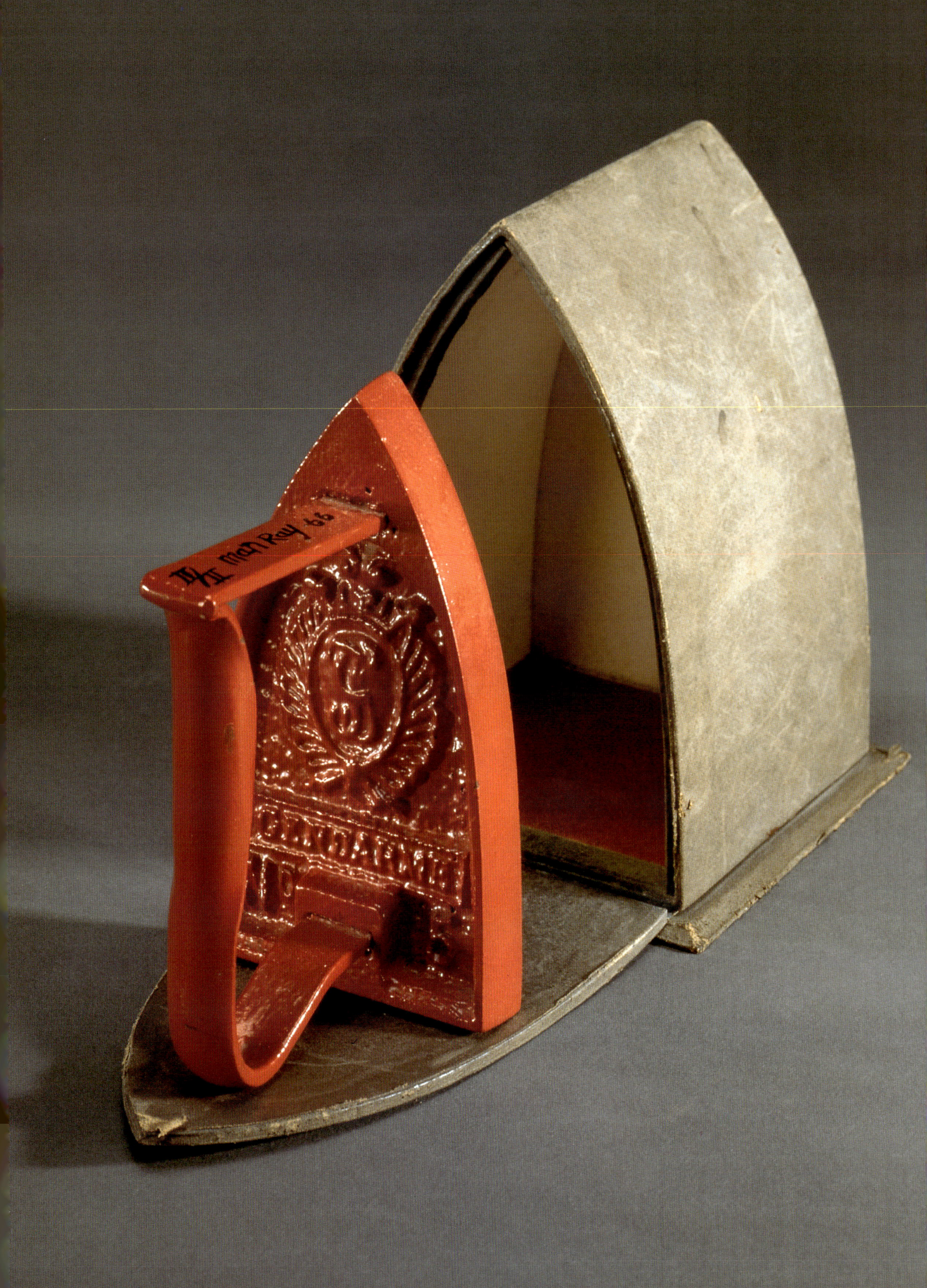
III/II man Ray 66

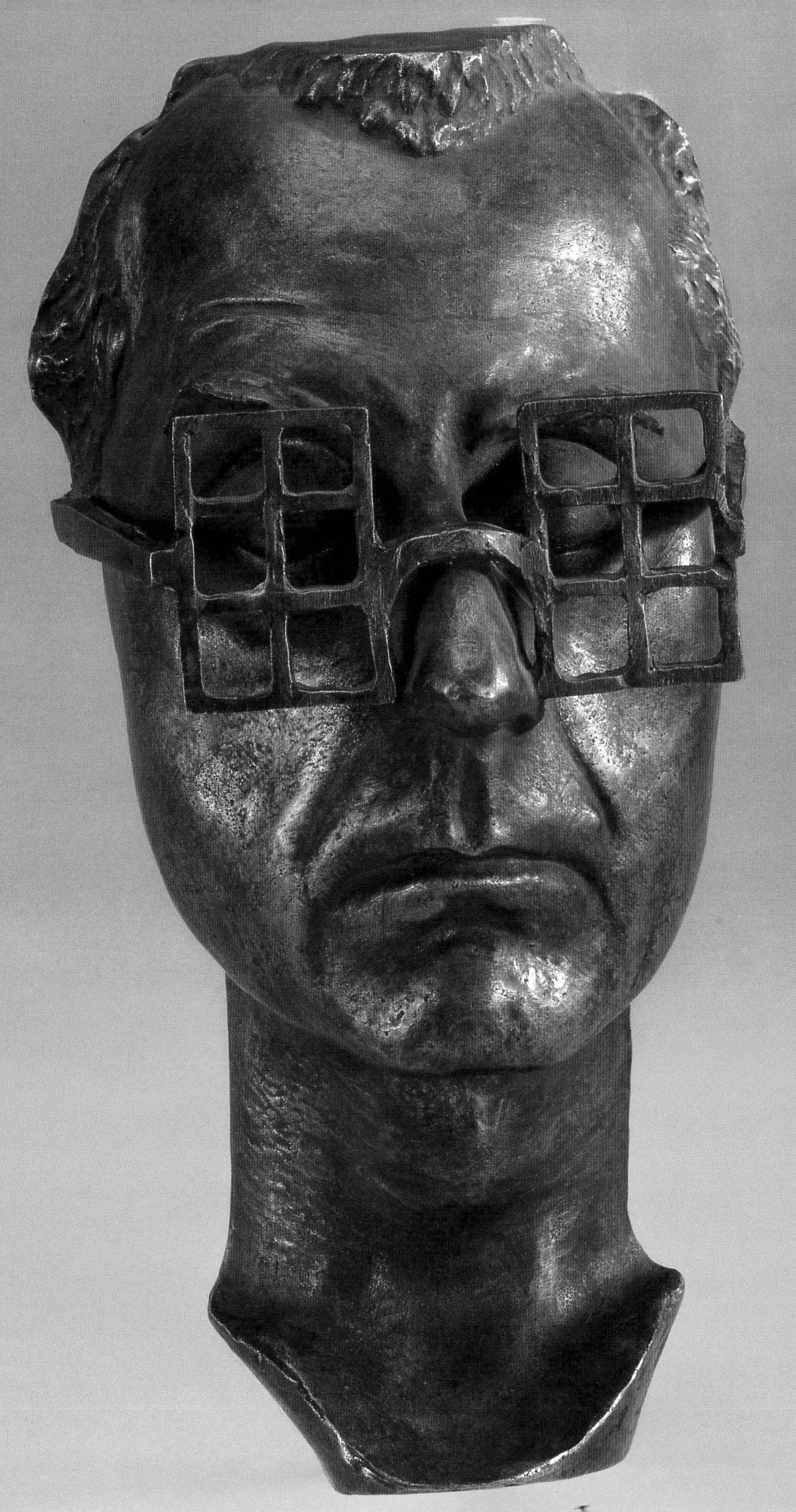

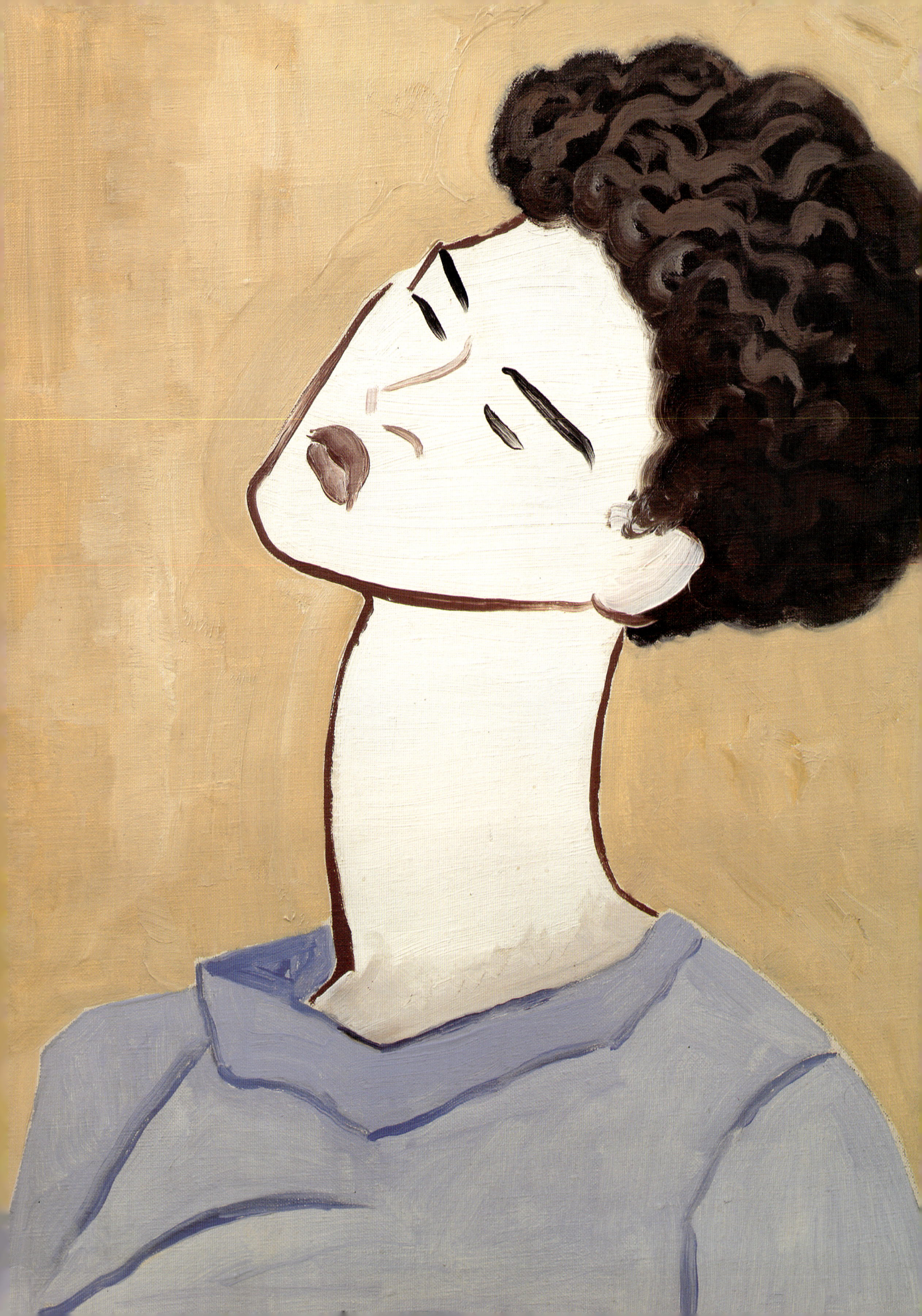

While Man Ray later recalled that the exhibition was well attended by the movie colony, nothing was sold. Even so, Perls had broken the ice, and other exhibitions were to follow. Perls continued to support Man Ray in June 1942 with an exhibition of his portrait photographs in tandem with the portrait paintings of George Biddle. In *California Arts and Architecture*, a progressive journal published locally, Perls acknowledged that the work on display was "artistically rather incongruous but that is exactly what this exhibition means to show." The pairing of Man Ray's photography and Biddle's painting would demonstrate "that a good portrait is predominantly original, personal, and creative and not simply a mechanical production."[25]

The academically oriented Biddle had run across Man Ray earlier in Paris and New York, but got to know him in Hollywood, where he came to respect "the clear cool intelligence which seemed lurking behind the extravagance of his art theories" (otherwise "pompous and irascible nonsense"). Their portrait exhibition at Perls gave Biddle a pretext to depict Man Ray in his Vine Street studio, posed on a sofa beside an "enormous horse's skull" from the Los Angeles County Museum as a Surrealistic accoutrement; hanging behind Man Ray was his recent oil, *Leda and the Swan*.[26]

Between the two exhibitions at the Perls Gallery, in May 1941 Man Ray also had an exhibition of paintings, drawings, and Rayographs at the M. H. de Young Museum in San Francisco. Invited to attend the opening, Juliet and Man Ray charged up the highway in his Graham-Page, and were warmly received by the museum's patrons. The exhibition itself was "very handsomely put up" and the occasion "a pleasant lark," he wrote Elsie, though he received a mixed review for his efforts. In September 1943, after a preview in his Vine Street studio, Man Ray's drawings and Rayographs went on view at the recently refurbished Santa Barbara Museum of Art, and in November 1943 he exhibited his paintings at the Los Angeles County Museum of History, Science, and Art, which would mount a more extensive exhibition of his work in 1945. There was no catalogue because of a war-caused paper shortage, but worse, there was little interest in his work.[27]

During the war years, Man Ray's visibility in Southern California peaked at the Pasadena Art Institute in the fall of 1944 when he was given his first retrospective (upon the recommendation of Antonin

Juliet, 1940 *Oil on canvas*

Heythum, who taught design at the California Institute of Technology). Before the opening on September 19th, the *Pasadena Star News* forewarned its readers that this "important show" would take contemporary art through "some of its most extreme paces." Man Ray was described as an "independent artist," despite his affiliation with the Surrealists.[28]

At the Art Institute six galleries were devoted to his work. Gallery A showed sixty-four oils dating back to 1913; galleries B and C displayed watercolors and drawings respectively, while his photographs were divided between Rayographs and portraits in two other galleries. (A final gallery was devoted to photographs of paintings left behind in France.) Jarvis Barlow, director of the Pasadena Art Institute, wrote a brief catalogue statement commending Man Ray as an "outstanding creative artist" and describing the variegated exhibition as "a panorama of creative pictorial art in general of the past thirty years."[29]

After the opening, Kenneth Ross reviewed the retrospective for the *Pasadena Star News*. In an apparent rhetorical ploy to win over confused viewers, he assumed their point of view and expressed bewilderment over Man Ray's "pure abstractions . . . nonsensical dreams, and deliberate distortions." He then quoted Man Ray's caveat, printed for the exhibition, that his work was "all designed to amuse, bewilder, annoy or to inspire reflection. . . ." On this basis, the critic argued that the exhibition was "entertaining and successful," even though he thought that Man Ray unduly emphasized novelty in his pursuit of artistic freedom. In the end, he praised the abstract paintings, especially the *Revolving Doors* series, as well as the photographs, portraiture and Rayographs alike.[30]

Displeased by what seemed to be a mixed review, and probably irked by Ross's preference for the photographs, Man Ray took the occasion of a lecture at the museum to go on the attack. He told the audience ("respectable and solid-looking") that "the pursuit of liberty and the pursuit of pleasure" were his prime motivations. Otherwise, "painting would become a bore." Rising from the audience, Ross countered by asking if Man Ray were more interested in being different and original, in enjoying himself, than in being profound. His query brought other questions from the audience, who were enlivened by this exchange. Man Ray tried to respond with sincerity

Revolving Doors I: "Mime", 1942 *Ink and watercolor*

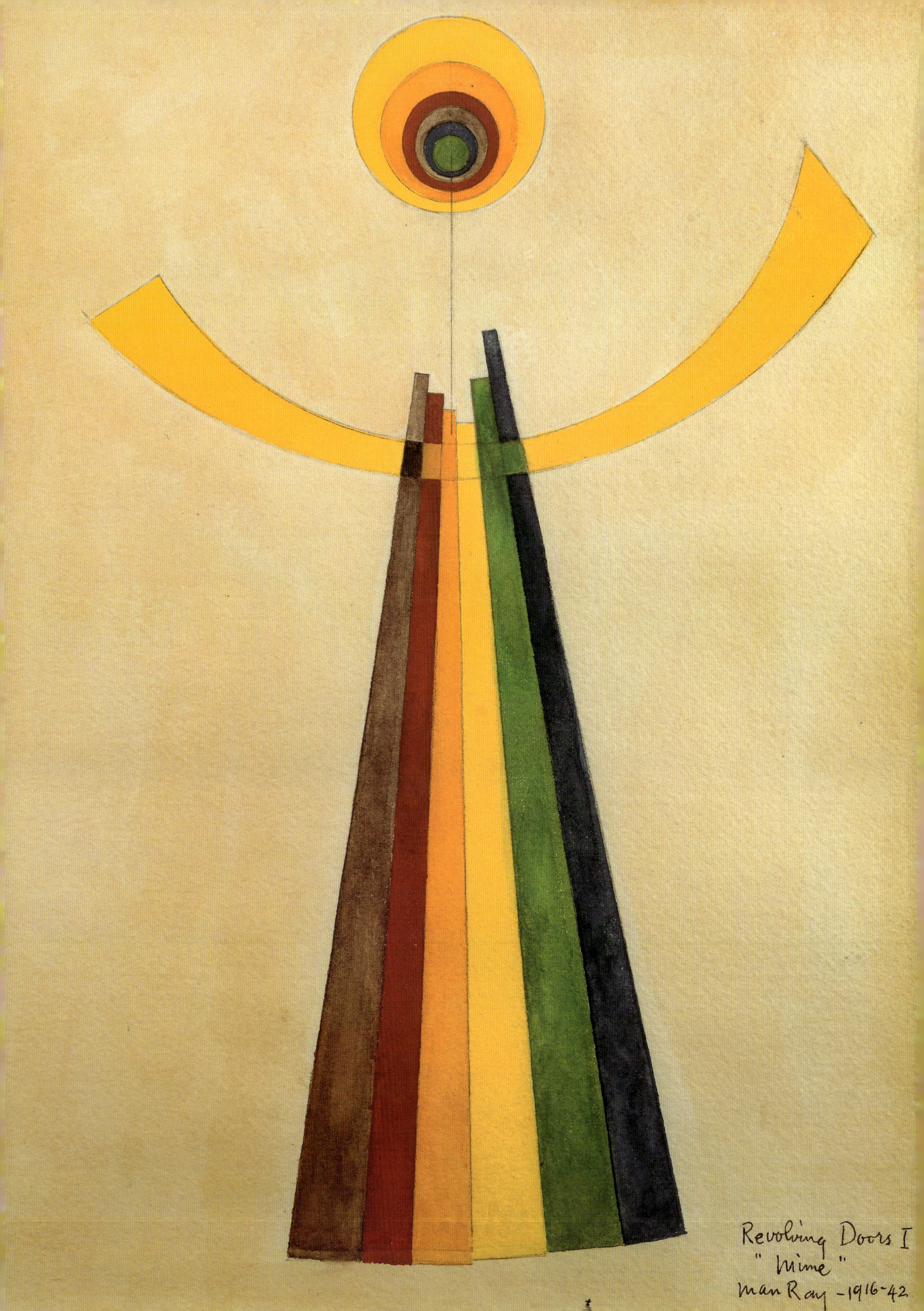
Revolving Doors I
"Mime"
Man Ray - 1916-42

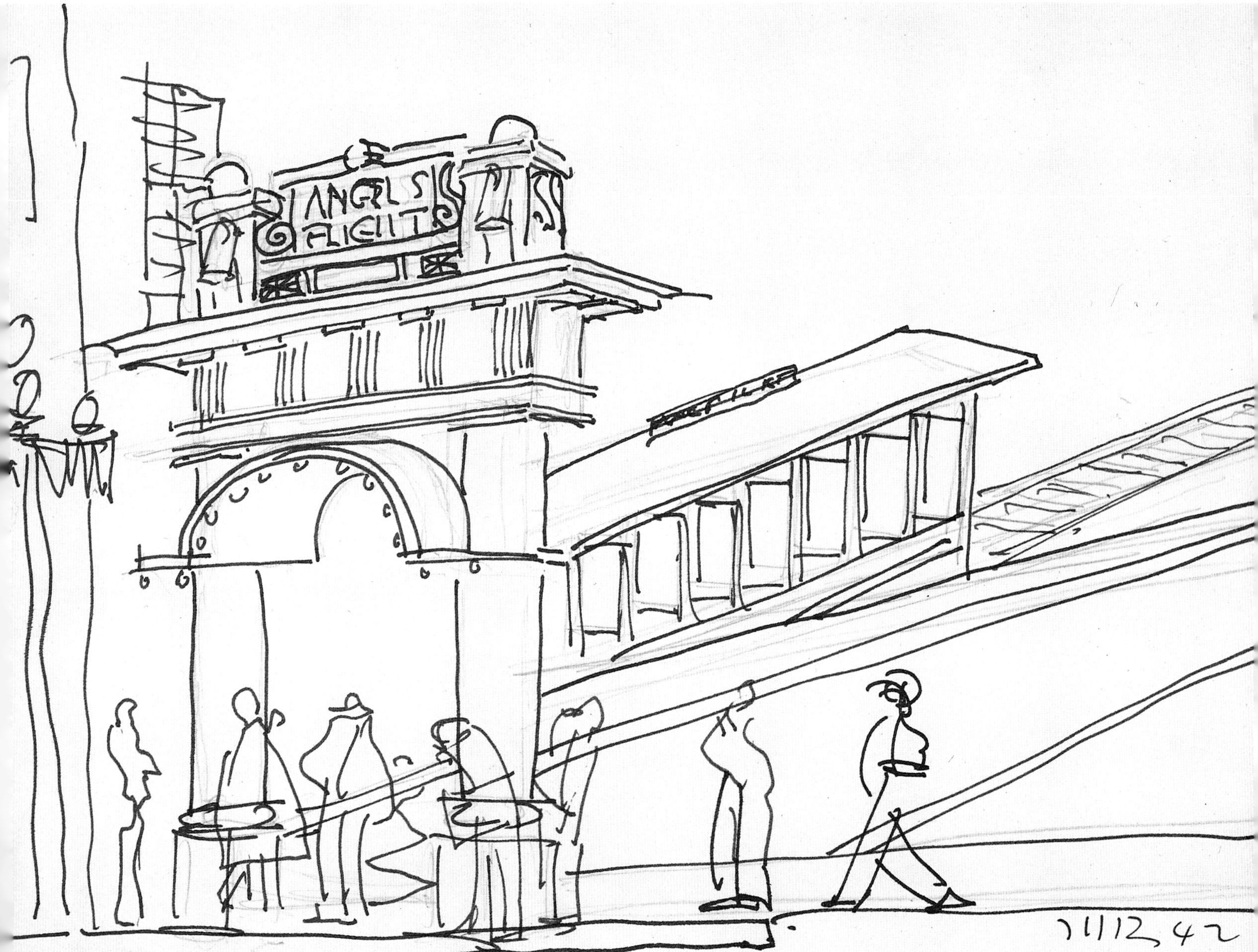

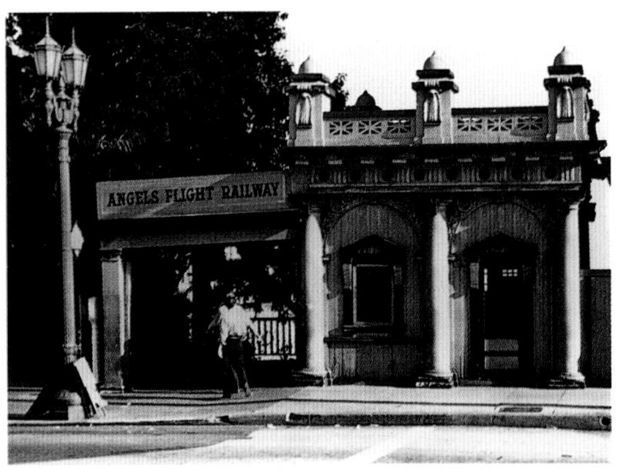

above:
***Angels Flight**, 1942 Ink on paper*

left:
***Angels Flight**, 1941–42 Gelatin-silver print*

and in a conciliatory way despite an urge to insult his audience. Even so, he found public speaking "exhilarating" and a way to promote self-dialogue. "Putting my ideas into words was like preparing canvases and paints for a new work," he claimed.[31]

The European war and its accompanying disasters taught Man Ray the urgency of speaking out on public issues. As early as December 1940, he took to the Santa Barbara airwaves to rebut the views of a group advocating "Sanity in Art" in a national campaign against an "insane" modern art. Reversing this slogan, Man Ray counter-punned with "Art in Sanity." (In January 1941 his talk was published in *California Arts and Architecture*.) Peyton Boswell, the conservative editor of the *Art Digest*, had dismissed the Sanity in Art movement for all the wrong reasons, reassuring his readers that "Ultra-modernism [was] . . . a feebly derivative echo in America." Man Ray, who was nothing if not "ultra-modern," spoke out against the "clamor for isolation in the arts." He reasonably asked that viewers make "direct contact with the work" with an "unbiased reaction." Speaking as an artist, he denied any intent "to fool or shock the public." Instead, he offered a courageous libertarian credo: "Only by laying aside ulterior motives, by accepting the unfamiliar and the unknown, by intensifying individual effort, can the artist hope to produce a great and healthy art."[32]

As Man Ray began to circulate in Los Angeles, he found like-minded individuals. In the summer of 1941, newlyweds Peggy Guggenheim and Max Ernst (who had escaped incarceration if not sure execution as a "degenerate" artist in Germany) flew to San Francisco from New York and then drove down to Los Angeles to visit Peggy's sister Hazel, also recently married. Man Ray knew Peggy: in the 1920s, he had photographed her in her Poiret evening gown, complete with cigarette holder and Vera Stravinsky headdress. Touring Europe to purchase art for her own collection when the war broke out, Peggy Guggenheim owned one of Man Ray's paintings and several Rayographs. She and Max stayed with Hazel for three weeks, and there in Santa Monica they were reunited with Man Ray, and met Juliet for the first time.[33]

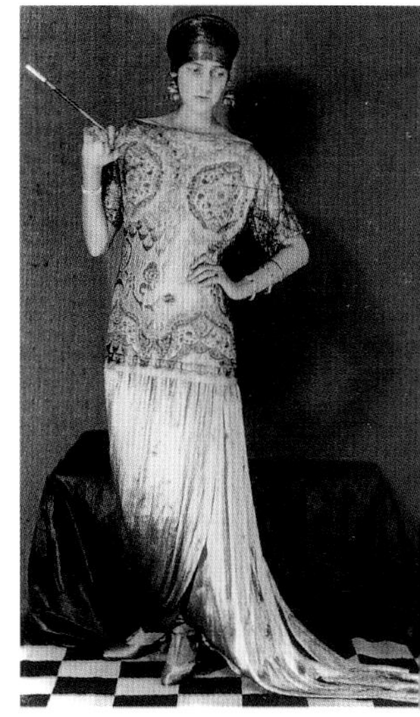

Margueret (Peggy) Guggenheim in a Poiret gown, 1925
Gelatin-silver print

There, too, Man Ray met Gilbert and Margaret Neiman, she an aspiring painter, he a translator of Federico Garcia Lorca and eventually a novelist. The Neimans lived downtown on South Bunker Hill

Avenue in the low-rent district. Their apartment was near Angels Flight, the funicular railroad, which Man Ray both sketched and photographed. They in turn introduced him to Henry Miller, the expatriate writer, just a year or two younger than he. Miller had landed in Hollywood after a cross-country trek by car with the painter Abraham Rattner. Having started out from Brooklyn in October 1940, Miller caught up with Man Ray in 1941 while working on *The Air-Conditioned Nightmare*, an account of his transcontinental misadventures.

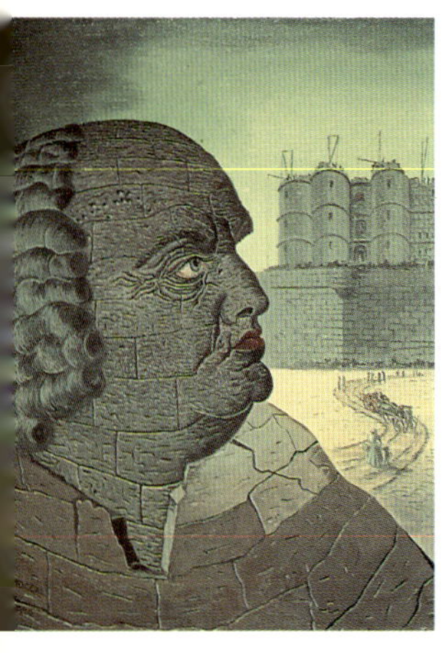

Soon after their first get-togethers at Vine Street, Miller wrote a note of appreciation to Man Ray and "Miss (the Countess) Julie" and asked for prints of photographs Man Ray had taken. In a tightly cropped version, Miller appears close up, and a finger can be seen on his head. In the uncropped versions, a nude but masked Margaret Neiman stands behind Miller, who is apparently unaware of her presence. In 1945, writing from Big Sur, Miller extolled the "sober clarity" of Man Ray's camera. "I can never determine," he claimed, "whether it's the magic box or the magic touch—probably both."[34]

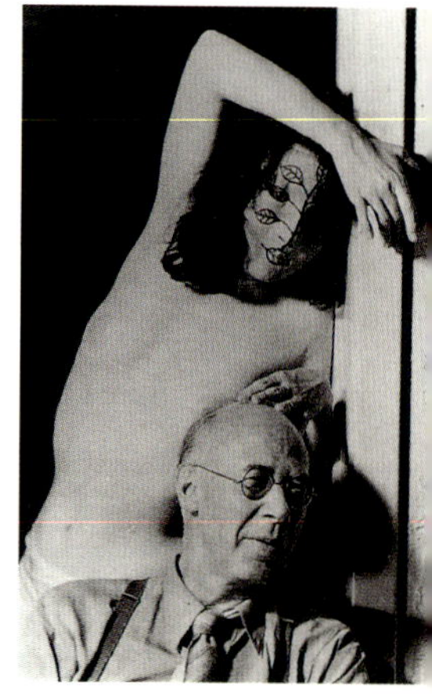

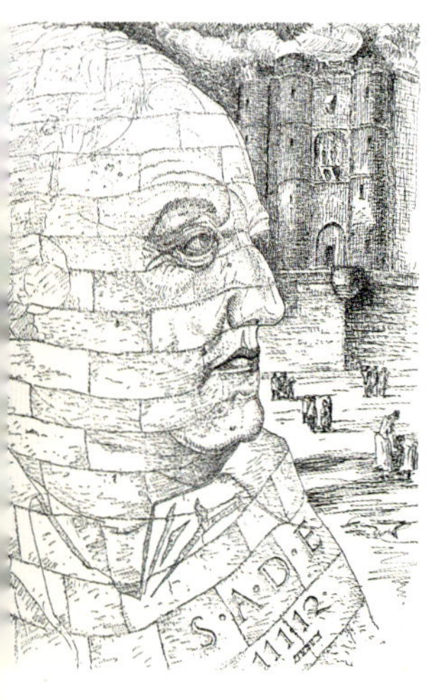

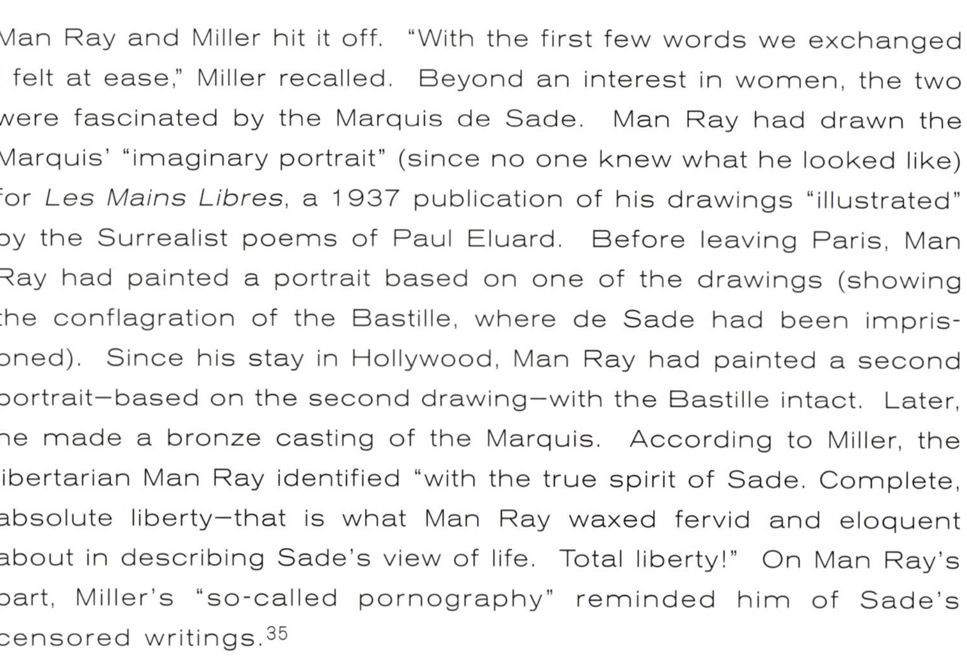

Man Ray and Miller hit it off. "With the first few words we exchanged I felt at ease," Miller recalled. Beyond an interest in women, the two were fascinated by the Marquis de Sade. Man Ray had drawn the Marquis' "imaginary portrait" (since no one knew what he looked like) for *Les Mains Libres*, a 1937 publication of his drawings "illustrated" by the Surrealist poems of Paul Eluard. Before leaving Paris, Man Ray had painted a portrait based on one of the drawings (showing the conflagration of the Bastille, where de Sade had been imprisoned). Since his stay in Hollywood, Man Ray had painted a second portrait—based on the second drawing—with the Bastille intact. Later, he made a bronze casting of the Marquis. According to Miller, the libertarian Man Ray identified "with the true spirit of Sade. Complete, absolute liberty—that is what Man Ray waxed fervid and eloquent about in describing Sade's view of life. Total liberty!" On Man Ray's part, Miller's "so-called pornography" reminded him of Sade's censored writings.[35]

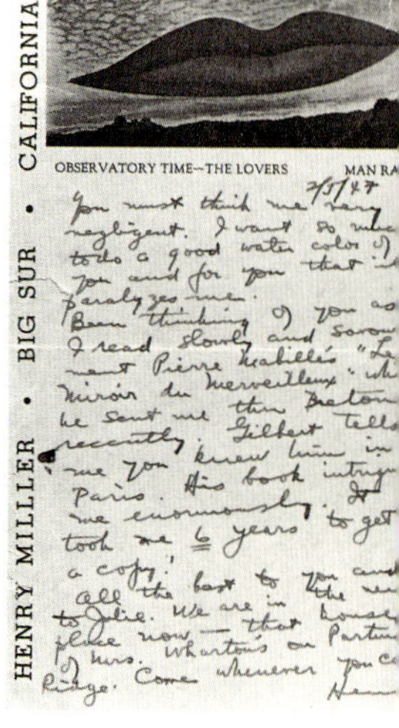
HENRY MILLER • BIG SUR • CALIFORNIA

OBSERVATORY TIME—THE LOVERS MAN RA

top:
Sade
(from Les Main Libres)
1936
India ink on paper

above:
Imaginary Portrait of D. A. F. de Sade, 1940
Oil on canvas

Man Ray and Juliet visited the impoverished Miller in his shack up at Big Sur, where they communally enjoyed the hot sulphur baths. "The sense of freedom was complete," Man Ray claimed. "And this open-air plumbing made a perfectly Surrealistic picture."

top:
Henry Miller and Masked Nude, 1945
Gelatin-silver print

above:
Letter from Henry Miller to Man Ray, 1947
Collection of The J. Paul Getty Museum, Malibu, California

opposite:
Henry Miller, 1945
Gelatin-silver print

overleaf:
p. 44
Juliet in Silk Stocking Mask,
c. 1945 *Gelatin-silver print*
p. 45
(detail) ***Imaginary Portrait of the Marquis de Sade***,
1971 *Bronze*

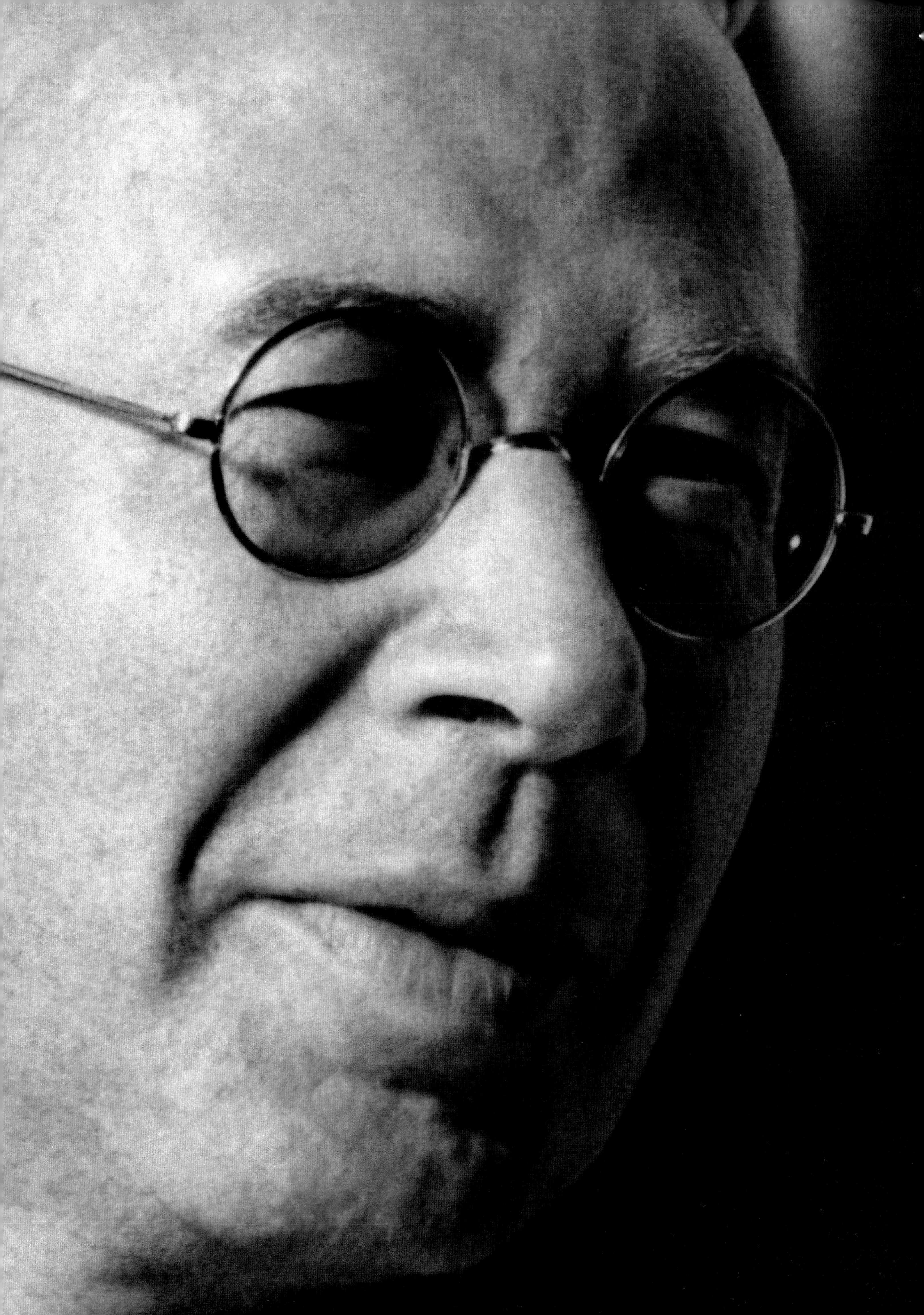

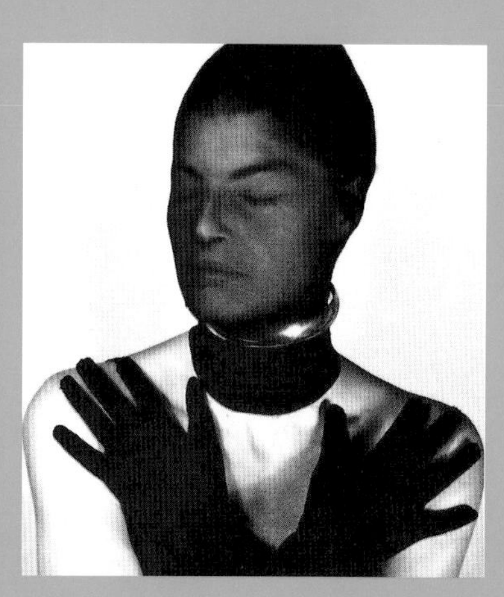

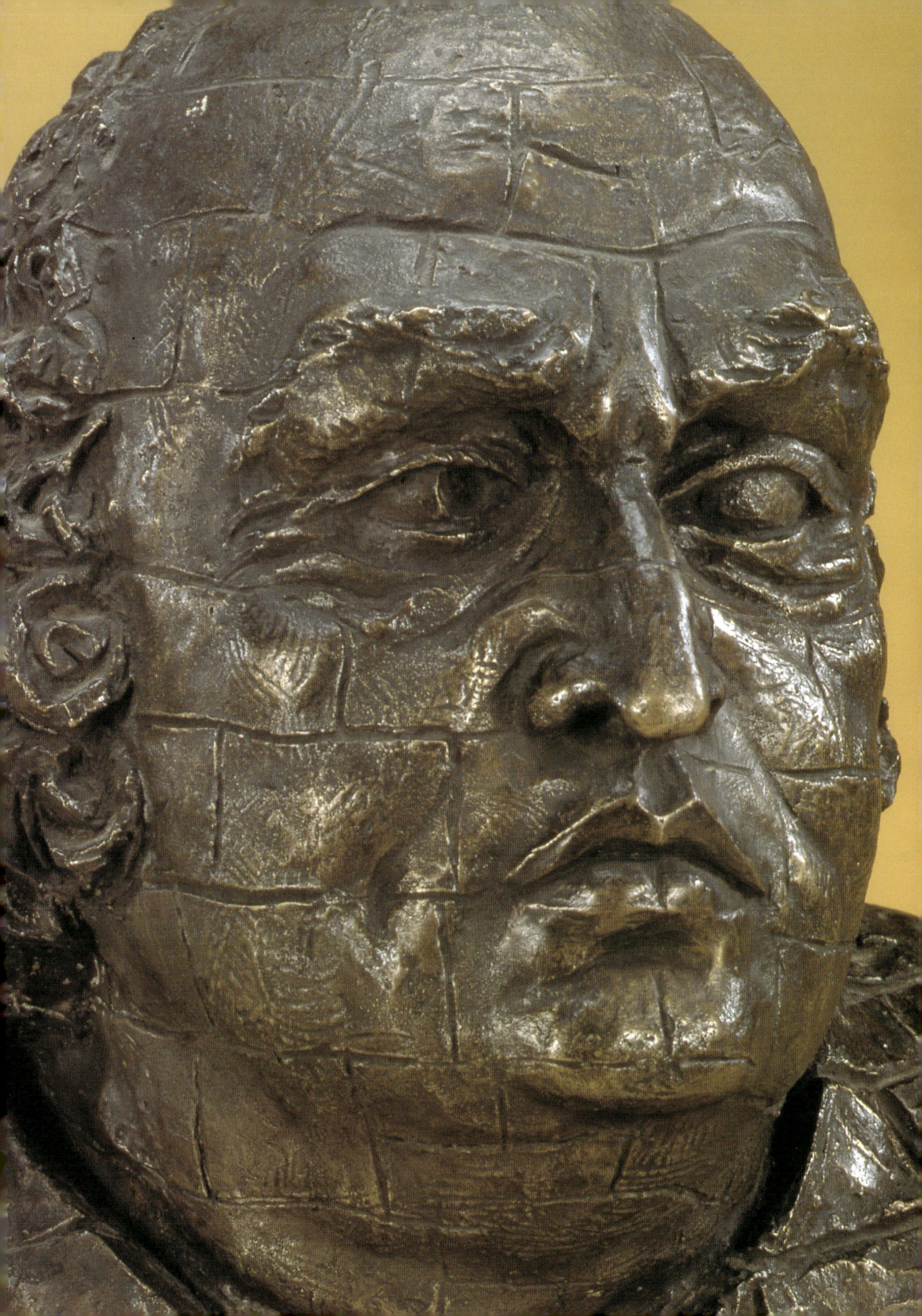

Miller planned a sequel to *The Air-Conditioned Nightmare,* which was to include Man Ray "and those days in Hollywood . . . the more enjoyable phases of that trip."[36] Miller paid perhaps the greatest compliment by printing postcards with Man Ray's 1934 *Observatory Time—The Lovers* reproduced on end, a small advertisement for the artist he admired.

Man Ray and Miller also converged in their admiration for Knud Merrild, a Danish painter relocated in Los Angeles. In 1944, Man Ray shot a portrait of Merrild, one version of which would be used on the cover of the catalogue for his 1948 retrospective at the short-lived Modern Institute of Art on North Rodeo Drive. Merrild's portrait was also published in *Circle*, an avant-garde magazine based in Berkeley, though without a conventional credit line since Man Ray wanted to quash the "legend" of "being a portrait photographer." Instead he asked for the intriguing caption, "Trial for television makeup on Knud Merrild by Man Ray," apparently a reference to their appearance on the Paramount Network to discuss modern art.[37]

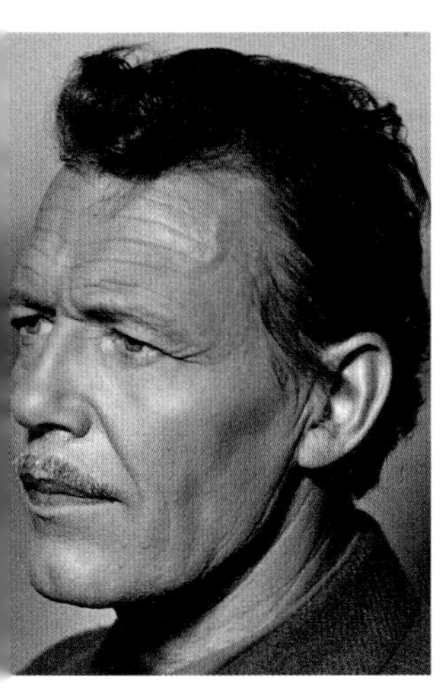

Knud Merrild, 1944
Gelatin-silver print

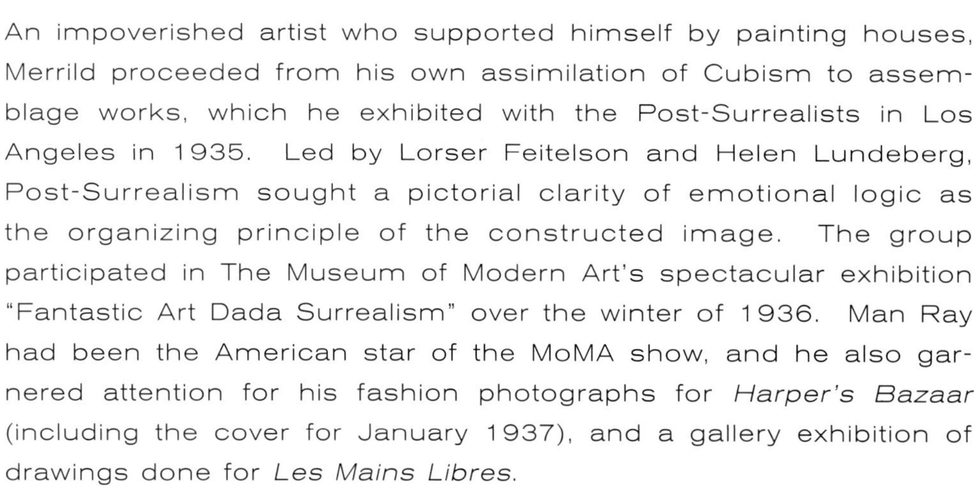

An impoverished artist who supported himself by painting houses, Merrild proceeded from his own assimilation of Cubism to assemblage works, which he exhibited with the Post-Surrealists in Los Angeles in 1935. Led by Lorser Feitelson and Helen Lundeberg, Post-Surrealism sought a pictorial clarity of emotional logic as the organizing principle of the constructed image. The group participated in The Museum of Modern Art's spectacular exhibition "Fantastic Art Dada Surrealism" over the winter of 1936. Man Ray had been the American star of the MoMA show, and he also garnered attention for his fashion photographs for *Harper's Bazaar* (including the cover for January 1937), and a gallery exhibition of drawings done for *Les Mains Libres*.

Now out of the limelight in Hollywood, Man Ray generously wrote "A Letter to the Artist" to the obscure Knud Merrild—which was published in *California Arts and Architecture* in January 1943. By this time Merrild had moved from assemblage to an extensive exploration of "flux" painting, a process by which he allowed paint to flow onto a surface. "When in motion," he explained, "incessant mutation of color and form ensue until arrested in a metaphor of its own flux." Merrild had clearly developed a variation on Surrealist automatism when he referred to his flux painting as "an automatic

pages 47-50:
Letter from Man Ray to Knud Merrild, 1942

Hollywood, December 20, 1942

My dear Merrild,

I am addressing you as one painter to another, something that happens very seldom amongst painters, because they are content, or not content, as the case may be, to look at each others work. In this case, looking at your work, has stimulated certain ideas in me which can best be put into words. Painters often feel this urge to resort to words, as you yourself have; just as your friend D.H.Lawrence felt the necessity of complementing his literary output, which was so complete and stimulating, with excursions into the domain of painting.

It is not inadequacy of the medium, or its lack of eloquence that will lead a painter into another field of expression, but his innate sense of economy that makes him choose the most direct medium for his thoughts. Even so , he will use words as if they were paint, just as the writer who turns to painting will make of it a literary vehicle.

I watched Picasso several years ago, in one of his prolonged moods of intense feeling and rage, turn out dozens of poems scrawled over large pages of white paper, that were good just to look at, even if one could not read the Spanish in which they were written. This finally culminated in the painting of the Guernica, which is black and white, and still bears indications of writing or print, that becomes entirely illegible.

When,in your painting, you break through the second dimension to give us additional planes in front or behind, your sense of reality, and the intensity of your feelings are satisfied by this symbol of free action. You are also continuing, or projecting into your painting your every day experiences, which gives you a sense of living to the fulness of your powers.

Every contemporary painter who has studied and reacted to the marvelous innovations and variations developed in painting during the last two generations, every such painter who has any sense of initiative, and the fearlessness indispensable to an explorer, has sought in one way or another to contribute to the accelerated tempo of an art that has practically been infused with new energy; this art of painting that has been the springboard for so many other developments in the realms of architecture, science, optics, chemistry and psychology. It would be easy, but it would take a whole book to show how many of our most prized discoveries and additions to living had their origin in the palette of the painter. In many instances it was the painter himself who turned his brush into a magic wand, to project into space, into the three dimensional world his dreams, and to give the more timid scientist his incentive to exploration. Leonardo da Vinci, Daguerre, Fulton, Morse, are a few of the names. The restless nights spent by Ucello to work out that perspective which was to enable him to penetrate the surface of his canvas, to permit him to enter a new world of space and illusion that would compete favorably with the most prosaic reality, and displace it; ~~findsxitx~~ this effort of Ucello was but a forerunner of your effort to create space in a two-dimensional plane, one of the most profound activities the human mind is capable of. It is the effort of the human mind ~~mind~~ to reduce the irrational and the inexplicable to a docile reason. Why shouldn't the artist be allowed to pursue ~~dix~~ this avowedly absurd activity, when the axioms of men who made a specialty of logic and reason, were found vulnerable.

Some may call your work tricky- I tell them that the tricks of today are the truths of tomorrow.

I cannot resort to criticism or praise; long ago my interest in another man's work was determined by the personality I was able to read in the work of art, and I was attracted or repelled accordingly. Once the personality became sympathetic to me, whatever the school or tendancies of the artist, I accepted without reserve all of that man's work. To have preferred one work of that man to another would have been a doubtful esthetic game, as practised by many critics, even dishonest. It would be as if one were to prefer your signature to a certain document, in preference to the same signature to another document.

Having first seen your work and then spoken with you, I have been fascinated and convinced. The consistency running through all your works, their appeal to my mind and to my senses, have given me a feeling of satisfaction that is best explained in your own words: "rather than seek to escape illusion, we must accept it as an integral part of painting--as its very nature."

Yes, there would be no question of problem or experiment in painting, for the spectator as well as for the painter, if we could only give ourself over completely to the created illusion as the door to enjoyment. If we did not resist or suspect the painter's motives. After all, we live in a world where we are daily forced to accept facts merely because they are facts; yet if they had been prophesied before they happened we would have been incredulous. Well,your paintings are accomplished facts, facts even underlined by the very precision oftheir realization, and I accept them eagerly, and in preference to so many other facts of daily existence, facts whose permanency I am much less sure of than I am of the permanency of your work. Of course, it may be destroyed or lost, as has happened to so many other intriguing works

(I leave the word "great" purposely to the historians), but it cannot be changed, or become the work of another personality than is yours.

Was it Kandinsky who struggled so hard to prove that his abstractions were the most concrete of manifestations? What a waste of time, just as the efforts of certain scientists or mystics to prove that all matter was non-existent. Who cares whether we live in a concrete or intangible world? They have even said that pain is an illusion. If that be true, then we must put our faith only into illusions, for it is by illusion that we react and continue to live, or die!

As long as you can continue to create the illusions, you are creating, you are the master of your destiny, and you have the edge on the critics and the doubters. If there be one other soul who believes in you, your work is justified; and even if that soul is lacking, your work justifies itself. If only for the reason that nothing can change it. There is a fact for you.

I have already implied that your personality as it expresses itself in your work, has great significance for me because it creates a complete illusion of a personality that provides me with enjoyment. This is a very rare event in one's life. It is the experience of having played a very satisfactory game with a friend, or had a very stimulating conversation free from argument, that opened new horizons, and gave one the courage to develop ones own powers.

I am very grateful to you, my dear Merrild, for having shown me your work, and for having told me things that one painter would like so much to tell another, but so seldom has the courage.

MAN RAY

creation of natural law, a kinetic painting of the abstract." Man Ray would have been attracted to Merrild's Surrealist variant, having photographed "space writings" of moving light in the late 1930s. Merrild speculated to Miller that "Man Ray has photographed the disintegrating movements of a drop of ink in a glass of water."[38]

Man Ray most likely remembered Merrild when he later returned to Paris and began to make "natural paintings" by an automatic process, integral to the Surrealist exploration of the unconscious. In *Self Portrait* he explained that "by spreading the colors according to the impulse of the moment," he "abandoned brushes and palette knives [as he had abandoned the camera in discovering the Rayograph process in the 1920s], and applied pressure with other surfaces, withdrawing them to produce a variation of the Rorschach test."[39] A specific example of Man Ray's method is the mirror image of impasto in a doubled-up *Ma bête noire et ma boite noire—A Pair of Natural Paintings*, beast and box brought together in 1965.

Man Ray demonstrated that the process could be controlled in a "natural painting" that became the catalogue cover for his 1966 retrospective exhibition at the recently reconstituted Los Angeles County Museum of Art on Wilshire Boulevard.[40] Comprised of an impasto "Man Ray 1966," the painting updated an early oil painting titled *Man Ray 1914*. The artist's signature, as Duchamp would claim, was sufficient in defining an artifact as a work of art.

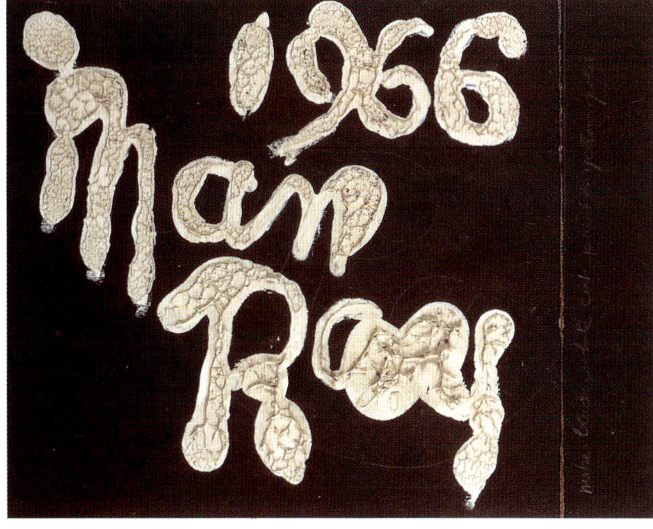

right:
***Natural Painting, Man Ray**, 1966*
Acrylic on card from a Kodak photographic paper box

overleaf:
***Ma bête noire et ma boite noire – A Pair of Natural Paintings**, 1965*
Acrylic on masonite in the artist's wooden box

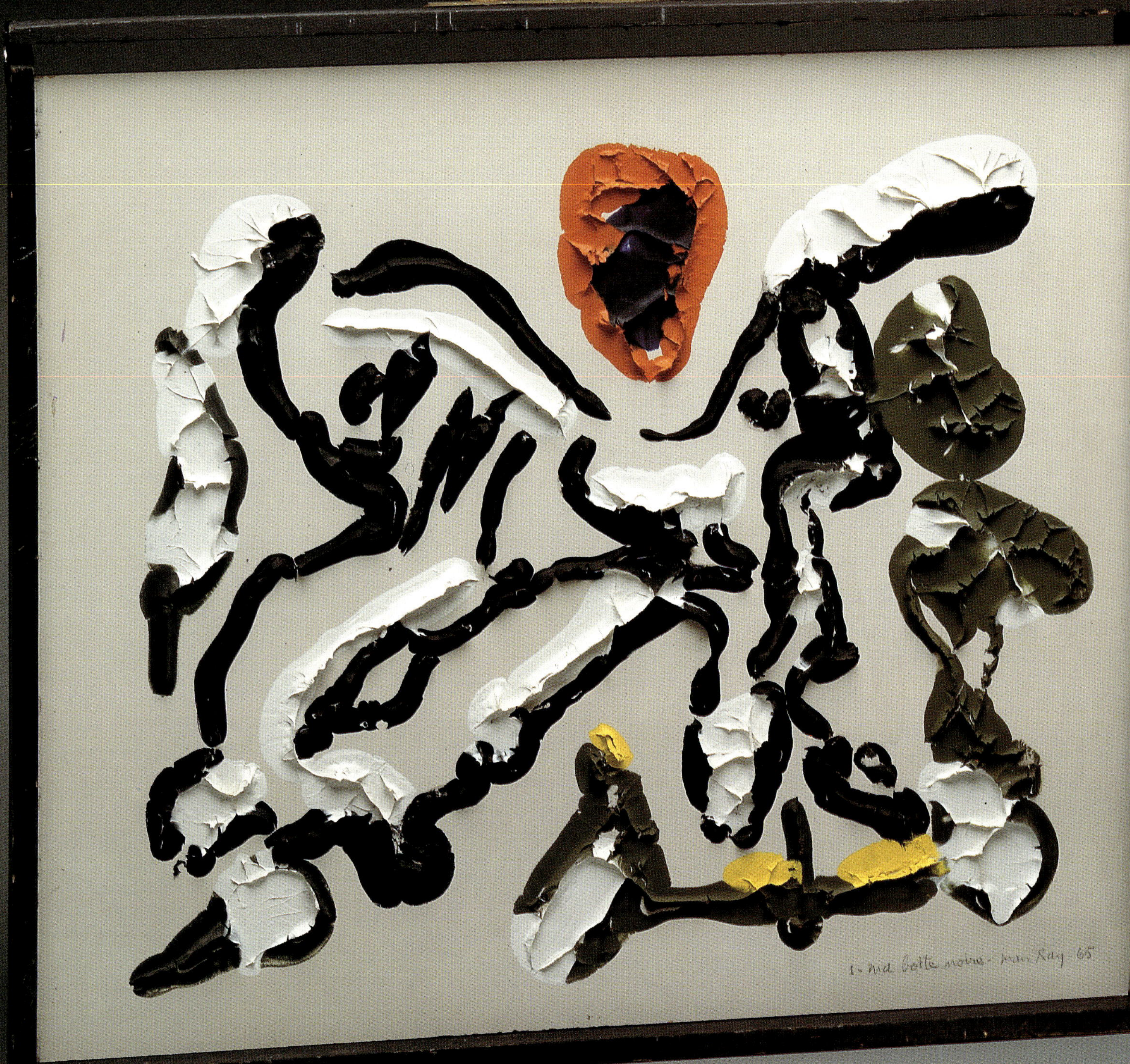
1 - ma boîte noire - man Ray - 65

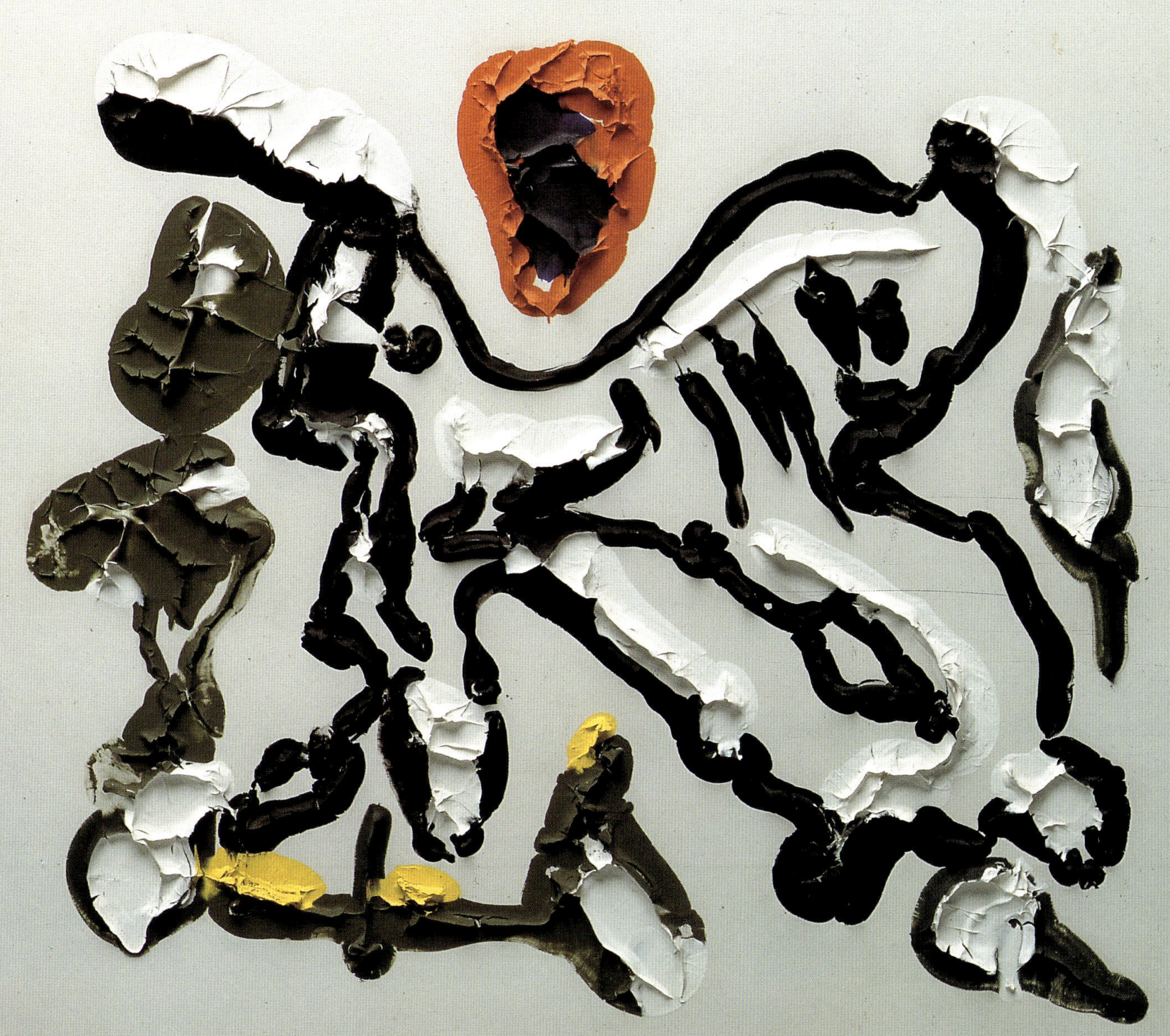
2- Ma bête noire - man Ray. 65

In 1943, however, Man Ray's admiration had less to do with any specific work or technique than with the example that Merrild set as an artist who had gone his own way over the years. As one *isolato* to another, Man Ray praised Merrild "for having told me things that one painter would like so much to tell another but so seldom has the courage." To continue alone, "to contribute to the accelerated tempo of an art [of painting] that has practically been infused with new energy," but above all to engage in the act of painting: he claimed that Merrild lived to the fullest of his powers.[41] These qualities gave Man Ray the courage to continue working in Southern California in the face of hostile criticism or, what was worse, misunderstanding and indifference.

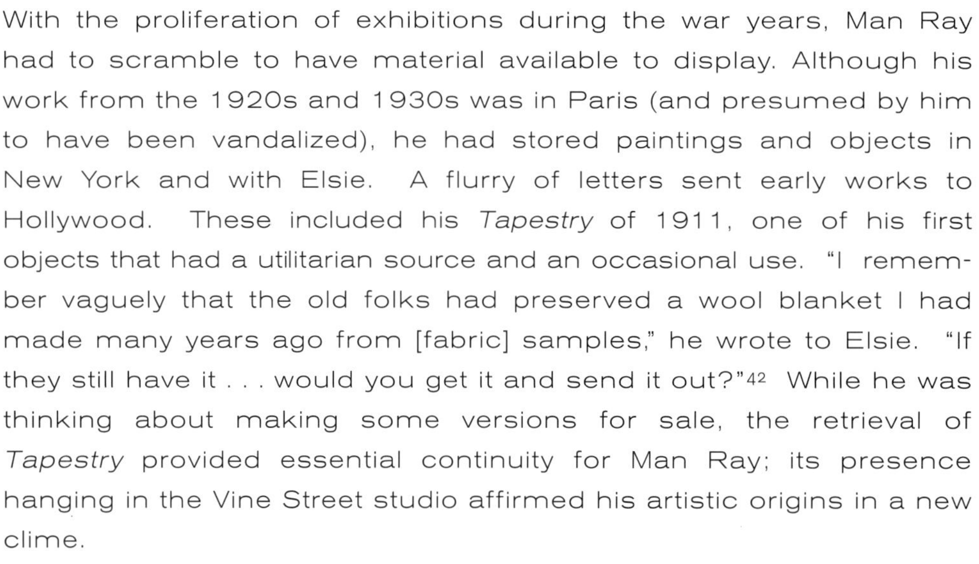

With the proliferation of exhibitions during the war years, Man Ray had to scramble to have material available to display. Although his work from the 1920s and 1930s was in Paris (and presumed by him to have been vandalized), he had stored paintings and objects in New York and with Elsie. A flurry of letters sent early works to Hollywood. These included his *Tapestry* of 1911, one of his first objects that had a utilitarian source and an occasional use. "I remember vaguely that the old folks had preserved a wool blanket I had made many years ago from [fabric] samples," he wrote to Elsie. "If they still have it . . . would you get it and send it out?"[42] While he was thinking about making some versions for sale, the retrieval of *Tapestry* provided essential continuity for Man Ray; its presence hanging in the Vine Street studio affirmed his artistic origins in a new clime.

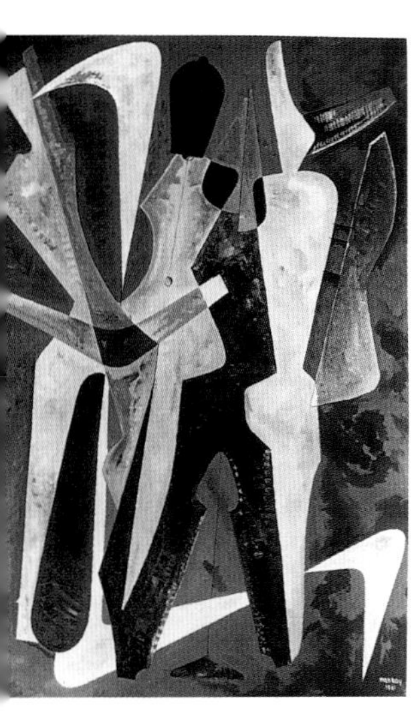

Promenade, 1941
Oil on canvas

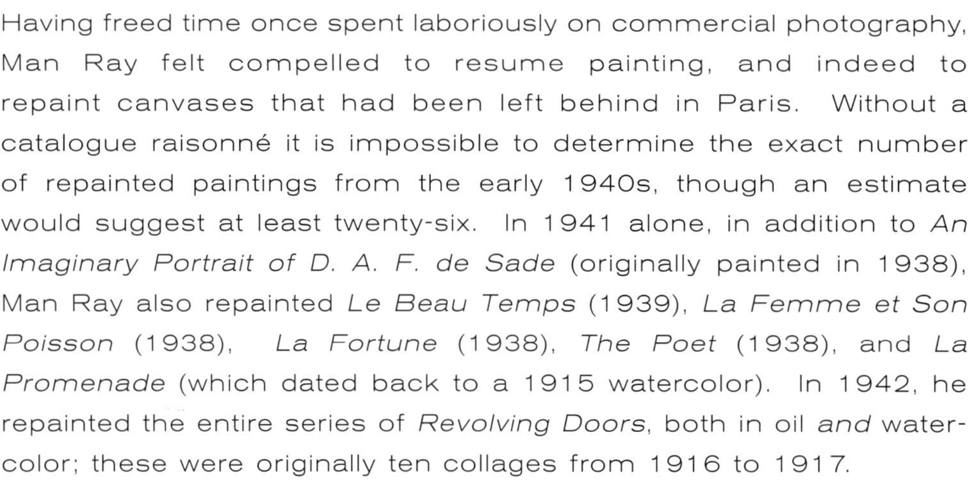

Having freed time once spent laboriously on commercial photography, Man Ray felt compelled to resume painting, and indeed to repaint canvases that had been left behind in Paris. Without a catalogue raisonné it is impossible to determine the exact number of repainted paintings from the early 1940s, though an estimate would suggest at least twenty-six. In 1941 alone, in addition to *An Imaginary Portrait of D. A. F. de Sade* (originally painted in 1938), Man Ray also repainted *Le Beau Temps* (1939), *La Femme et Son Poisson* (1938), *La Fortune* (1938), *The Poet* (1938), and *La Promenade* (which dated back to a 1915 watercolor). In 1942, he repainted the entire series of *Revolving Doors*, both in oil *and* watercolor; these were originally ten collages from 1916 to 1917.

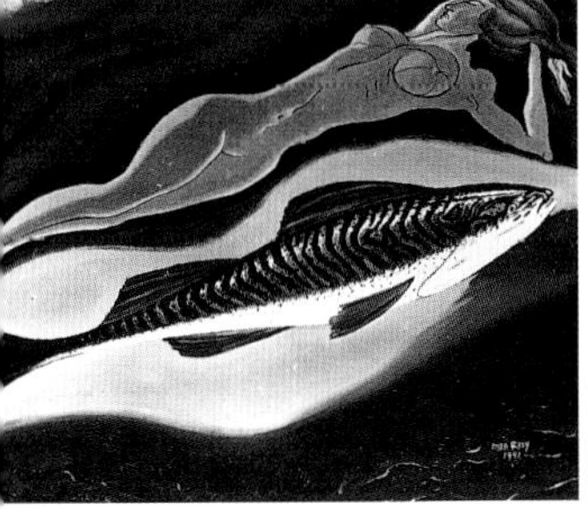

On a sheer practical level, the repainted paintings served to replenish the work Man Ray thought vandalized by war; at the very least, the project was necessary to provide a hoped-for source of income. Yet the process of repainting had many layers of meaning, covering over the ruptures in Man Ray's life. The repaintings were, above all, his effort to stave off the destruction of war, to deny that it had the power to destroy his work back in Paris. Though at the time he was pessimistic that the work had survived, the act of painting became an affirmative gesture that would heal the trauma of war.

Using photographs that he had managed to carry with him out of Paris, he repainted *Le Beau Temps*, a large compendium of brightly colored symbols, an uneasy mix of the geometric and the organic, an anxiety-ridden melange of monsters, fierce beasts, and lovers. The visual image ironically suggests the worst of times, but could Man Ray eventually cut through the irony to find his fair weather once again in California?

In a much smaller version (as though to distance the war, assuage the pain), the repainted *Beau Temps* can be seen along with *The Poet* in a photograph of Juliet lying on a divan. *La Fortune*, of course, could also be ironically construed, though in its reincarnation it might have become a talisman of good luck: in its final version, as an object, it became a wheel of fortune. And *La Femme et son poisson*, woman and fish in embrace, retraced a drawing from *Les Mains Libres*, which in turn echoed a superimposition of Lee Miller's lips on Kiki's, floating over Paris in *Observatory Time—The Lovers*.

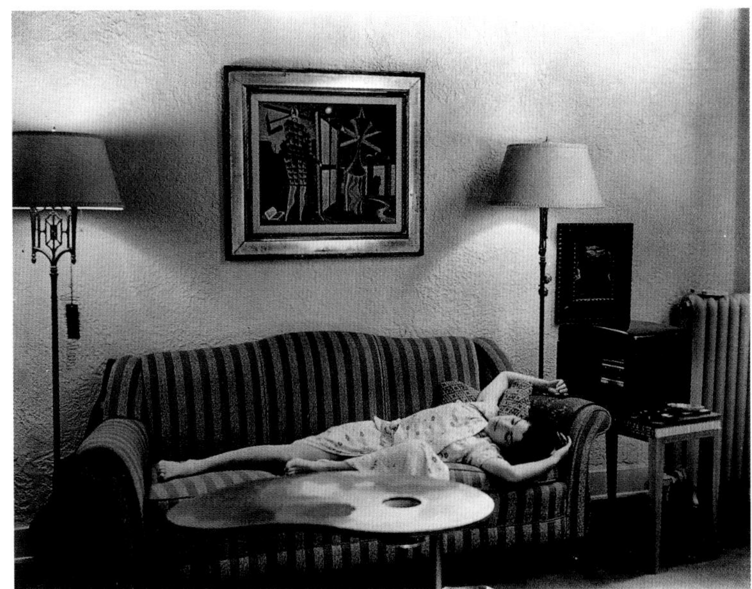

top:
La Femme et son poisson II, 1941 *Oil on canvas*

right:
Juliet on couch at 1245 Vine Street, c. 1945
Gelatin-silver print

Le Beau Temps, 1939 *Oil on canvas*

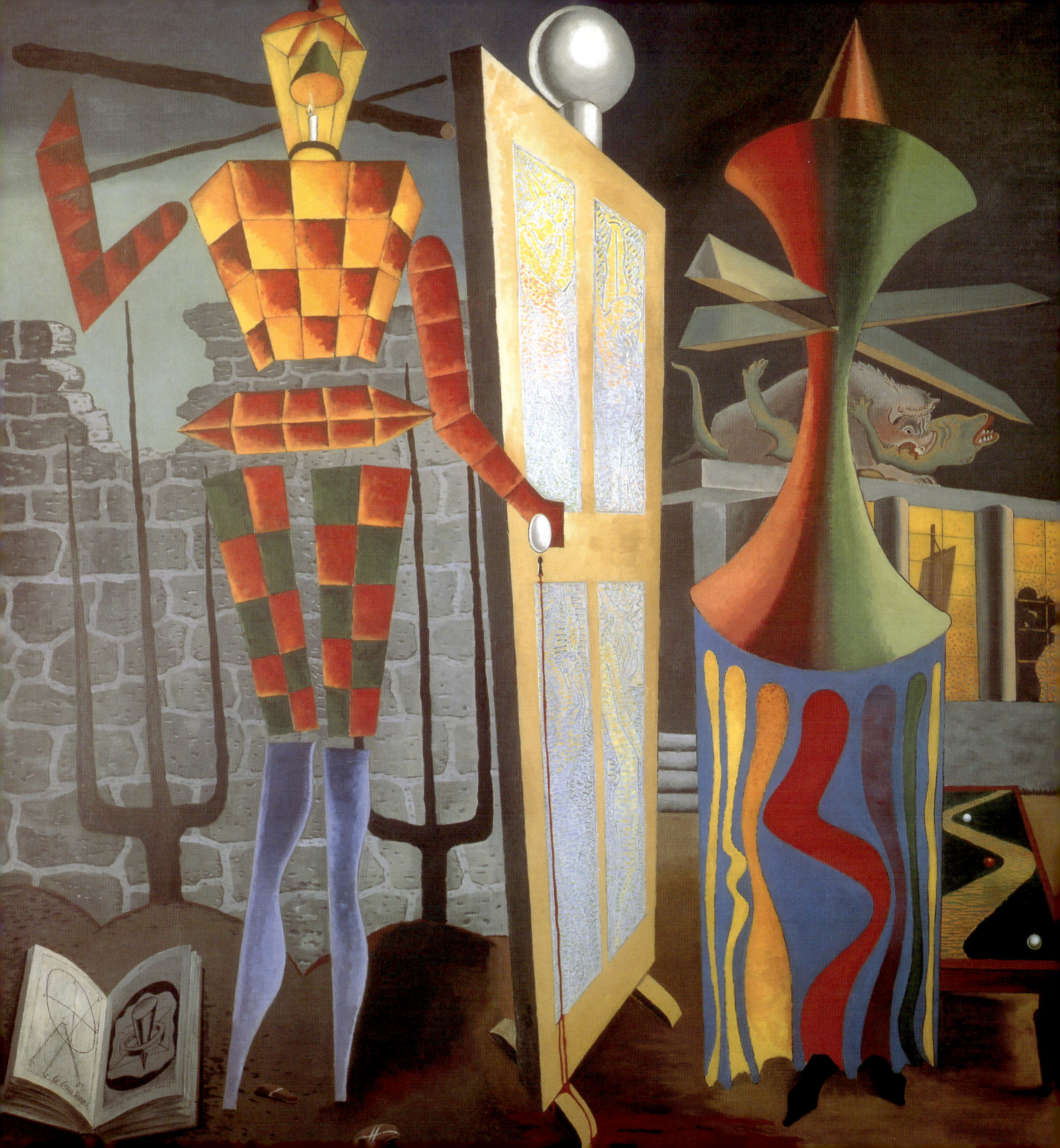

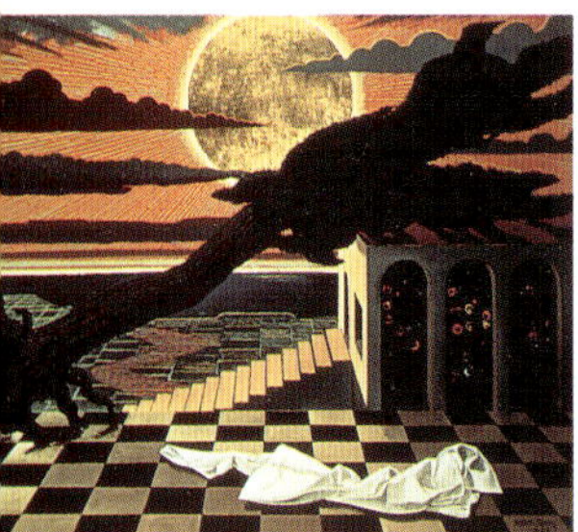

In repainting as an act of reliving life in the familiar environ of the studio (thereby recalling a phase of his life in Paris), Man Ray had fashioned an aesthetic rationale for this project. His efforts demonstrated a paradoxical contempt for the medium (in this instance, painting): the virtuosity necessary to duplicate the work denigrates the medium (and technique)—look how easy it is—while the very need for virtuosity exalts the medium. Man Ray's (often heated) insistence that he had never painted a recent painting, that he did not repeat himself, was ultimately the flip side of Duchamp's idea of the readymade and duplications: a close or even an exact copy of a painting or its variation is no less unique than the original oil painting from which it is generated—just as a mass-produced object, a bottle rack, for instance, can be transformed into a work of art by the artist and his signature.[43]

Man Ray also painted some new canvases in the early 1940s. These included *Leda and the Swan* (1942), *Infinite Man* (1942), whose depiction of a mechanistic figure subverts the optimistic title, and *Night Sun—Abandoned Playground* (1943), which suggests the deadly serious inversions of war. His mood was not entirely bleak, however. He also painted *Apple, Knife and Legs* (1941), which appeared in his first exhibition at the Frank Perls Gallery (and later mystified Kenneth Ross at the Pasadena retrospective). The disparate body parts (cheesecake) and objects (still life) may have been inspired by *Noire et blanche*, his 1926 photograph of a disembodied Kiki set against an African mask—a photograph that he had requested from Elsie soon after his arrival in Hollywood.[44]

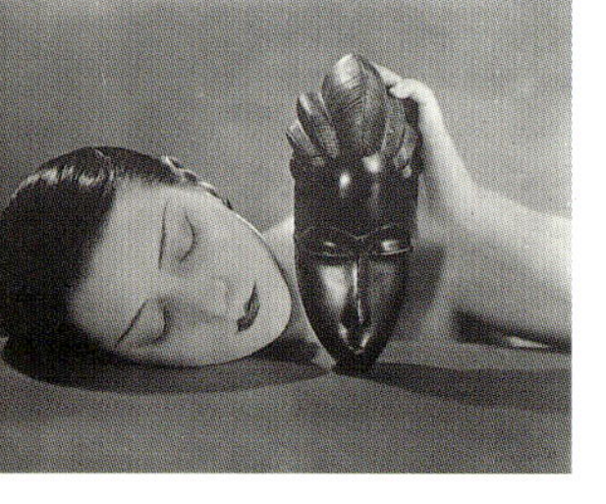

top:
Night Sun – Abandoned Playground, 1943
Oil on canvas

above:
Noire et blanche, 1926
Gelatin-silver print

Man Ray did not completely abandon photography while in Hollywood, and there were certainly several reminders of his photographic work in traveling exhibitions that passed through California. Nevertheless, Man Ray expressed strong antipathy toward the medium. In an unpublished meditation on "Black," he observed that "nearly every painter has a mood when he decides against black—when he feels that his work must eliminate black." After citing the Impressionists and their heightened palettes, he went on to develop the metaphorical implications of black, arriving at the "black swastika, final expression of man's lowest descent!" Well, almost, for in the next sentence he claimed that "there is nothing more depressing than work in a photographic darkroom. Or coal mine!"[45]

At the same time, however, Man Ray soothed this unexpected vehemence with a "Calm Diatribe," which concludes:

> And now the blackening by light
> Of a silver sheet
> Confounds our most precious proverbs.

That both expressions ring true suggests that his loathing came from the darkroom labor associated with commercial photography, despite the economic freedom he gained from it, and no matter his obvious pleasure in photographing beautiful women. When Julien Levy passed through Hollywood with his "caravan of modern art" in November 1941, he recalled that Man Ray insisted that he was not a photographer but a "*faute*grapher," a complex pun that played on the notion of false photography as well as photography based on accident. Manipulation rather than "straight photography," which Man Ray "despised," was his way of sustaining visual innovation.[46]

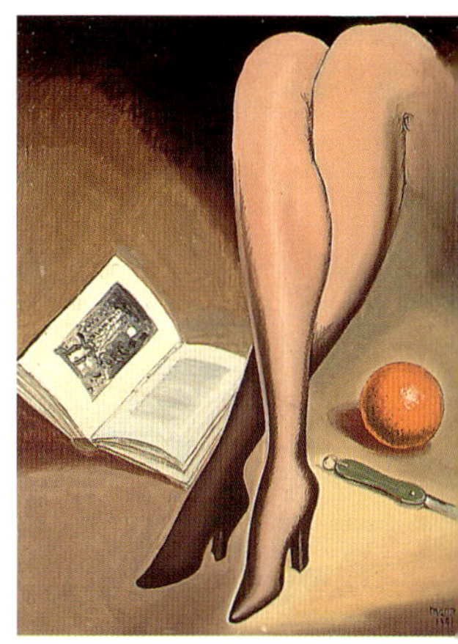

Apple, Knife and Legs, 1941
Oil on canvas

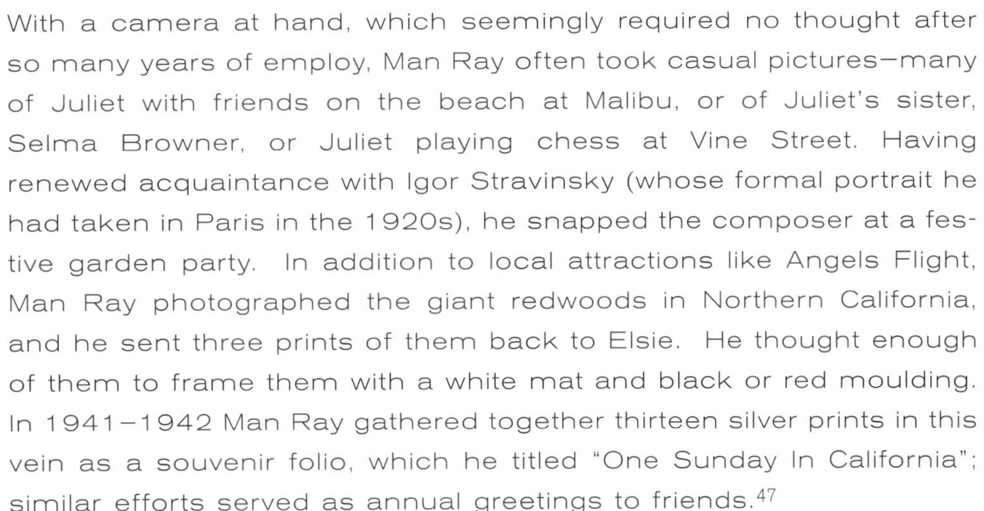

With a camera at hand, which seemingly required no thought after so many years of employ, Man Ray often took casual pictures—many of Juliet with friends on the beach at Malibu, or of Juliet's sister, Selma Browner, or Juliet playing chess at Vine Street. Having renewed acquaintance with Igor Stravinsky (whose formal portrait he had taken in Paris in the 1920s), he snapped the composer at a festive garden party. In addition to local attractions like Angels Flight, Man Ray photographed the giant redwoods in Northern California, and he sent three prints of them back to Elsie. He thought enough of them to frame them with a white mat and black or red moulding. In 1941–1942 Man Ray gathered together thirteen silver prints in this vein as a souvenir folio, which he titled "One Sunday In California"; similar efforts served as annual greetings to friends.[47]

Other photographs were predicated on deliberate compositions, based on "deformations" exercised by a "fautegrapher." In March 1942, for example, *California Arts and Architecture* published a solarized still life of "California objects." For the cover of the June 1943 issue of *View*, an independent Surrealist journal edited by the young poet Charles Henri Ford in New York, Man Ray contributed a solarized still life of a broken chair, a stump, and ballet shoes—such an unlikely group of objects that Ford was led to write, "Your cover has had a great success—even with those who weren't enthusiastic before it *became* a cover!" The October 1943 issue of *Minicam Photography* presented a "Man Ray Folio" of five photographs with his commentary. Included was *The Dying Leaf*, a dramatic image that caught Man Ray's attention because of its "poignant quality": "the dying leaf would be completely gone tomorrow."[48]

In 1944 Man Ray unwrapped a package and accidentally dropped the twine on the floor. Fascinated by the design, and unable to preserve the actual entanglement, he took a photograph and made a solarized print.[49] Mordantly titled *Enough Rope*, the image played a variation on Duchamp's exercise in establishing a new unit of measurement, based on chance, for his monumental *Large Glass* project. (Duchamp's *Three Standard Stoppages* preserves in glass the curvatures of three threads one meter in length dropped from a height of one meter.)

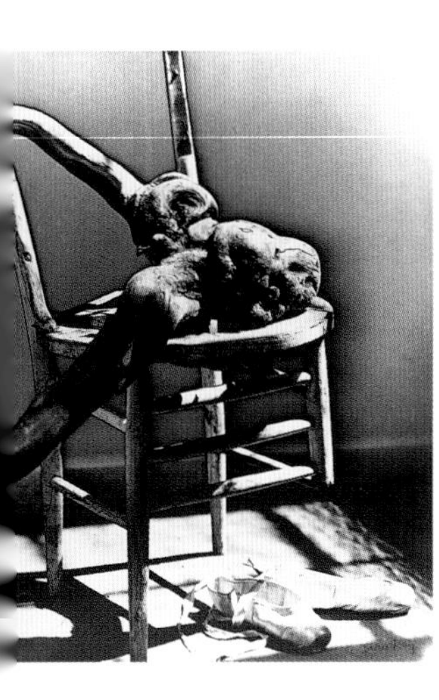

For a special issue of *View* devoted to his work, Duchamp sought Man Ray's assistance in 1944. The invitation amounted to a *carte blanche*: Send photographs of Rrose Sélavy (Duchamp's female alter ego), for example, write a long caption or a short note, whatever might pass through your head. Along with several photographs of Duchamp and a 1923 portrait, Man Ray sent his photograph of Duchamp's *Large Glass* construction titled *Élévage de poussiére* (Dust Raising), on which he superimposed Charles Henri Ford's "Flag of Ecstacy" to create a lyrical *homage à trois* to Duchamp. "Didn't we raise the dust, though, old boy!" Man Ray exclaimed in an accompanying "Bilingual Biography," which entwined their friendship in a double chronology. Man Ray's recall moved from the early days in 1915 when they played tennis without a net in Ridgefield, New Jersey, to their departure from France to New York and Hollywood in 1945, united once again by their game: "yes, and chess. Au revoir!"[50]

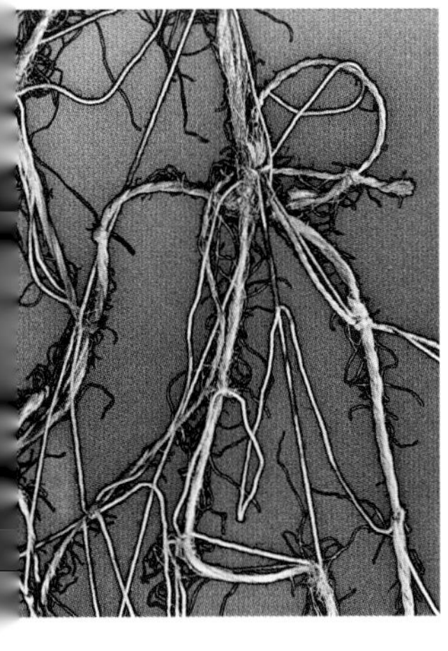

top:
Broken chair with stump and ballet shoes*, 1942*
Solarized gelatin-silver print
Collection of The J. Paul Getty Museum, Malibu, California

above:
Enough Rope*, 1944*
Solarized gelatin-silver print
Collection of The J. Paul Getty Museum, Malibu, California

right:
The Dying Leaf*, early 1940s*
Gelatin-silver print
Collection of The J. Paul Getty Museum, Malibu, California

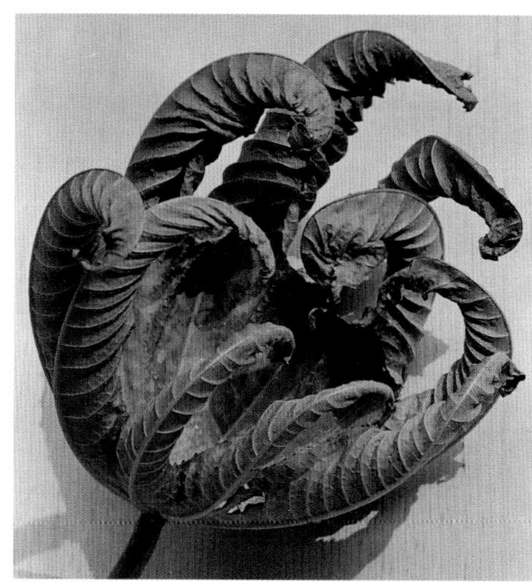

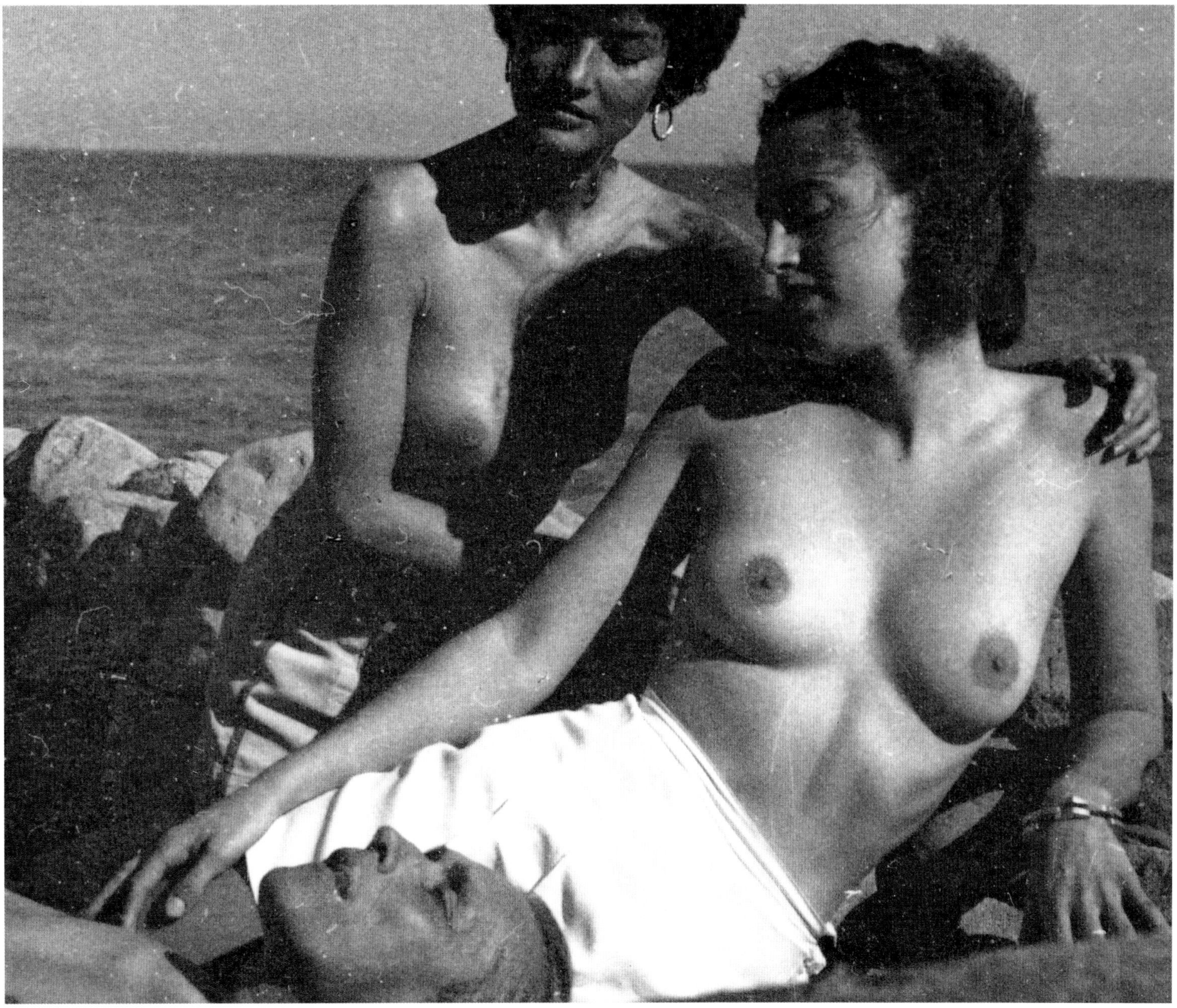

above:
***Juliet and friends**, Malibu,* early 1940s
Gelatin-silver print

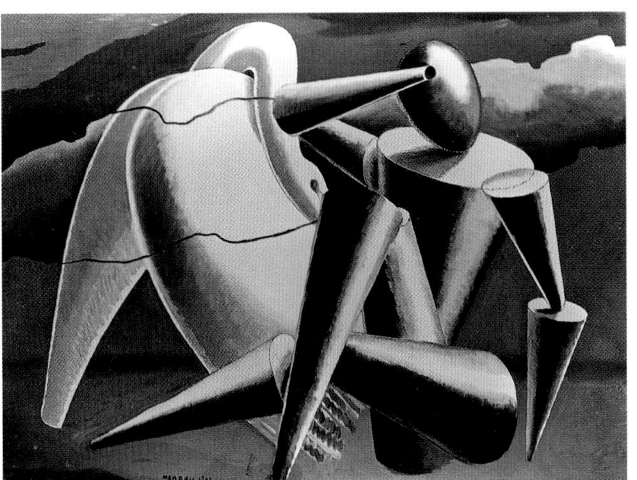

left:
***Leda and the Swan**,* 1941
Oil on canvas

counterclockwise from below:
Portrait of Selma Browner, c. 1945 *Textured gelatin-silver print*

Malibu, c. 1945 *Gelatin-silver print*

Party in Los Angeles, *Selma and Juliet Browner, and Igor Stravinsky in foreground*, 1940s *Gelatin-silver print*

opposite:
Untitled (*Redwood tree*), 1940s *Gelatin-silver print*

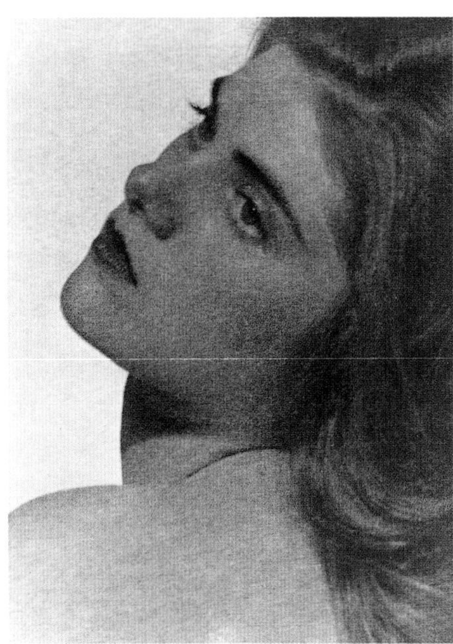

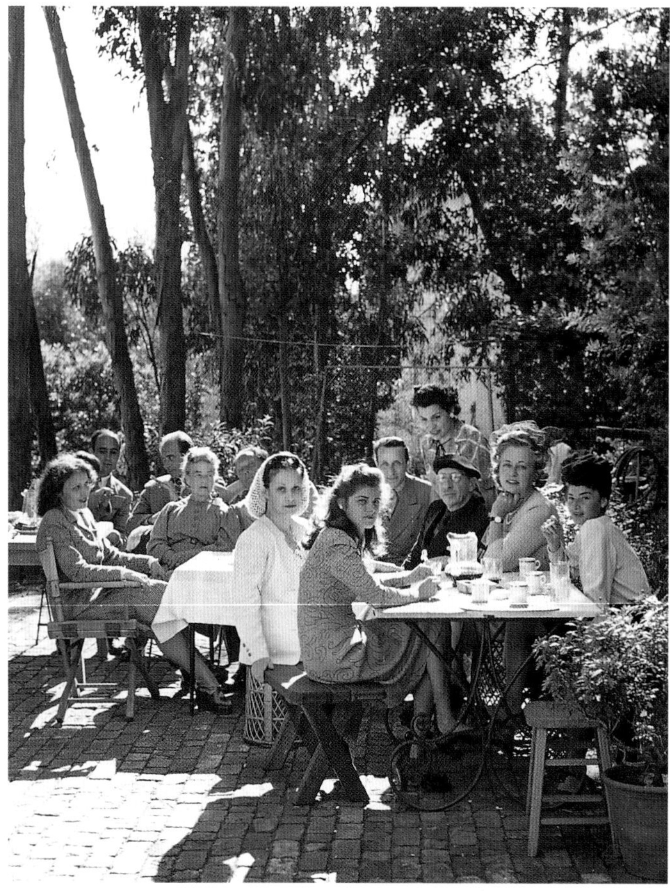

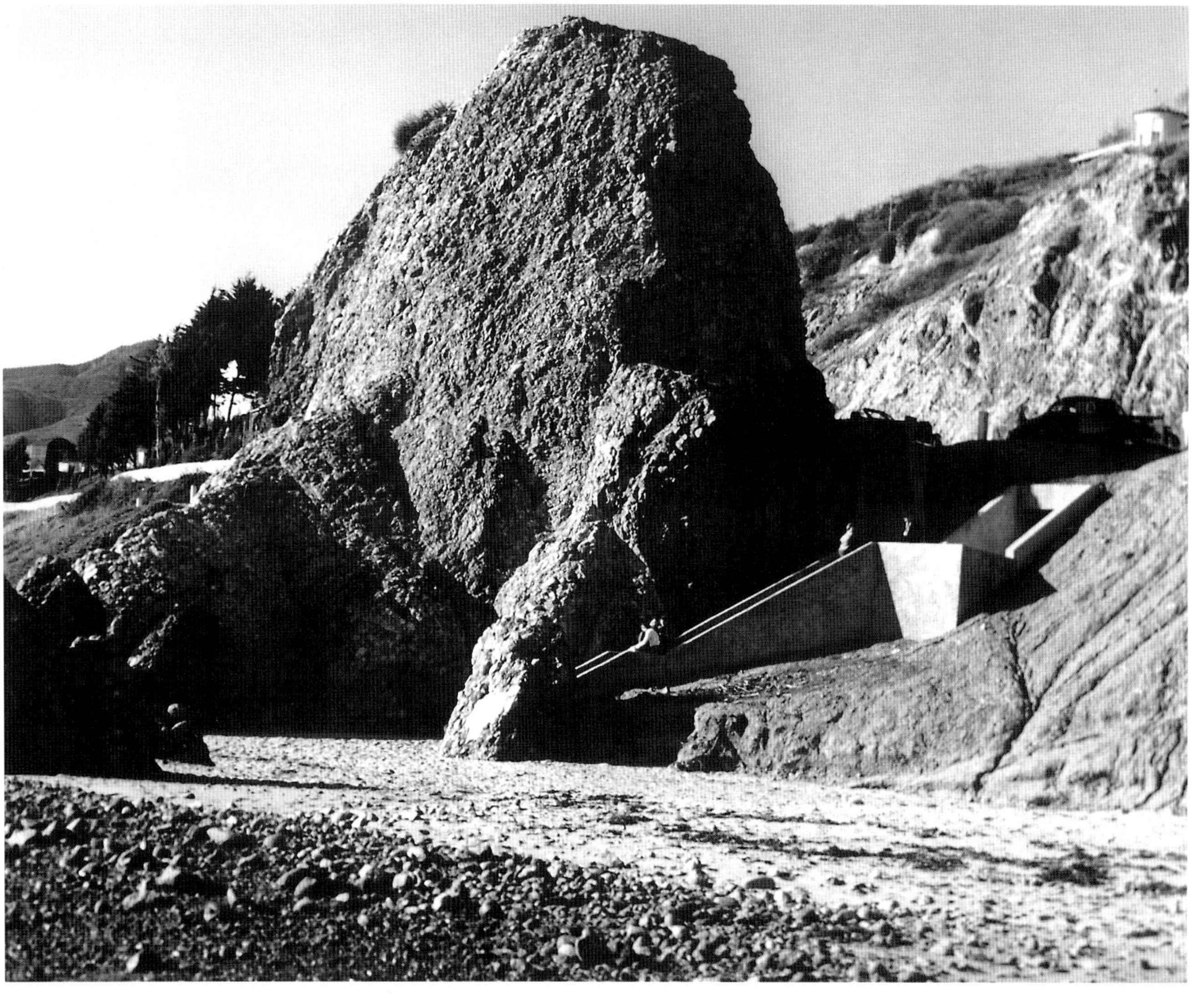

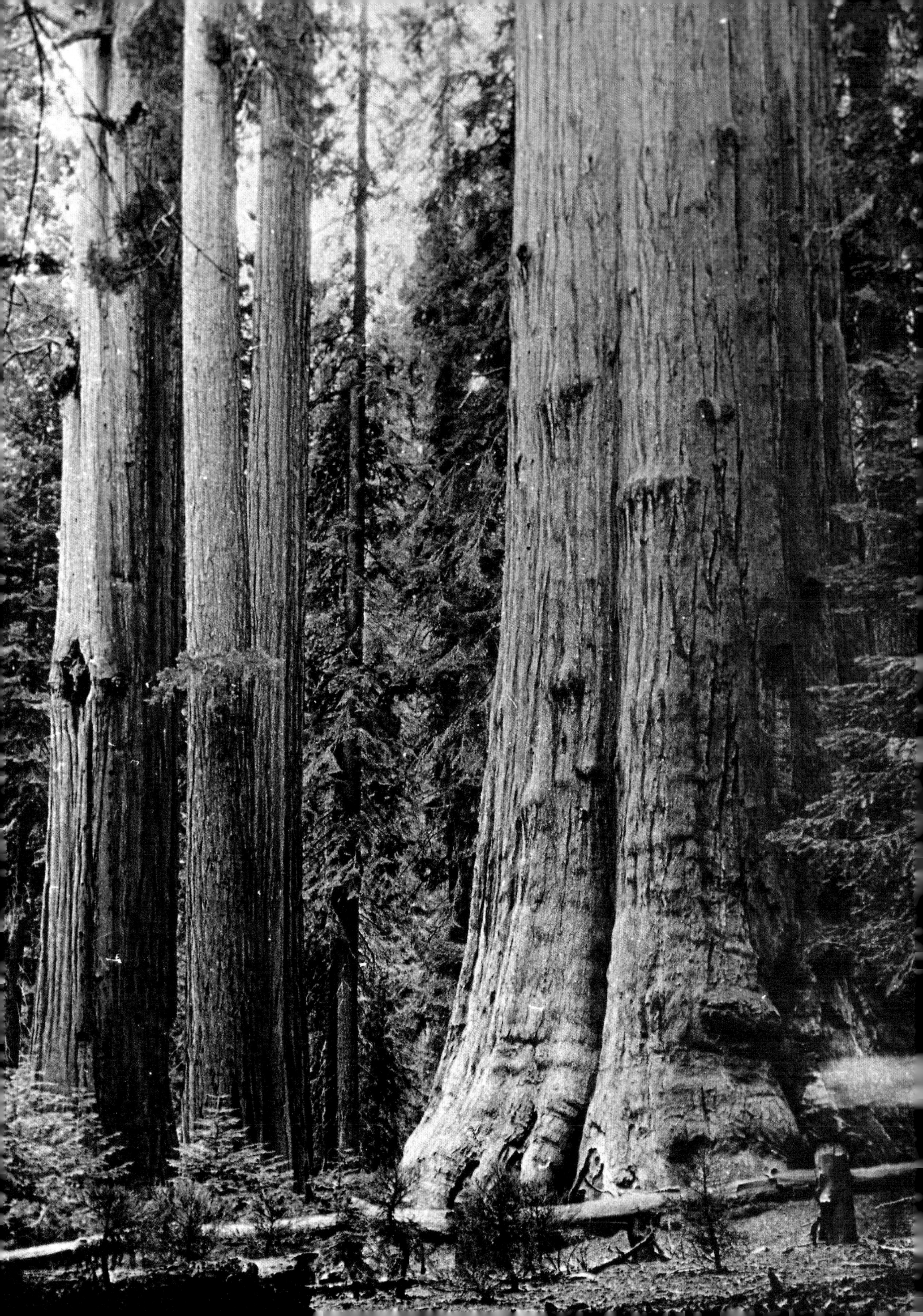

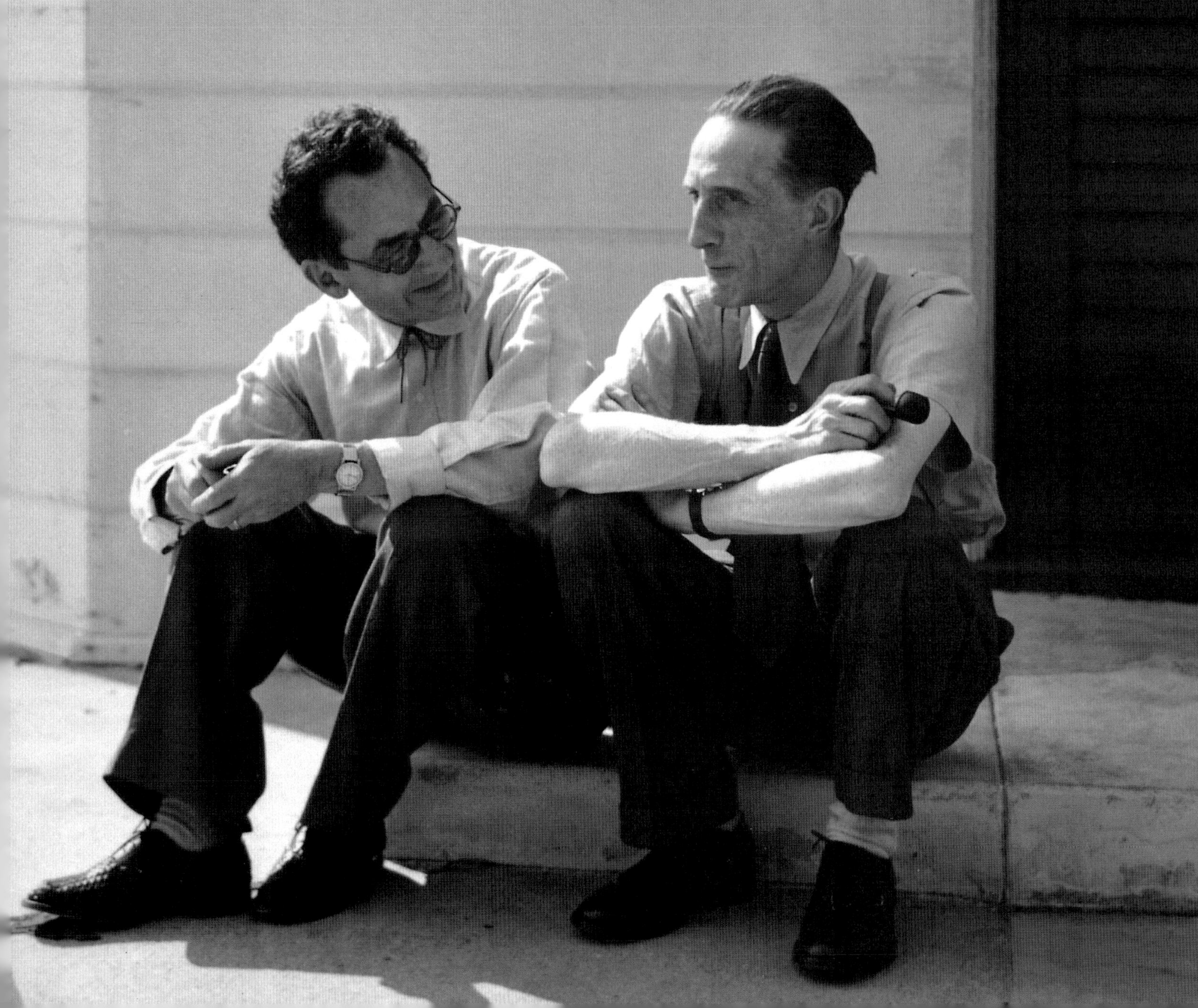
RUE
DE LA
VIEILLE LANTERNE

At Duchamp's suggestion, Julien Levy had decided to mount an exhibition of chess sets designed by artists in December 1944. Duchamp, of course, was a chess fanatic whose enthusiasm had spread to his friends, Man Ray among them. Viewing chess at the very least as a social event—he took countless photographs of Juliet and his friends at play—Man Ray considered chess a metaphor for the creative process. "Find in the chessboard the origin and goal of all graphic art," he wrote to himself, "field for clear thinking, impromptu imagination, surprise, planning for the abstract, solid ground to walk on. . . ."[51]

Not only did chess become a recurrent motif in his painting, photography, and objects, but Man Ray the inveterate craftsman also designed several different chess sets and boards, the earliest dating back to 1921. Making use of his student training in mechanical drawing, he sketched many diagrams with careful specifications for sets he wanted to design. These ranged from early wooden chess pieces (one out of maple and walnut, designed in 1942), to sets he had cast in 1947 out of aluminum. In some versions the opposing pieces were anodized in silver and gold, or a deep red, a process he enthusiastically dubbed "alchemical" (echoing the Surrealists' interest in alchemy). Duchamp became Man Ray's New York agent for these sets, which provided a minor source of income; they sold among the Hollywood crowd, including the big band leader and clarinetist, Artie Shaw.

In some versions of these sets, the king bears an "R" on his crown, designating "*roi*" or "Ray." In all versions, the pieces were based on simple geometric forms—spheres, cubes, and cones deployed in variant combinations to make up pawns, rooks, and bishops. Man Ray eventually simplified the head of the horse from its initial shape derived from the scroll of a violin to create an abstracted knight formally consonant with the other figures. Many of these sets were signed along the exterior edges of the accompanying board. His chess sets, as he had enthusiastically written to Elsie as early as 1930, were "a work of art!"[52]

opposite:
***Man Ray and Marcel Duchamp in Hollywood with French street sign**, 1948*
Gelatin-silver print

overleaf:
*(detail) **Photograph by Man Ray of one of his chess sets**, c. 1943*
Gelatin-silver print

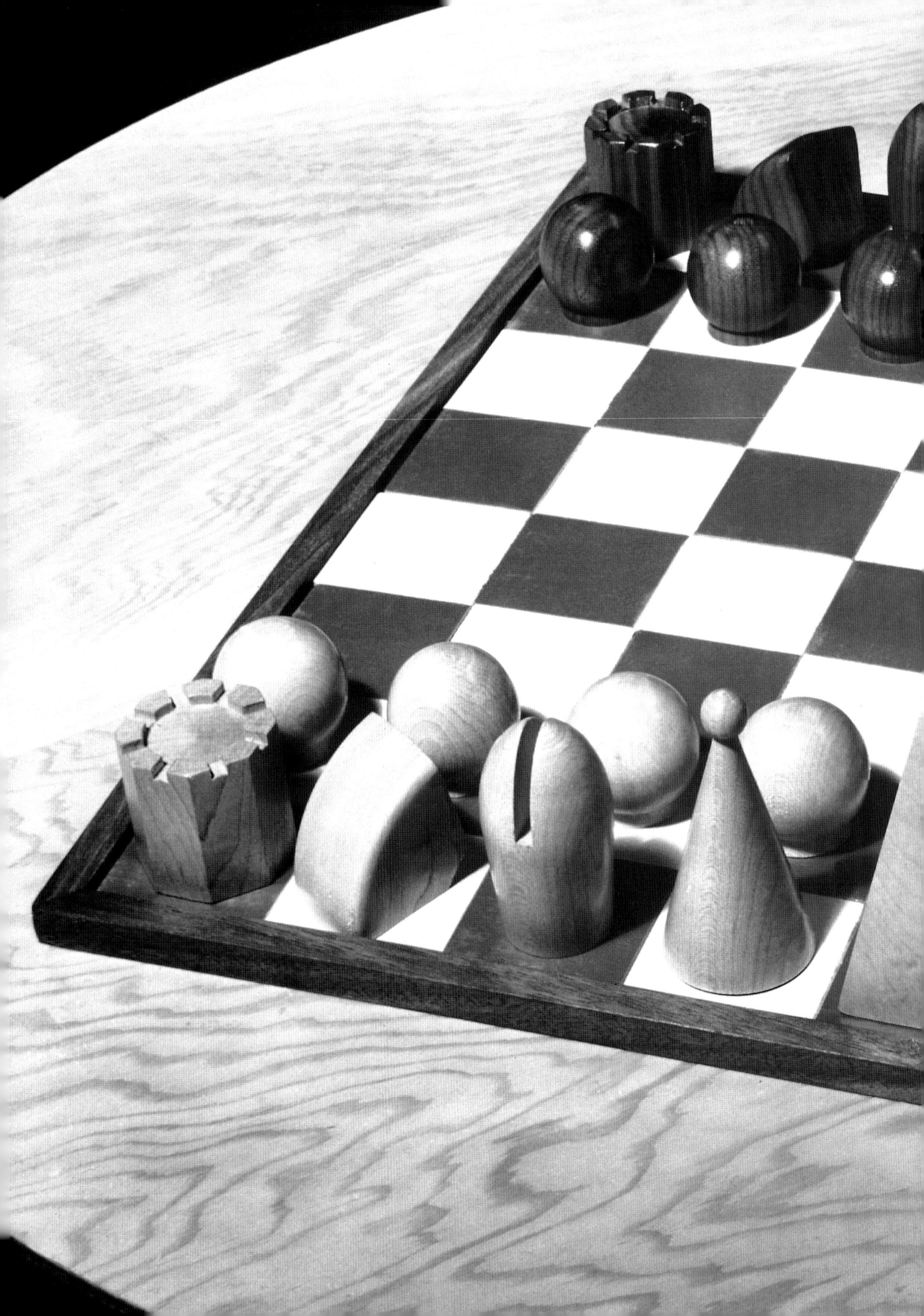

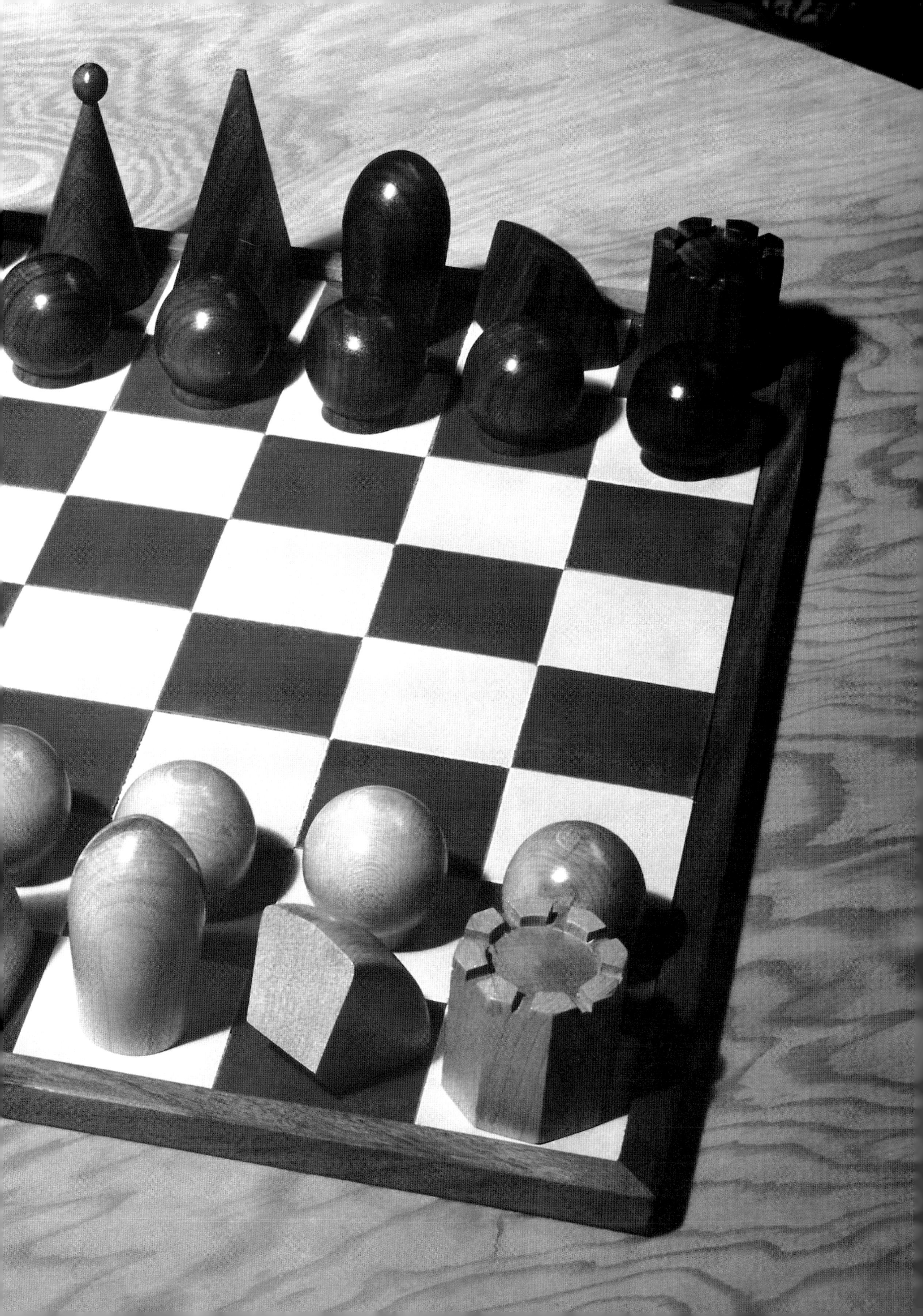

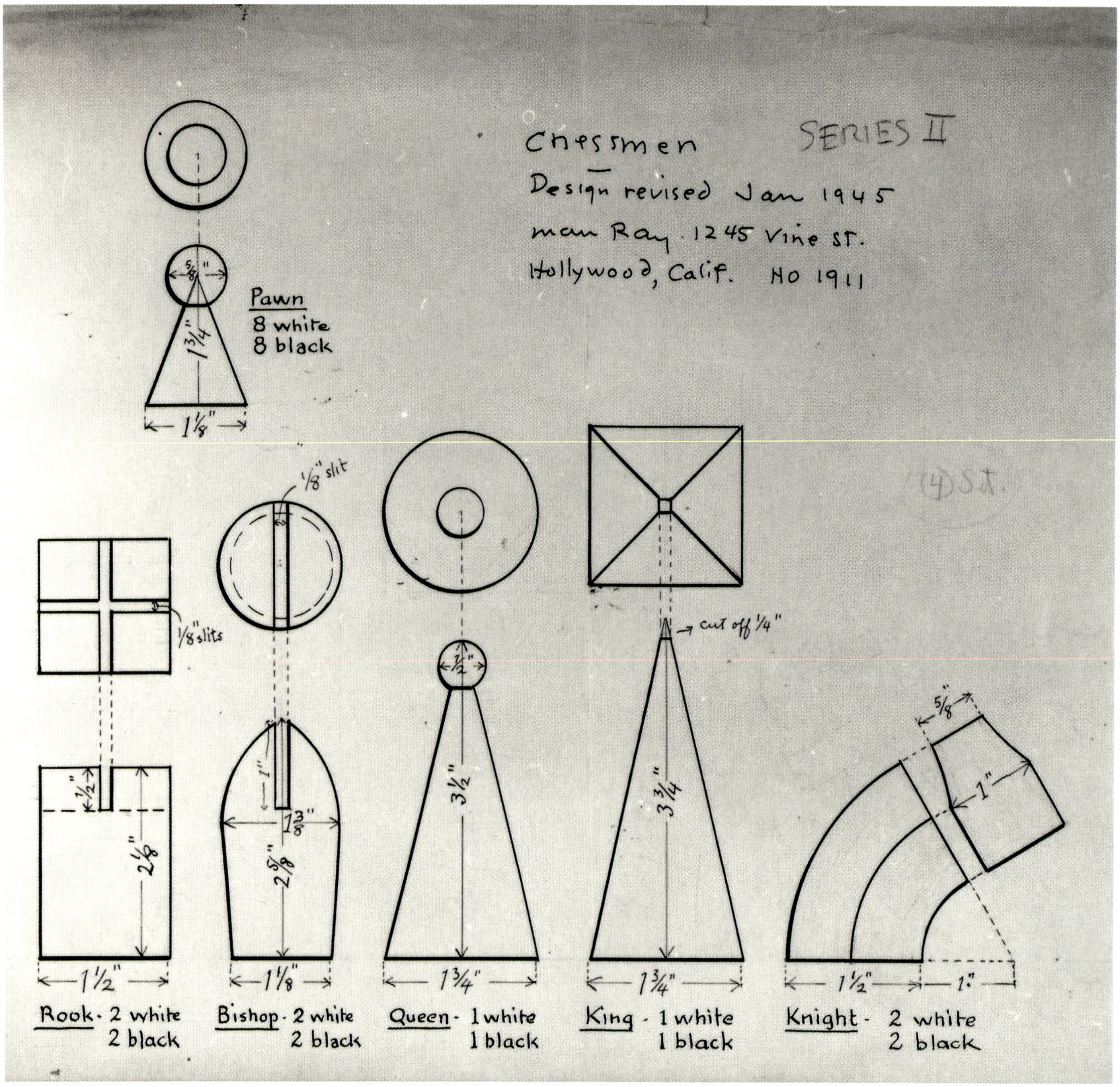

Chessmen SERIES II
Design revised Jan 1945
man Ray. 1245 Vine St.
Hollywood, Calif. HO 1911

Pawn
8 white
8 black

Rook - 2 white
2 black

Bishop - 2 white
2 black

Queen - 1 white
1 black

King - 1 white
1 black

Knight - 2 white
2 black

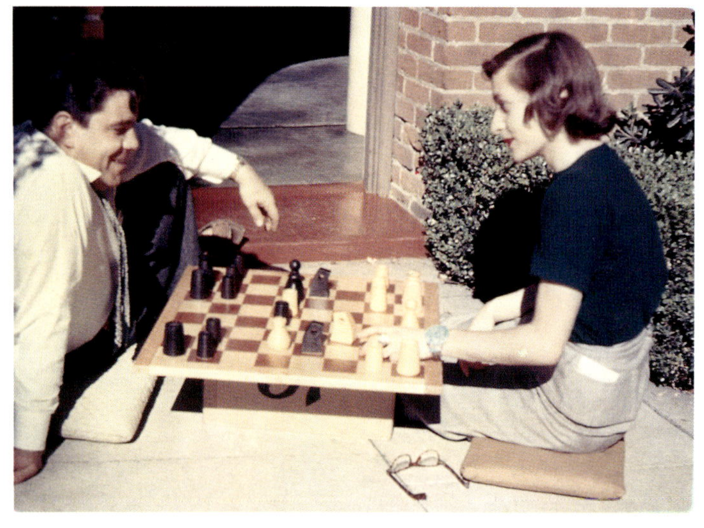

above:
Working design of chess set, 1945
Pen and ink with instruction in blue crayon

left:
William Copley and Gloria de Herrera with a Man Ray chess set, c. 1949 *Ektachrome print*

opposite:
Dr. Alexander Alekhine, *chess champion*, c. 1928 *Gelatin-silver print*

overleaf:
Chess Set, c. 1950 *Thirty two aluminum chesspieces, 16 red and 16 silver, on glass and aluminum chessboard*

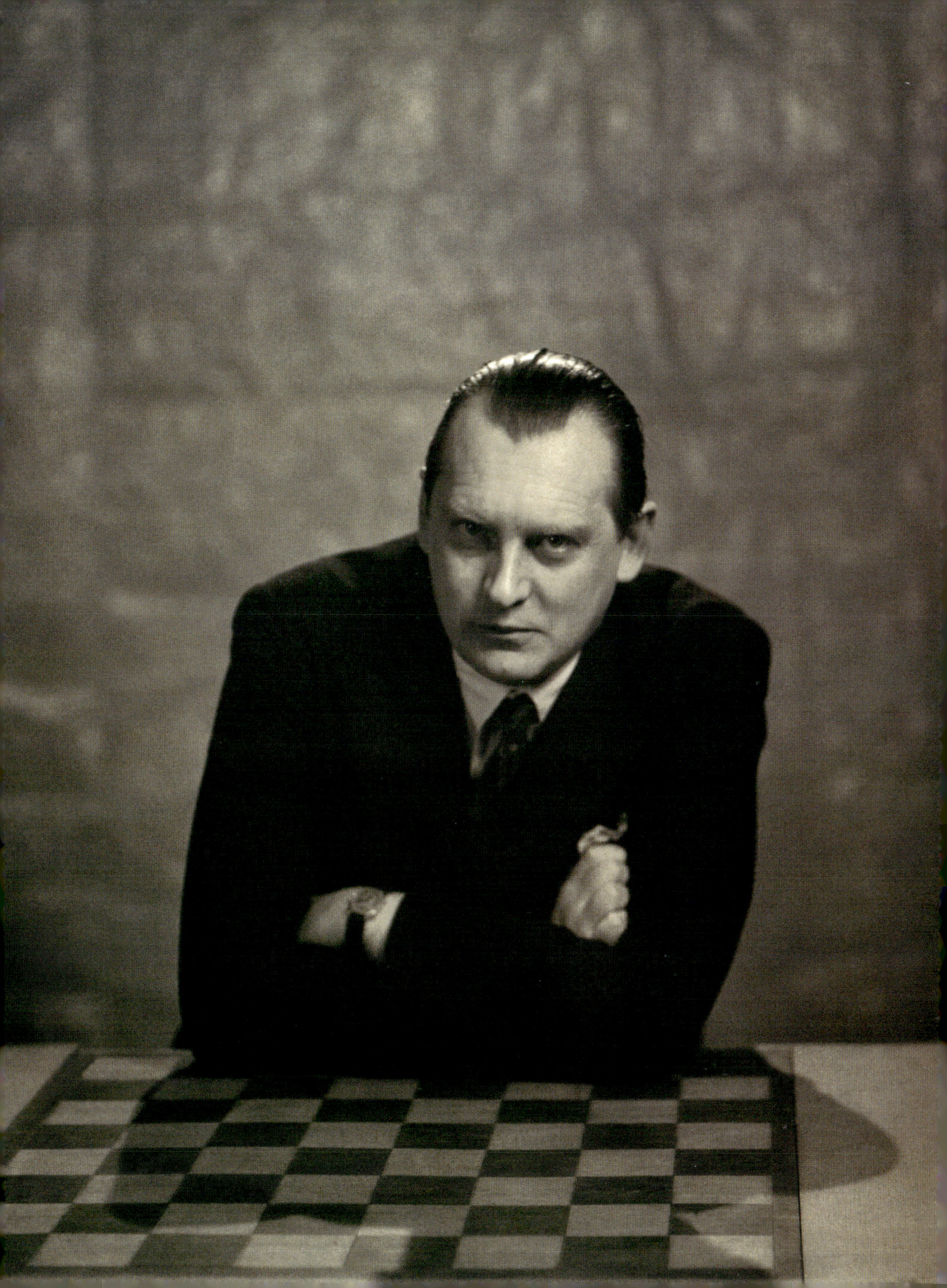

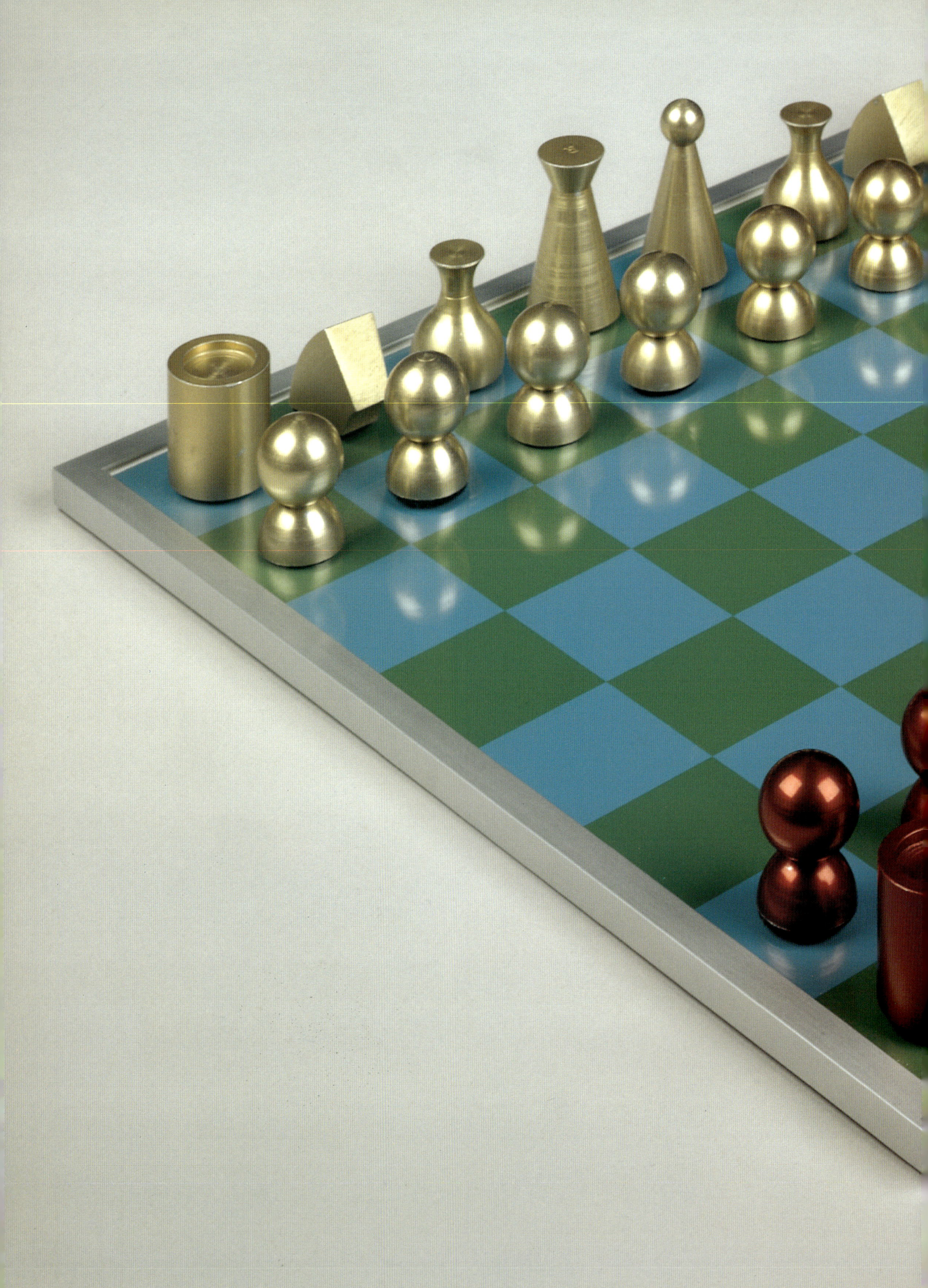

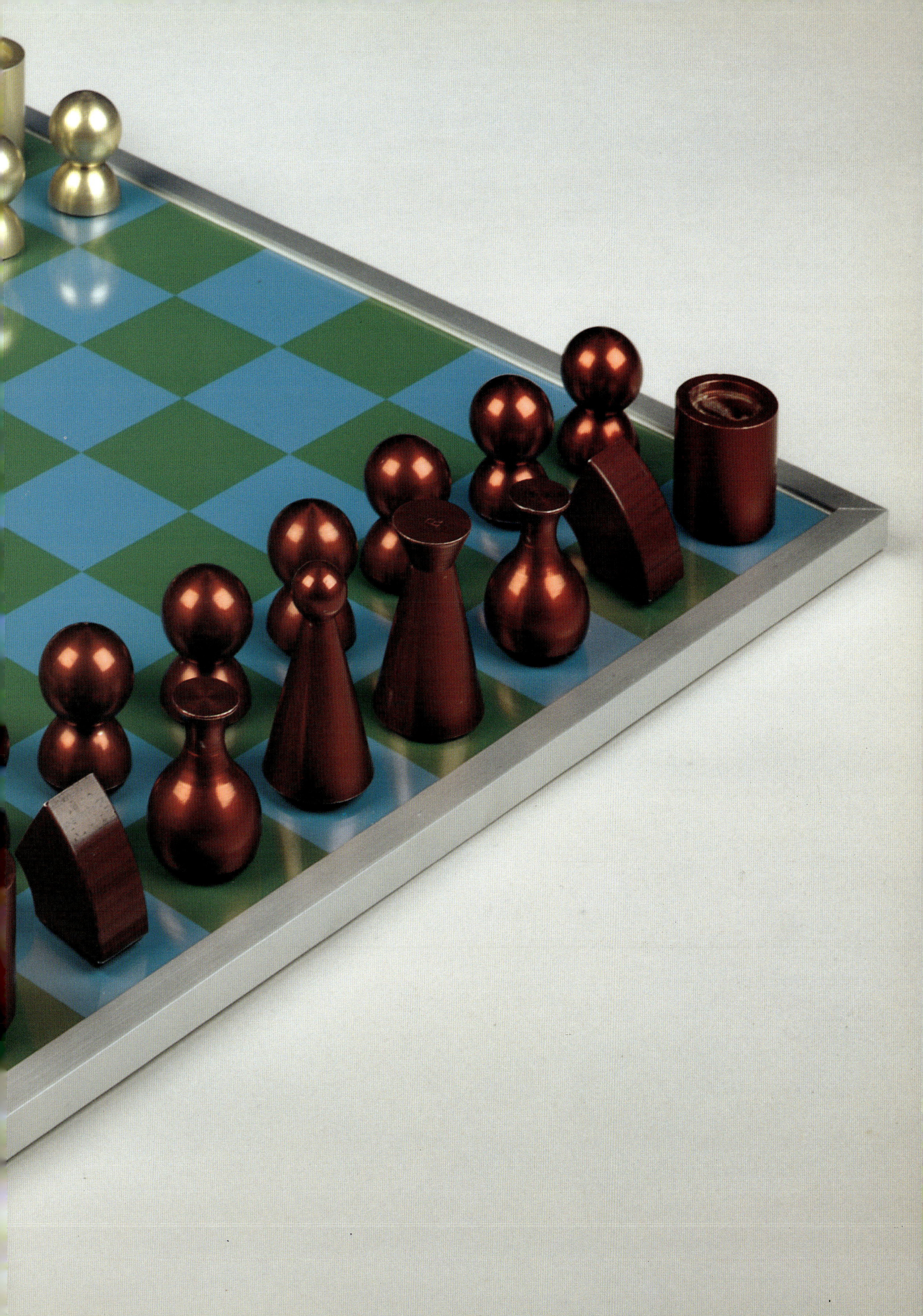

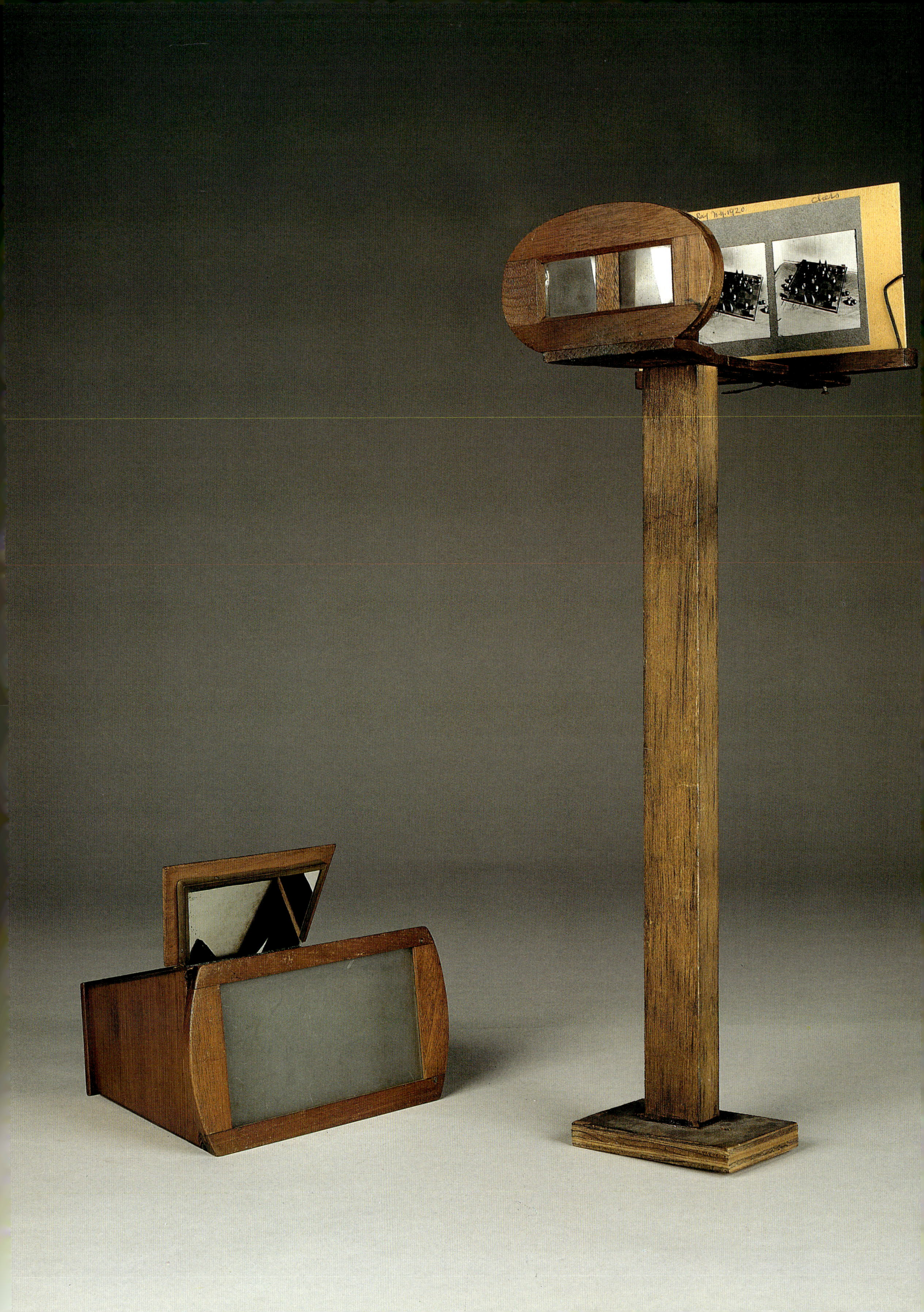

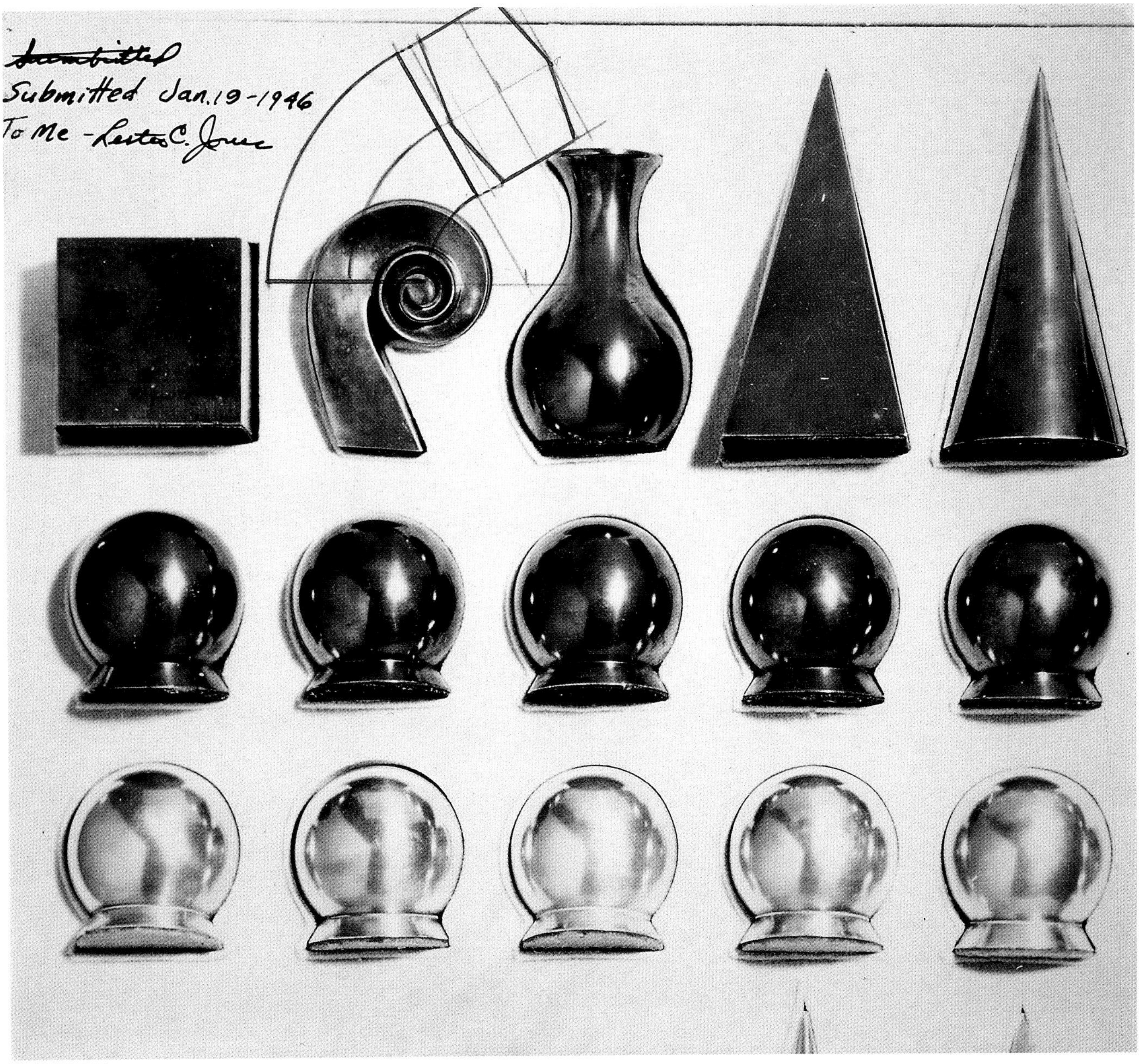

Submitted Jan. 19-1946
To Me - Lester C. Jones

counterclockwise from right:
William Copley and Gloria de Herrera with a Man Ray chess set, c. 1950
Gelatin-silver print

Juliet with a Man Ray chess set and portrait in background, 1940s
Gelatin-silver print

Photograph of chess pieces, c. 1946
Gelatin-silver print with ink

opposite:
1870 Brewster-type Stereoscopic viewer *and a part of another viewer with a* ***Man Ray stereoscope photograph of a 1920 chess set,*** c. 1940s

overleaf:
Chess Set, 1962–66
Chess set comprising 32 polished bronze chess pieces on an enamel and metal inlay chessboard mounted in wood with storage drawersfor chess pieces

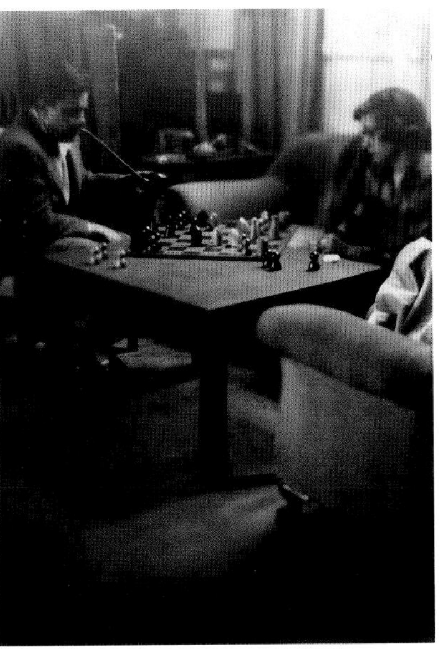

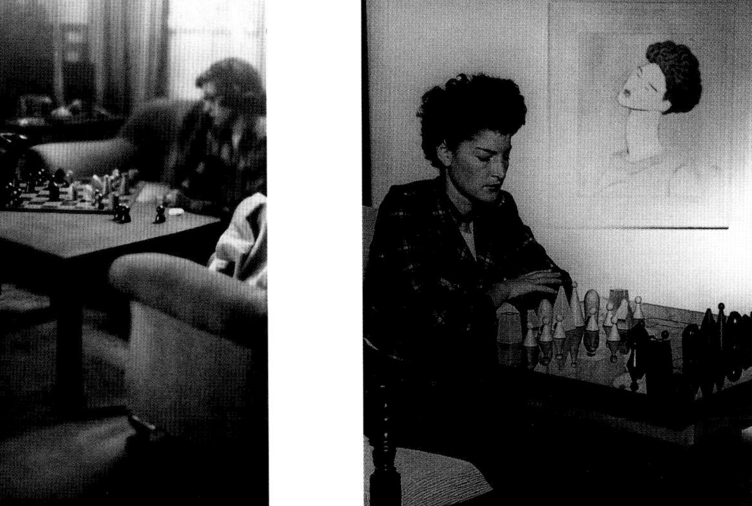

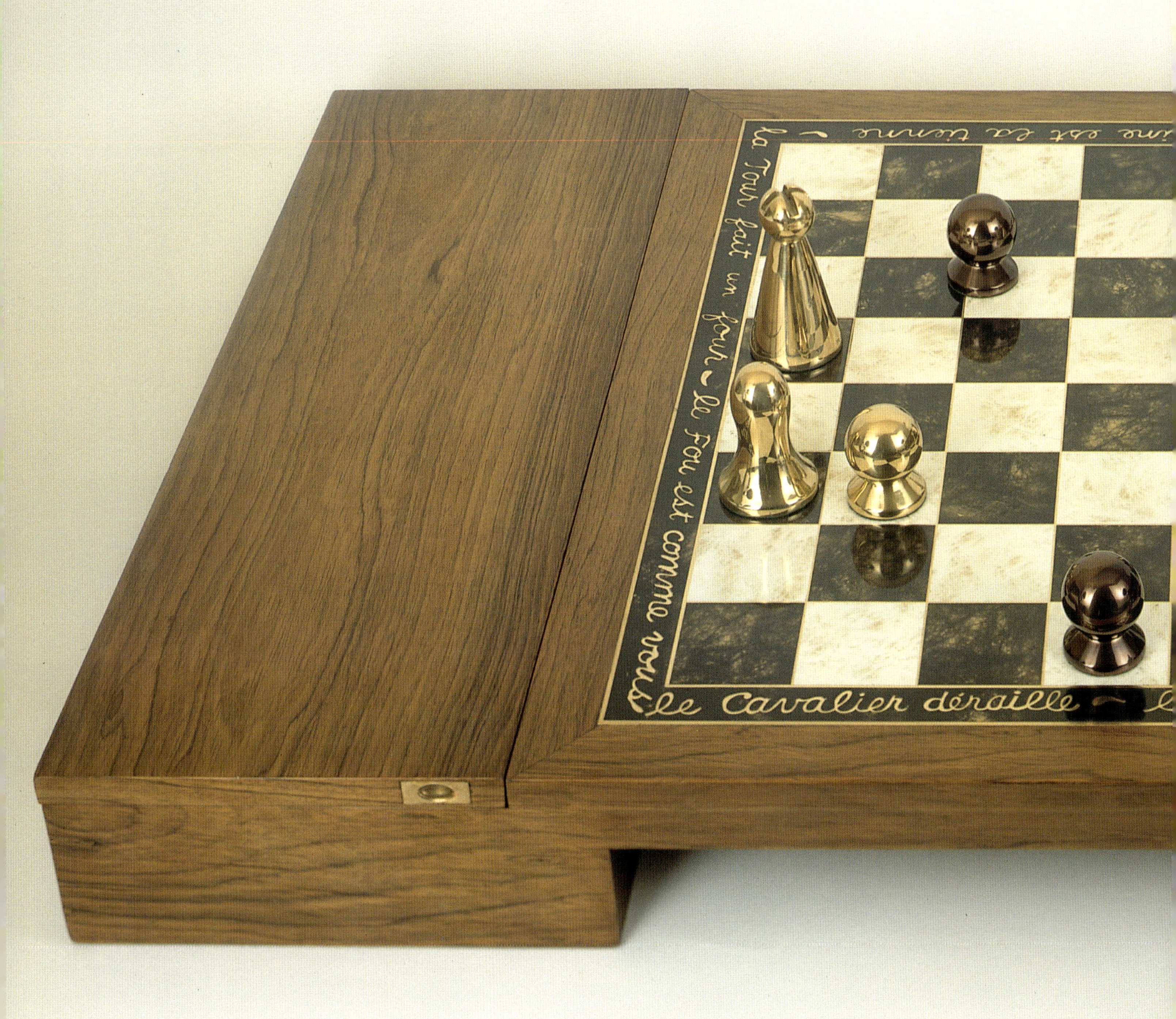
la Tour fait un four – le Fou est comme vous
le Cavalier déraille –

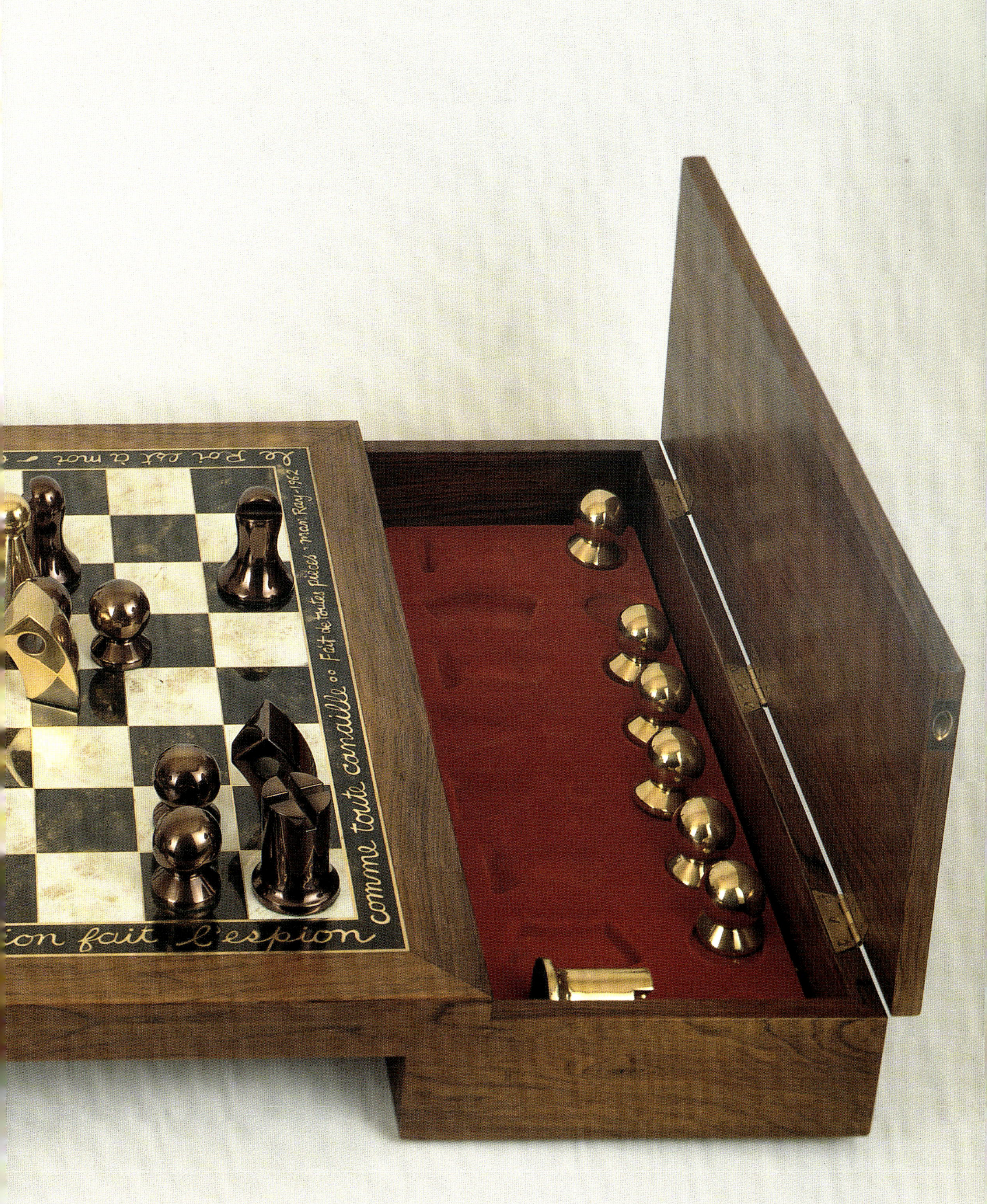
Le Roi est à moi
Fait de toutes pièces · man Ray · 1962
comme toute canaille
fait l'espion

Soon after the group exhibition "The Imagery of Chess," Levy mounted "Objects of My Affection," Man Ray's first major one-man show in New York, in April 1945. With a catalogue cover of a silhouetted couple kissing (reminiscent of a Rayograph of Man Ray and Kiki kissing), designed by Duchamp, the exhibition displayed a mix of drawings, watercolors, Rayographs, and oil paintings that extended back to 1915, and included new paintings as well as repaintings. With its title, however, the exhibition emphasized the assemblage that Man Ray had been making since his arrival in Hollywood. Included in the catalogue were his comments on the ten pieces displayed. Thus his generic *Self-Portrait*, "reflected in a flexible mirror, is capable of infinite variations simply by the pressure of a finger to the surface of the mirror. . . ." Or his *Table for Two* (1944), enigmatically described as "casseroles in the role of personages."[53]

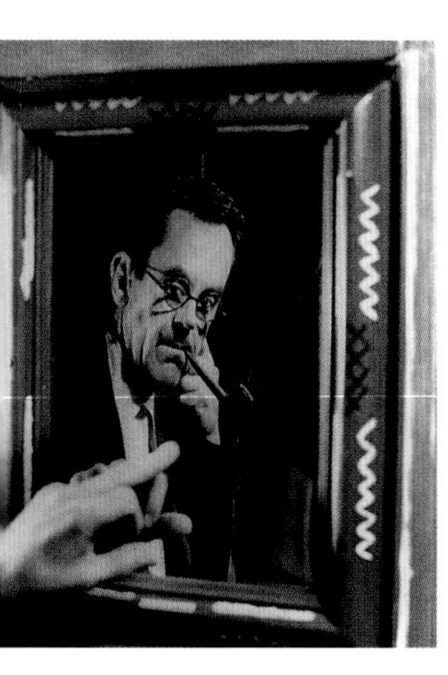

Autoportrait, *self-portrait of the artist's reflection in the 1944 object*

Man Ray and Juliet had made a quick trip to New York for his exhibition at Julien Levy's. Coming back through Chicago, he lectured at Moholy-Nagy's school and turned down a teaching position, one of several that he had been offered while in Los Angeles. With the end of the war in August 1945, Man Ray's life took an upswing. By year's end, he resumed relations with the Société Anonyme, Inc., which had been founded by Katherine Dreier in 1920. He became its Vice-President once again, succeeding Kandinsky (who had died the previous year), and he donated *Promenade* (repainted in 1941) to the Société's collection of modern art recently bequeathed to Yale University.

In September 1946 the Circle Gallery at 7623 Sunset Boulevard held an exhibition devoted mainly to Man Ray's objects. Visitors were greeted by *Lampshade*, which hung in the doorway; this reincarnation of the 1921 original would undergo yet another transformation as a "painting in three dimensions" in 1956, after Man Ray's return to Paris. *Palettable*, one of the first objects that he made in Hollywood in 1940, was a large artist's palette mounted on legs to become a table. As a place setting, *Mr. Knife and Miss Fork* makes literal reference to the title of the first chapter of *Babylon*, René Crevel's 1927 Surrealist novel, (illustrated by Max Ernst). Returned from the New York exhibition was *Life Saver*, made out of cork and driftwood that Juliet and Man Ray collected on their visits to Mary and Herbert Stothardt (she a painter and he a composer for film), whose house was on the beach in Santa Monica. Playing literally with optical illusions engaged by a swinging ball and large magnifying glass, one of the more complex objects was *Optical Longings and Illusions*, its title a variation on *Hopes and Optical Illusions*, a 1938 drawing that had graced the cover of Man Ray's Pasadena catalogue.[54]

Finally, on view was Man Ray's *Last Object* (transformed from being a "Lost Object," as it was misspelled in the show at Julien Levy's), a metronome mounted with a swinging eye. Man Ray first made this object in 1922 as *Object to Be Destroyed.* After its destruction, Man Ray drew another version in 1932, titled *Object of Destruction*, the eye of which was clearly intended to be that of the departed Lee Miller. Some of Man Ray's sexual jealousy had dissipated, even though he claimed, "It is still my earnest desire, some day while the eye is ticking away during a conversation, to lift my hammer and with one well-aimed blow to completely demolish the metronome."[55]

Soon after this exhibition, Dorothea Tanning and Max Ernst (who had divorced Peggy Guggenheim) came from Sedona, Arizona, to visit. When the two decided to get married, with Man Ray and Juliet as witnesses, they all agreed to a double ceremony at City Hall in Beverly Hills. "Yes, Julie and I officially married on the 24th [of October, 1946]," Man Ray rather casually wrote his sister. "We had been together six years now, so it was not such a revolutionary step."

His efforts "to get on with a minimum of publicity" were not successful, as photographers converged upon them; a frosty Ernst with a dismayed Tanning appeared in the *Los Angeles Times* local section under the headline "Surrealists Get Licenses to Marry." Parties followed at the Arensbergs and champagne flowed at the gallery of Earl Stendhal, who had recently moved next door to the collectors, and Florence Homulka, one of Man Ray's few students in California, took a more congenial and intimate portrait of the two couples. Later Dorothea Tanning mocked their newfound respectability but conceded that, despite their jokes, it was "rather pleasant being married".[56]

With the war's end came the news that Man Ray's property and belongings in Paris were safe. He later realized that he had been "subconsciously under a strain through the years."[57] Though he was eager to return to Paris, he was warned of all the postwar difficulties

overleaf:
p.78
Mr. Knife and Miss Fork,
1944–1973 *Mixed media*

p. 79
Peinture en trois dimensions,
1956 *Oil on white prepared aluminum*

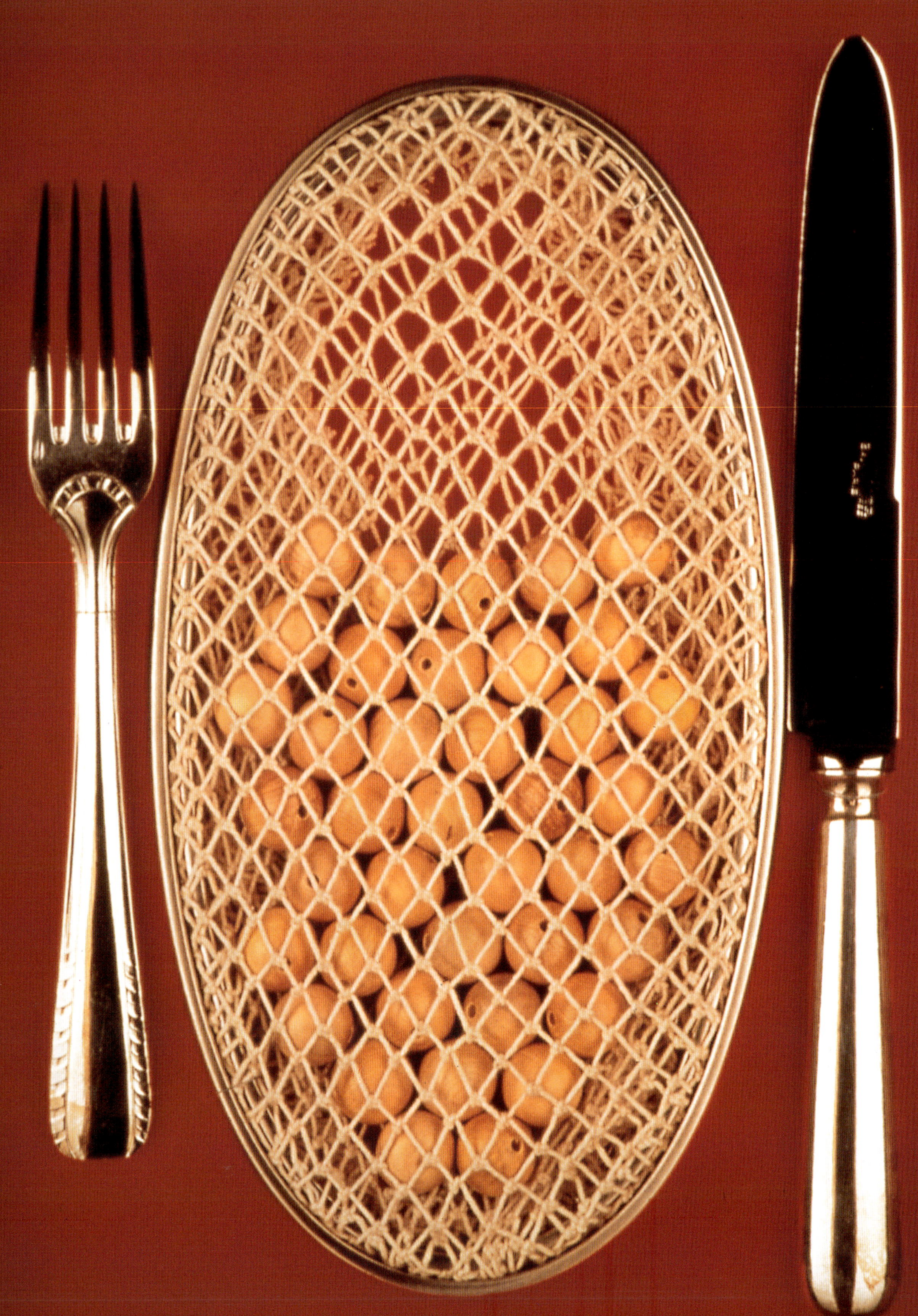

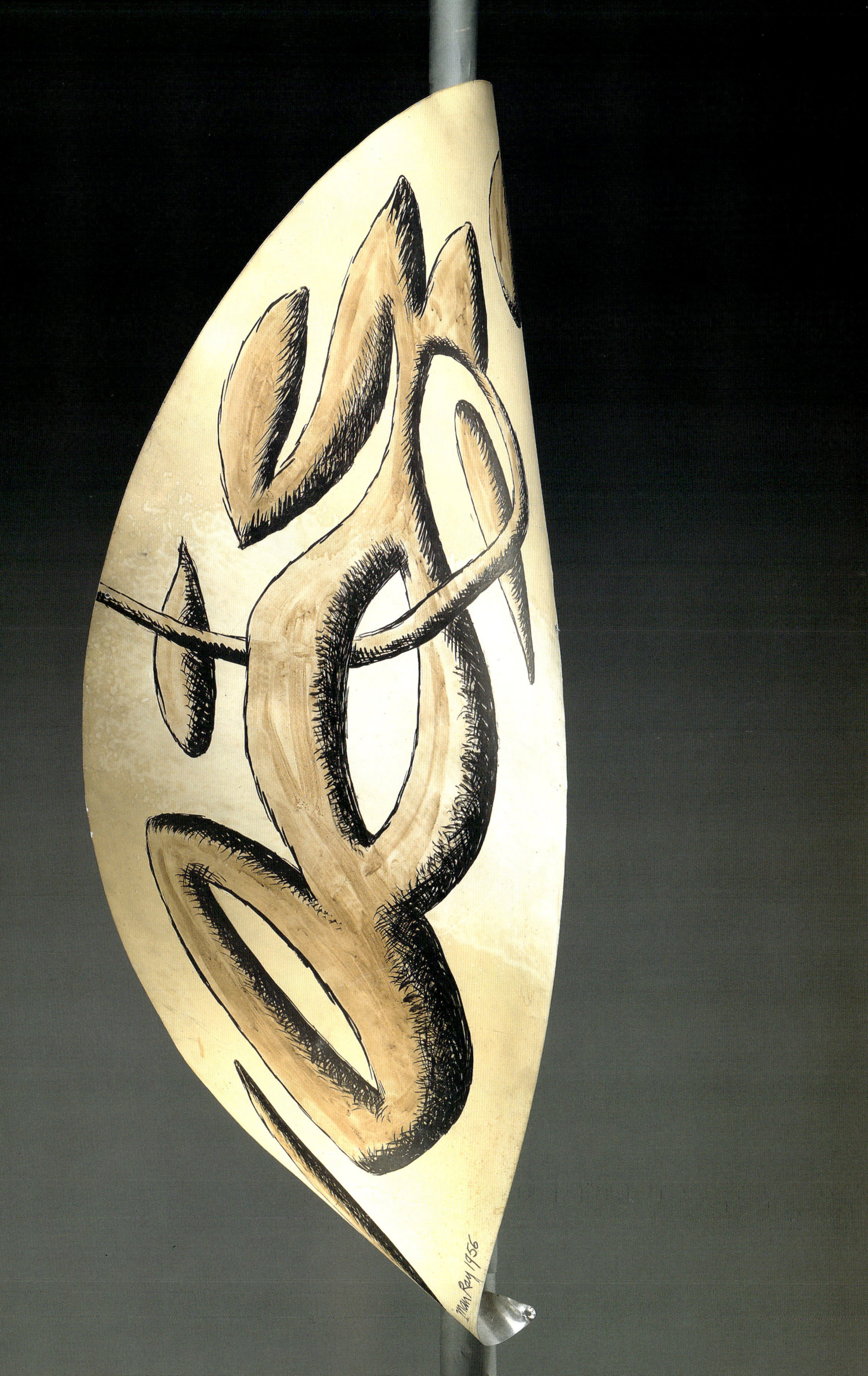
Man Ray 1956

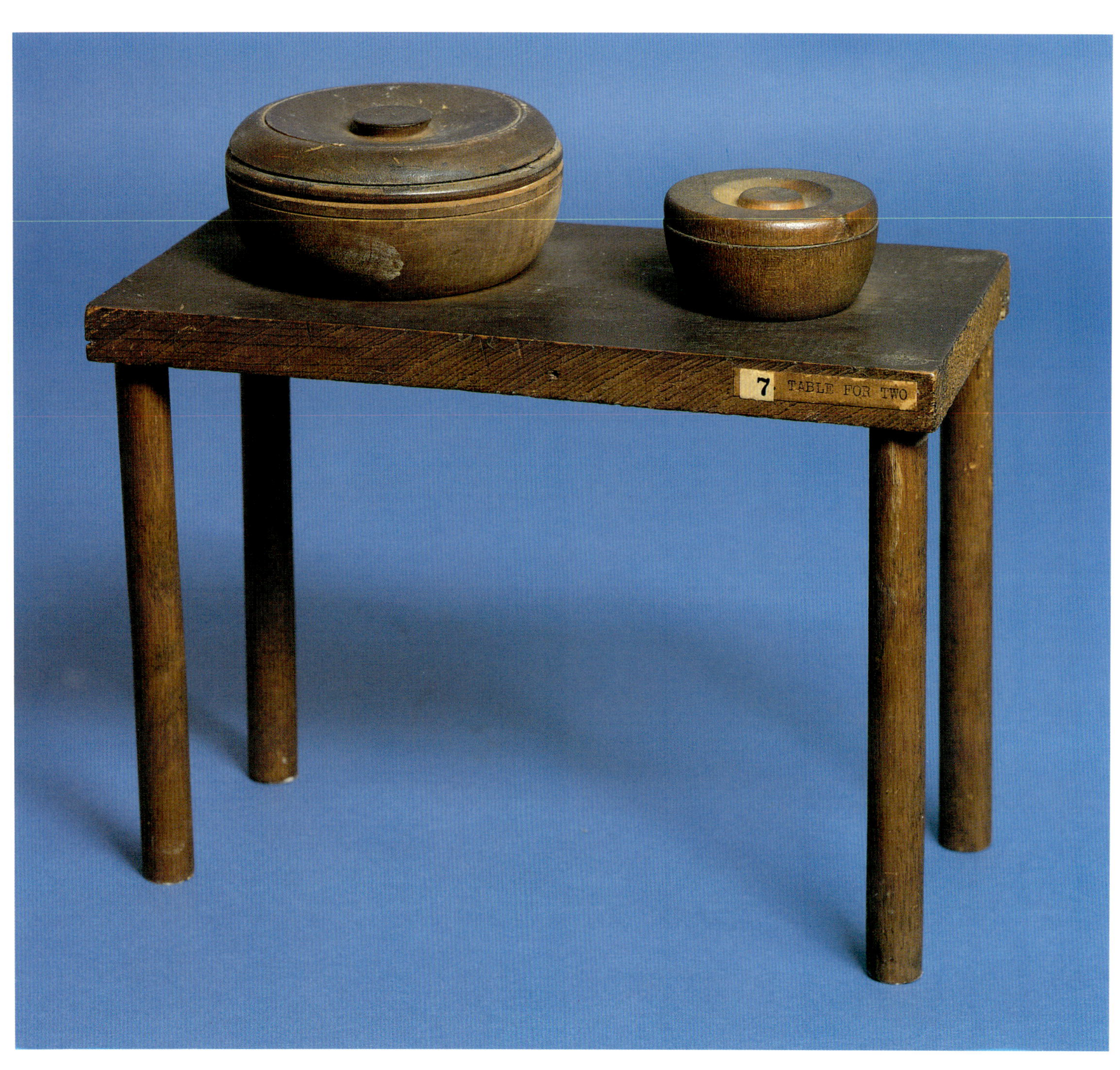

above:
Table for Two, 1944
Wood table with two wooden bowls affixed, original object

opposite:
Object Indestructable, 1923–1975
Readymade wooden metronome with photograph of an eye

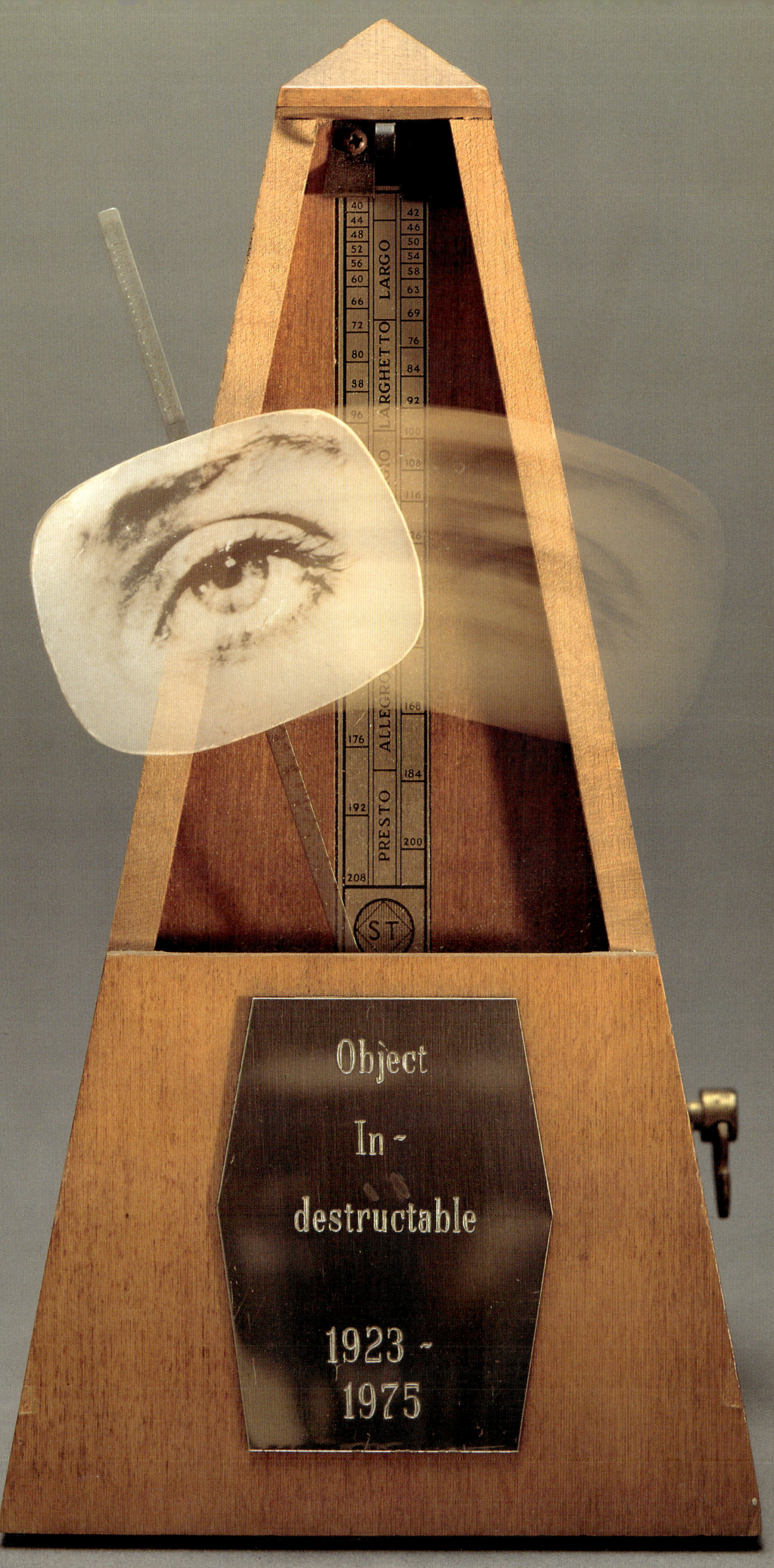
LARGO
LARGHETTO
ALLEGRO
PRESTO
ST
Object
In-
destructable
1923 -
1975

besetting France, and it was not until 1947 that he and Juliet flew to Paris from New York. That he had referred to his house in Saint-Germain-en-Laye as his "bungalow" to Elsie perhaps suggests the extent to which he had become settled in California. Writing from rue Vavin in Paris, where he was staying with friends, he told Elsie that he was "not quite used to the shift" on his "French keyboard machine," which he had retrieved from his house.[58] A larger shift to Paris, intimated by this slip, was not in yet in the cards. He cleaned out his house, shipped work back to the States, and managed to sell his property to an English major stationed in Paris. In the process he made a minor windfall with the sale of a cache of his 1932 albums of photographs to an American dealer. He returned to California relatively prosperous.

Having settled in glamorous Hollywood, Man Ray received the inevitable queries from his young nieces back in mundane Jersey City. "No, I haven't met any 'stars,'" he wrote to Elsie, "as I don't go out to people much." Eventually he managed to frequent some of the Hollywood glamour spots. On one occasion he was exuberantly greeted by Mike Romanoff, whose restaurant at 325 North Rodeo was a favorite of the stars. "We fell into each other's arms," Man Ray recounted in *Self Portrait*, and he and Juliet were treated to a "sumptuous lunch" complete with obligatory champagne. Man Ray had known Romanoff, a self-proclaimed "illegitimate son of the czar," in Paris, where the Russian was eventually *persona non grata* for lacking a passport.[59]

Man Ray also sent his niece Naomi a gaudy postcard advertising Bob Brooks's Seven Seas restaurant on Hollywood Boulevard opposite Grauman's Chinese Theater. "They have real rain falling in the landscape in back of the bar!" Man Ray marveled. Here was proof positive that "there was more Surrealism rampant in Hollywood than all the Surrealists could invent in a lifetime," as he once told William Copley, whose attempt to run a Surrealist gallery in Beverly Hills must have seemed like bringing coals to Newcastle.[60]

As an avant-garde filmmaker in his previous life, Man Ray was occasionally approached by younger filmmakers like John Whitney, Sr., who sought some commentary on his abstract efforts. And he did keep at least half an eye on the film industry, which pervaded southern California. At that same lunch at Romanoff's, he was courted by an agent and a producer to become a cameraman. Fixated on the division of labor in the film industry, they could not understand that Man Ray wanted to be a star in his own one-man production company. "Wasn't that a better-paid job?" he asked, tongue-in-cheek, knowing from the outset that he would not be hired. In an informal talk he gave in 1943 at the American Contemporary Gallery on the occasion of a film screening, he argued that "the movies will become a great art one day," but only when film production "will really be in the hands of one mastermind."[61]

In a letter to George Leite, editor of *Circle*, an avant-garde magazine published in Berkeley, Man Ray argued that he was "interested only in the one-man's medium, like painting, for instance." As a staunch libertarian, he was incapable of collaboration: "Any vehicle that gets beyond the control of one, becomes a social effort, and that is another thing entirely." He wanted to keep his hands clean because "the chances of taking chances diminished" in "complicated collaboration." He also wanted to avoid at all cost the possibility of censorship and misinterpretation, which could occur through someone else's editing.[62]

Man Ray also found that the studio system violated one of his most basic operating principles, the deployment of an economy of means. "Most films," he noted in an unpublished meditation on cinema, "involve the same disproportion of effort and result. This film that required a fortune for its realization, the drudgery of thousands of men, two years of sustained effort, perhaps a few catastrophes and some deaths . . . all this is destined to appear only during a few months until it has regained its cost plus a sufficient profit. . . ." The dispiriting result was a "distracted" public, "aroused" by "hopeless envies and desires." To George Leite, he implied that he was constitutionally incapable of making a Hollywood movie. "I'm afraid that is out of the question," he claimed. "It is like asking me to set up a new religion in a country swarming with cults and temples."[63]

Needless to say, Man Ray had no takers in Hollywood; even European filmmakers like René Clair and Luis Buñuel, both with a more substantial track record than Man Ray, had difficulties working in Hollywood during the war years.[64] In his memoirs Buñuel recalled seeing "the enormous two-mile-long Los Angeles garbage dump, with everything from orange peels to grand pianos to whole houses."

overleaf:
Letter from Man Ray to George Leite, *editor of* ***Circle*** *magazine, November 1944*

1245 VINE STREET
HOLLYWOOD, CALIF.

November 16 -44

My dear Leite,

I am as sensitive to praise and appreciation as I am refractory to adverse criticism; in this respect I admit a common bond even with my detractors. So when a letter like yours comes along, my first impulse is to reel off a book of 500 pages, and expand on my sentiments.

Words have never been my true fort, not because I doubt my ability to exprss myself, but I have been so much more seduced by the plastic or optical image, that I prefer giving most of my time in this direction. Since pleasure is the guiding principal in my creative activity, I have never had much patience with the process of supplementing it with explanation, which to me is a drudgery.

Now and then I am cornered, as I was in making the little talk you reeeived, which talk was a summing up of a series of anecdotes in connection with the showing of some old avant-garde films. It was all very polite and informal, and tolerant on my part for a sincere but misguided Hollywood audience which works in the studios or has made a fetichism out of some abstract idea of what they vaguely hope the cinema might be. Or some secretly hoping to get some for them new angles which they might "apply" in the studios.

I have always been revolted by the demand as to <u>how</u> I did something, as if it were a trick; I am less impatient when asked <u>why</u>, but just as much at a loss to answer. There is no bottom to the ignorance or stupidity of questioners. Wasn't it sufficient that it was <u>done</u>? I am never on trial for anything I've done, it is the spectator that is on trial; according to his receptivity he acquits or convicts himself.

The talk I gave, I think answers most of your questions regarding my opinion of films and the movie industry in general. I cannot enter upon a diatribe, anymore than I could criticize any of the other great commercial industries simply because they do not come up to my ideas of what they should be. I am interested only in the one-man's medium, like painting, for instance. Any vehicle that gets beyond the control of one man, becomes a social effort, and that is another thing entirely. I don't deny it. But I want to keep my hands clean. I find Courbet so admirable because there is no trace in his work of the revolutionary turmoil in which he participated so effectively. At least I want to wash my hands between operations. Some may think me as begging the question or simply being cryptic, but even in a cheap technicolor Hollywood production I saw the other night, these words slip out of the actor's mouth, "Most people try to live, I try to live <u>and</u> paint." I've dreamed of it for days. Here and there someone agrees with me!

This is the real eclecticism for me. For twenty years my studio in Paris was the center of a diversified activity. Moving-pictures, painting, photography branching out in new directions, contraptions dadaistic, surrealistic. They called me the pre-surrealist, which may be a hint that I have not borrowed from all the contemporary schools so much as they have borrowed from me. The painters and writers that streamed through my studio did not hesitate to adopt any idea they saw on the walls or in the publications, hoping to make it more legitimate- and valuable- by giving it the final touch.

I was very careless with my ideas. Here in this country, they know only the names sanctioned by dealers,museums, and editors, and so it is natural that I am considered a follower. -By the local critics, who do not know what has been going on in this world for the past thirty years, in spite of the facilities of present day communications. I have been very careless, and still am, for I am very busy enjoying myself, and have no time for putting myself over. I can assure you whatever notoriety I've attained has been purely incidental, and without any effort on my part.

Yes, I got interested in the moving-picture at the time it was still silent and capable of manipulation by one man; when it became a matter of complicated collaboration, the chances of taking chances diminished, and I returned to my little one-man jobs. My short films were sketches for more ambitious projects, but even when the opportunity offered for making a more ambitious picture(by the same patron who sponsored Cocteau and Bunuel) I refused because I could not be assured of its distribution. Not for the sort of thing I would have liked to do. And see what happened to the others.

I still have a feeling that an insignificant static drawing, painting or photograph can outlive a million-dollar film. It is always accesible, and there is no risk involved in the making. Yes, for me the artist is the real economist, he takes no chances, if the result is uncertain, or if the effort is out of all proportion to the result.

On the several occasions I have been approached since my stay in Hollywood, by the studios with the object of getting me behind a camera, I balked; I demanded to be placed <u>in front</u> of the camera. I am here for the beautiful climate, and to enjoy myself, and to continue perpetrating all those creations which the supers would like to censor or destroy. I,also,have the distinction of being classed among the "degenerates" by the nazis.

Besides doing my chosen work, all I can do is sit back and wait until someone comes along and asks me for a contribution, as you did, for then only am I sure that I am wanted and will be accepted.

Thank you for your kind appreciation.

Sincerely Man Ray

MAN RAY

P.S. I enclose a couple of prints which you may reproduce with my talk, as well as anything from this letter.

The landscape took on a surreal quality: "Smoke from the fires rose here and there; and at the bottom of the pit, on a small piece of land raised slightly from the piles of garbage, stood a couple of tiny houses inhabited by real people." He enlisted Man Ray to make a film about a young girl whom Buñuel imagined "involved in a love affair in this infernal decor."[65] There were no financial backers.

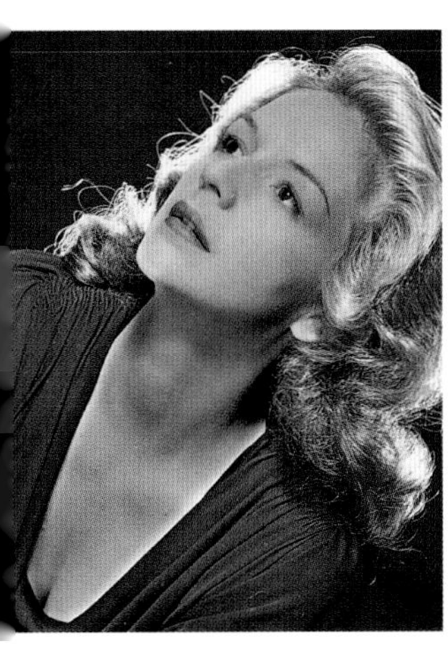

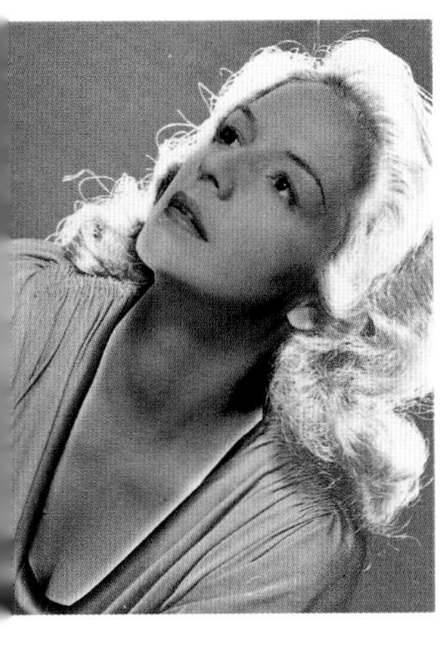

top:
Ruth Ford, 1940s
Gelatin-silver print

above:
Ruth Ford, 1940s
Manipulated gelatin-silver print

As a consequence, Man Ray maintained a low profile on the fringes of the movie industry—unlike Dalí, whose notoriety in the United States gave him some clout among the studios, first with Disney, and then with Alfred Hitchcock to devise the dream sequences for *Spellbound* (an intrigue among psychiatrists). At most, Man Ray undertook occasional assignments from the studios to take glamour shots. And so he shot Gypsy Rose Lee on set and became reacquainted with Paulette Goddard, who he posed with her screen lover in *Diary of a Chambermaid,* Hurd Hatfield. (In 1936 he had photographed her for *Harper's Bazaar* after her successful debut in Chaplin's *Modern Times.*) There were also conventionalized publicity stills of Dolores del Rio in stereotypical Latin American regalia, and a close-up of the beautiful young actress Ruth Ford, sister of the poet Charles Henri Ford. Man Ray included Ford's portrait in *Minicam Photography* (whose readers were always eager to learn how to shoot cheesecake), and explained the "two-time" print process that turned her blond, "without having to make the doubtful experiment upon herself."[66]

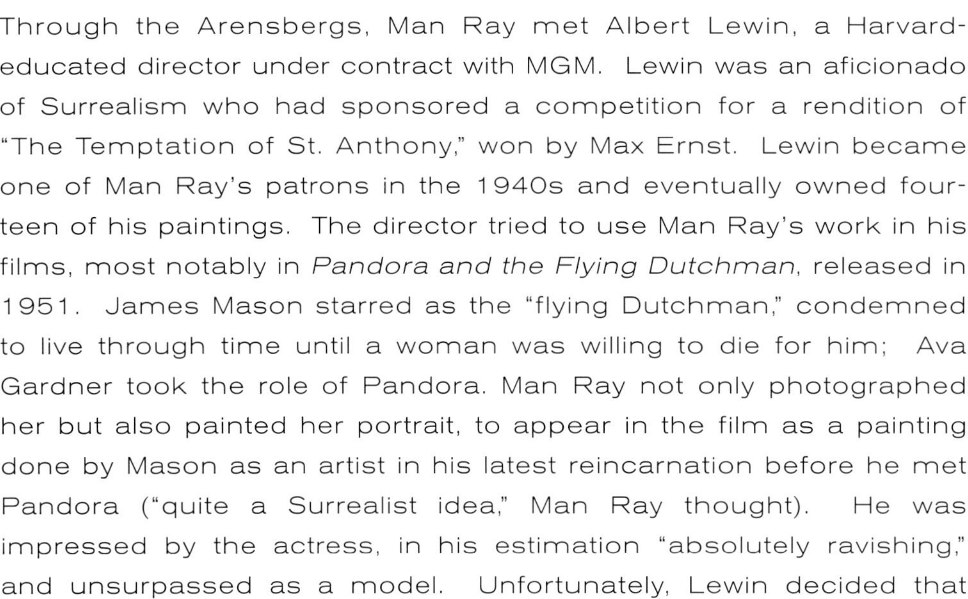

Through the Arensbergs, Man Ray met Albert Lewin, a Harvard-educated director under contract with MGM. Lewin was an aficionado of Surrealism who had sponsored a competition for a rendition of "The Temptation of St. Anthony," won by Max Ernst. Lewin became one of Man Ray's patrons in the 1940s and eventually owned fourteen of his paintings. The director tried to use Man Ray's work in his films, most notably in *Pandora and the Flying Dutchman*, released in 1951. James Mason starred as the "flying Dutchman," condemned to live through time until a woman was willing to die for him; Ava Gardner took the role of Pandora. Man Ray not only photographed her but also painted her portrait, to appear in the film as a painting done by Mason as an artist in his latest reincarnation before he met Pandora ("quite a Surrealist idea," Man Ray thought). He was impressed by the actress, in his estimation "absolutely ravishing," and unsurpassed as a model. Unfortunately, Lewin decided that

Man Ray's portrait did not depict a sufficiently "innocent" Pandora, so he had the image redone in London before the film was shot on location in Spain. Staying with Lee Miller and Roland Penrose, Lewin borrowed one of Man Ray's chess sets, which avoided the cutting-room floor and appeared as a prominent prop in the film.[67]

Not surprisingly, Man Ray's most notable cinematic achievement occurred outside Hollywood, involving a collaboration from which he absented himself. As early as 1942, the German filmmaker Hans Richter, director of the Institute of Film Technics at City College of New York, wrote to Man Ray about the prospect of putting together an anthology of avant-garde films that had been made before the war began. Eventually, Richter asked Man Ray to participate in an entirely new film with segments made by Max Ernst, Marcel Duchamp, Fernand Léger, and Alexander Calder.[68] Richter was to contribute a segment of his own as well as produce and direct the final amalgam. Made on a shoestring despite the generous financial backing of Peggy Guggenheim, Richter shot the 95-minute film in color in a loft in the garment district of Manhattan. With the assistance of volunteers, including students, Richter worked on site with Duchamp, Léger, Ernst, and Calder; Ernst, for example, acted in his segment, along with Julien Levy.

Titled *Dreams That Money Can Buy*, the film was a spoof on psychiatry: Joe, a "bum" with his own psychological problems, rents a room and hangs out a shingle to provide his clients with personalized dreams. As the blurb on a small throwaway claims, Joe is "a heavenly psychiatrist" who "looks into their eyes and finds there on the inside of the retina the images of their dreams and wishes." This conceit provides the thread that holds the seven dream sequences together. "Desire," Ernst's opening sequence, is followed by Léger's "The Girl with the Prefabricated Heart" ("Oh Venus was born out of sea foam / Oh Venus was born out of brine / But a goddess today / If she is Grade A / Is assembled upon the assembly line," sung by Josh White). Man Ray's segment followed, then Duchamp's "Discs and Nudes Descending the Staircase" (with the ballerina Ruth Sobotka, who would marry film student Stanley Kubrick); a mobile "Ballet" and wire "Circus," Calder's two sequences; and the film concluded with Richter's "Narcissus." Paul Bowles, John Cage, and Darius Milhaud provided original musical accompaniment.

the following pages in order:

p. 88
Untitled, 1940s
Gelatin-silver print

p. 89
Dolores del Rio, 1940's
Gelatin-silver print

p. 90
.ee Miller with midget, c. 1930
Gelatin-silver print

p. 91
Ava Gardner, c. 1950
Gelatin-silver print

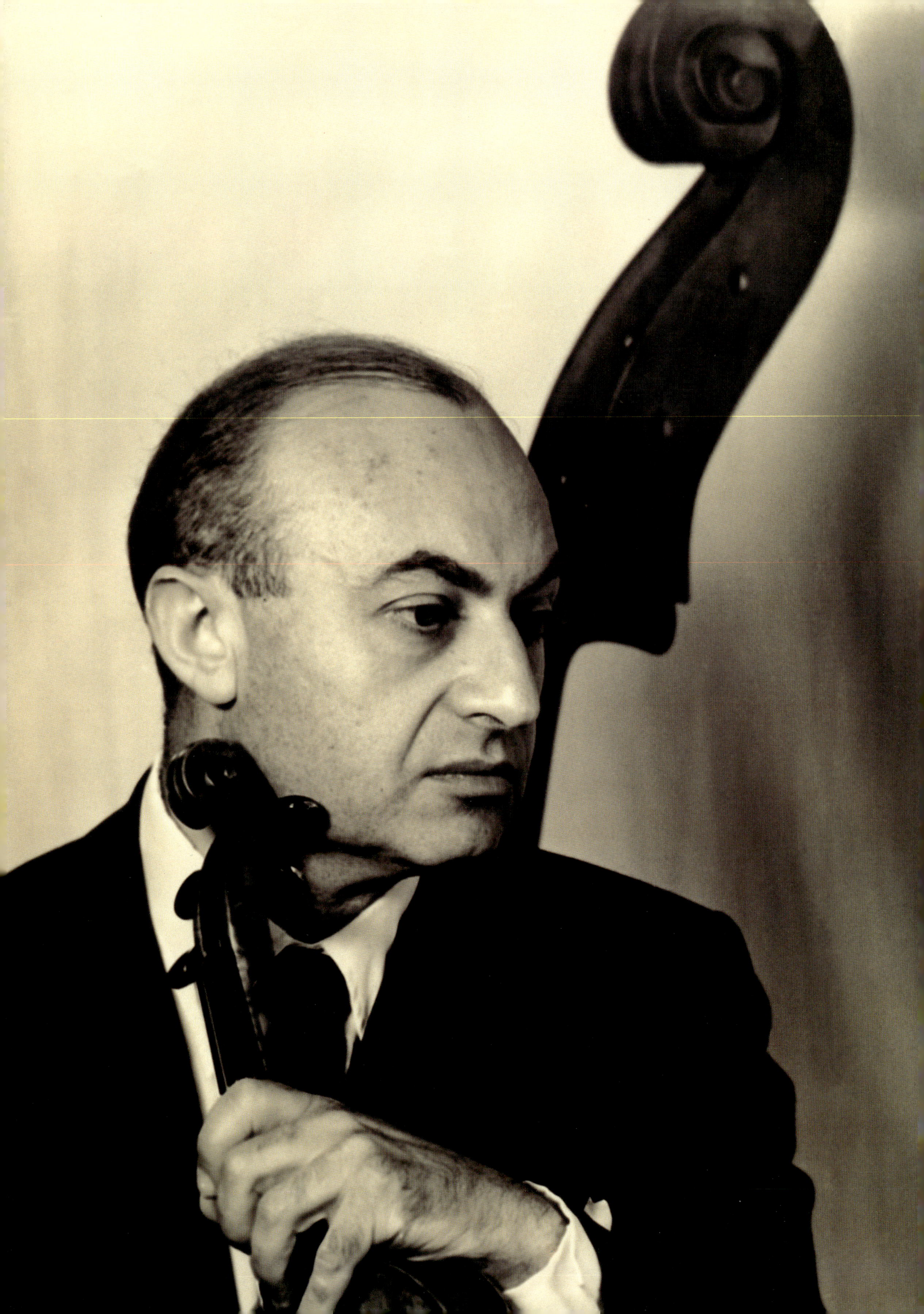

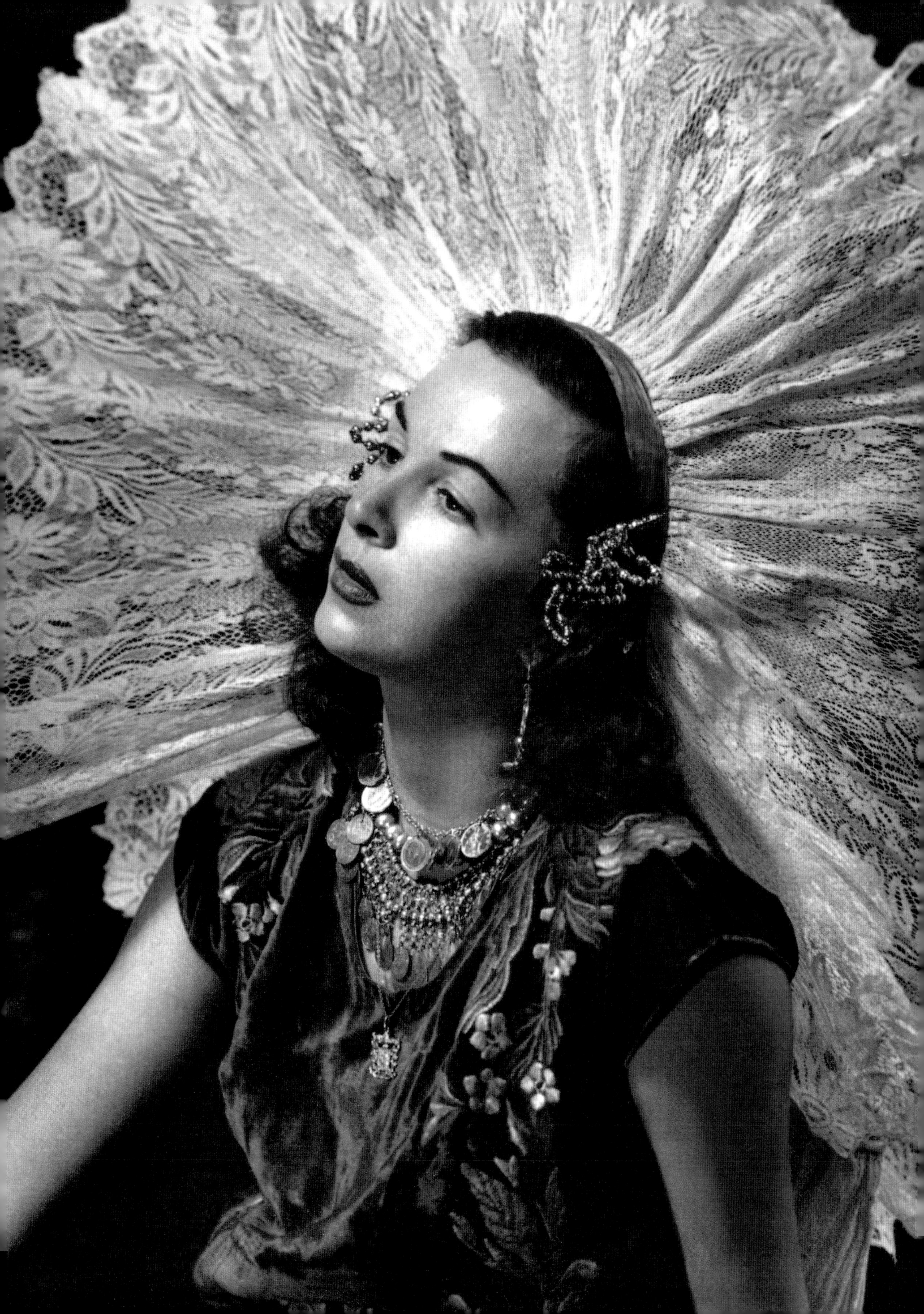

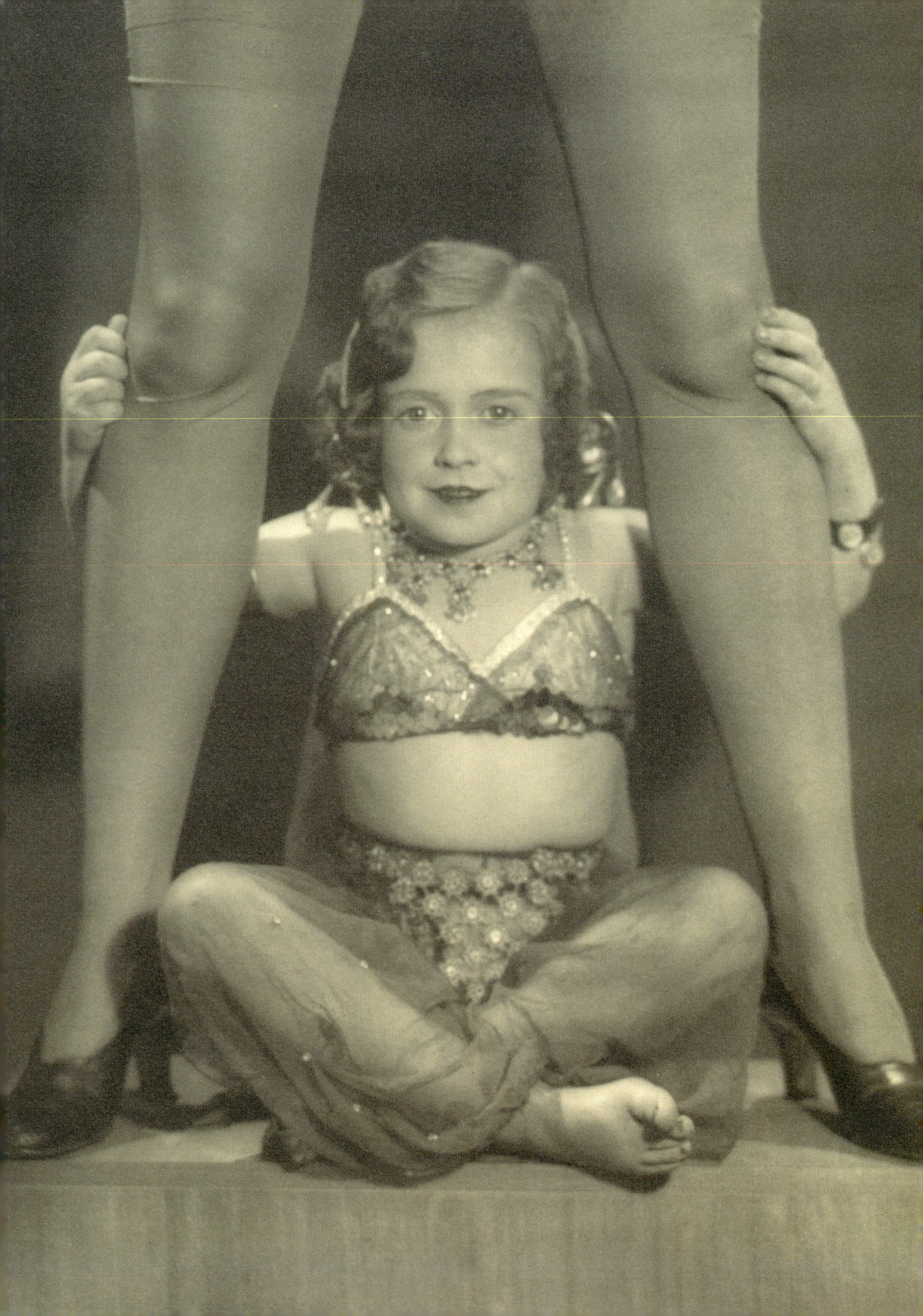

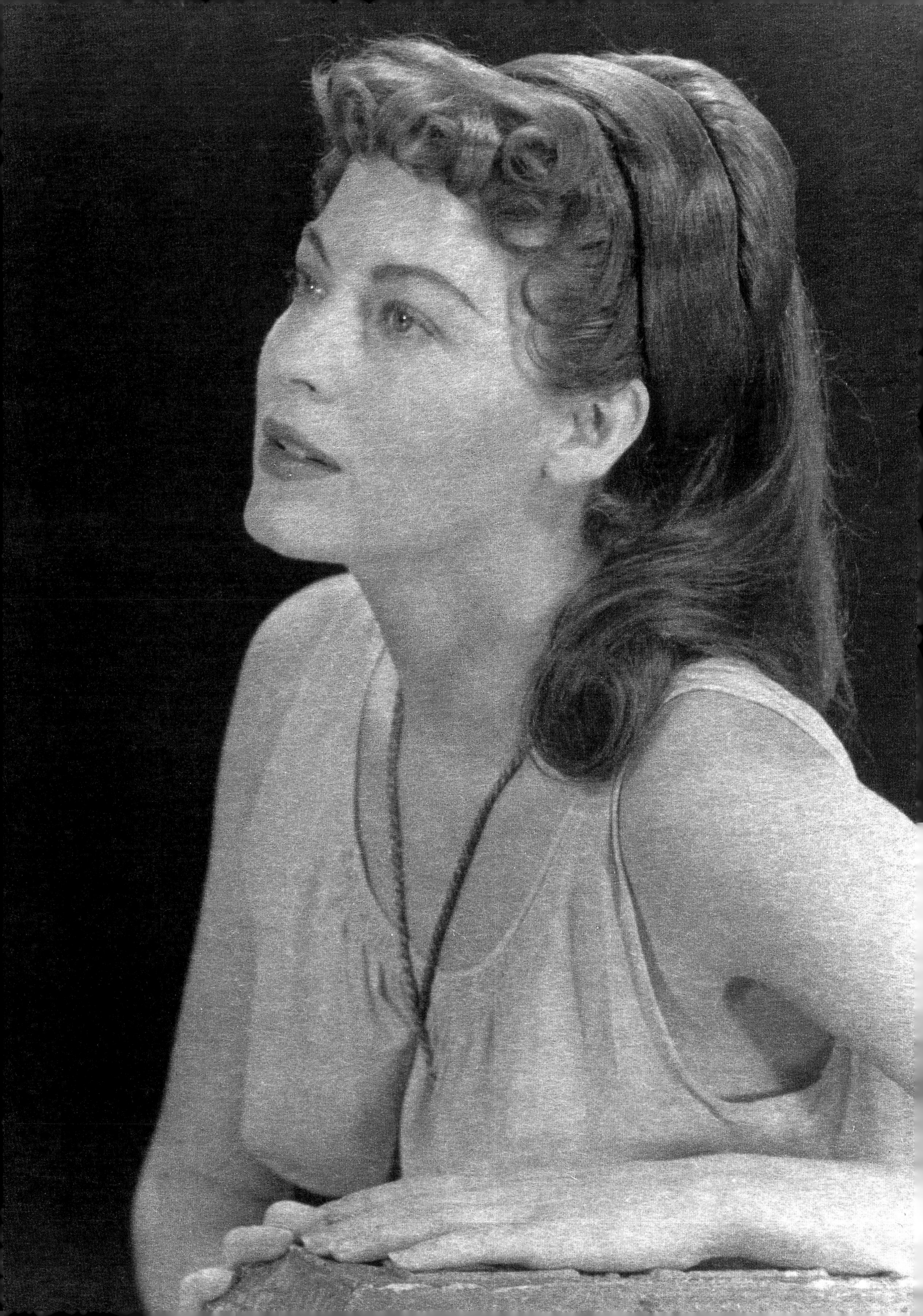

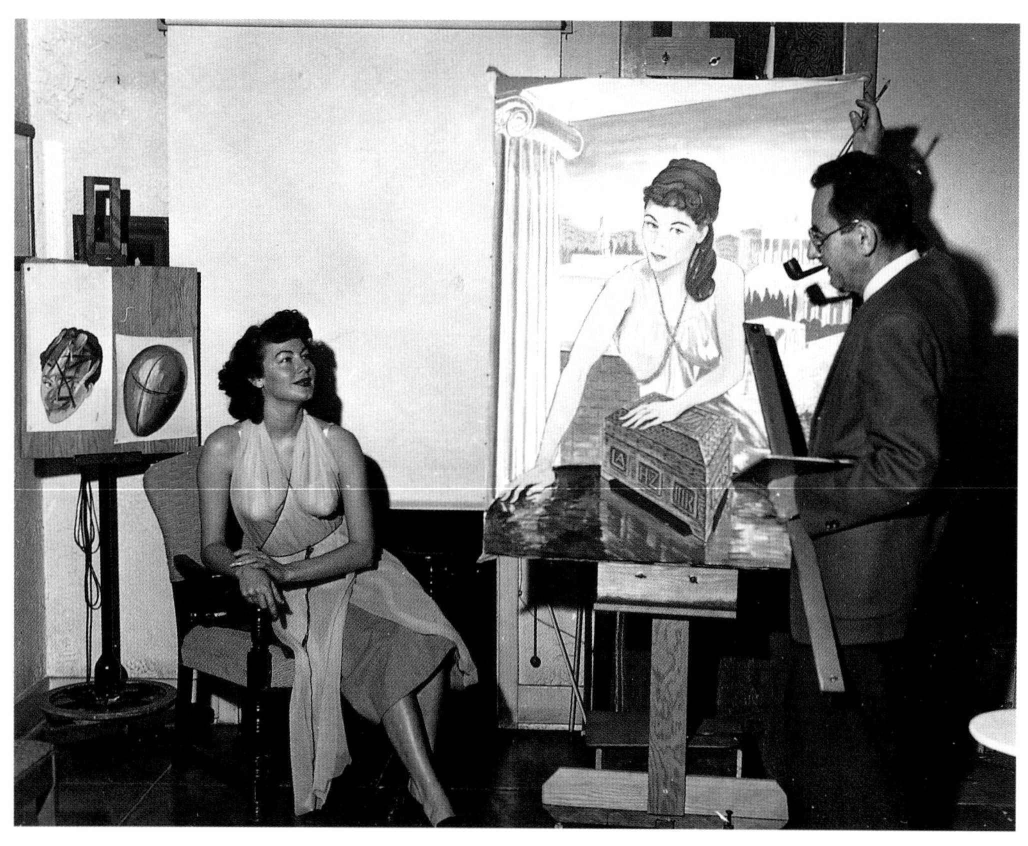

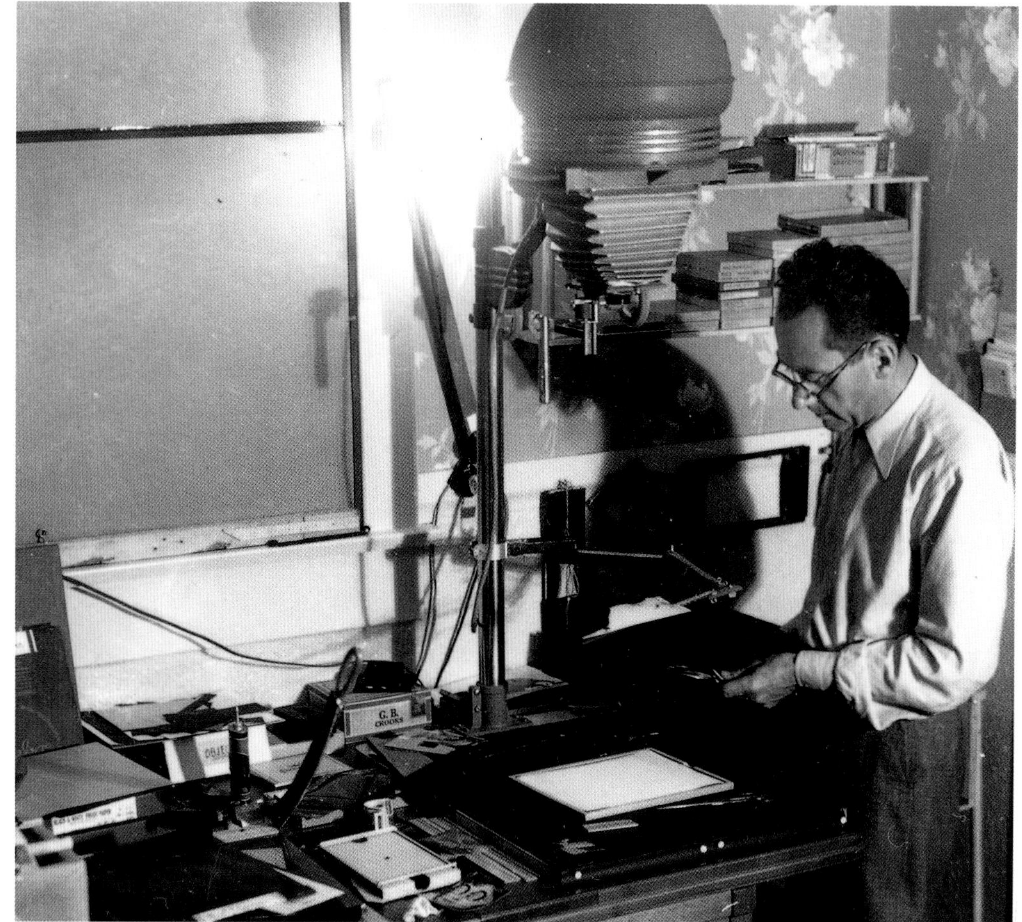

top:
Man Ray painting
***Ava Gardner** for the movie*
Pandora and the
Flying Dutchman, 1950
Gelatin-silver print

left:
Man Ray in his darkroom,
Hollywood, 1948
Gelatin-silver print

Man Ray's sequence is titled "Ruth, Roses and Revolvers," described as "a Surrealist fantasy;" it was originally published in Charles Henri Ford's *View* magazine in December 1944. He wrote this piece in celebration of the recent liberation of Paris: "I swore to you," he begins, "I would not paint another picture, photograph a pretty woman, nor make love to her, until the day of the liberation of Paris. Today I shall do all three." The main body of the narrative, accompanied by portraits of Juliet and Ruth Ford, served as the basis for Richter's shooting script. Before entering a small movie theater with Juliet, the protagonist (Man Ray as narrator in the version for *View*) leaves a book beneath a tree. In the theater, Ruth introduces the film: "Good evening. We are going to have the privilege tonight of witnessing one of the most unusual films ever produced."[69]

Upon this parody of every pretentious "art" film presentation, Man Ray has Ruth then urge audience participation, as he had urged it the year before in his talk at the American Contemporary Gallery. "Whatever it may lack in the way of sound and color you may supply out of your own conversation and by looking at me," Ruth says, adding what becomes an ironic twist: "But for the real success of this presentation, you are earnestly requested to collaborate even more actively. You all know the principal character in this film, you have every confidence in him, and in the economy of his gestures. To give these gestures their full meaning I earnestly implore you to follow, and to repeat these gestures as they occur."[70]

Subsequent participation by members of the audience, hilariously mindless in their contortions, is, however, hardly the sort of collaboration that Man Ray had sought in his earlier talk. Then he had hoped that "the spectator . . . would desire to rush out and breathe the pure air of the outside, live his own life, be the leading actor and solve his own dramatic problems." In stark contrast, his fictive audience in *Dreams That Money Can Buy* reveals its conformity to the banal dreams of Hollywood movies. As the reviewer for *The Hollywood Reporter* was quick to point out, though rather huffily, "One dream, apparently aimed at Hollywood, ridicules the readiness with which most people accept the impressions of others."[71]

the following pages in order:

p. 94
Ihagee folding plate camera

p. 95
Man Ray in Cannes holding Ihagee camera, 1930s *Gelatin-silver print* on carte postale *paper* (unknown photographer)

p. 96
Thorton-Pickard folding field camera, English, c. 1900 *Mahogany body, black fabric bellows, brass fittings, and ground-glass screen*

p. 97
Untitled *(painted mask),* c. 1960 *White painted cardboard mask with black fabric eye mask*

Man Ray's collaboration with Richter was not without its complications. In August 1945, after some delay, the filmmaker requested some suggestions from Man Ray for a shooting script based on "Ruth,

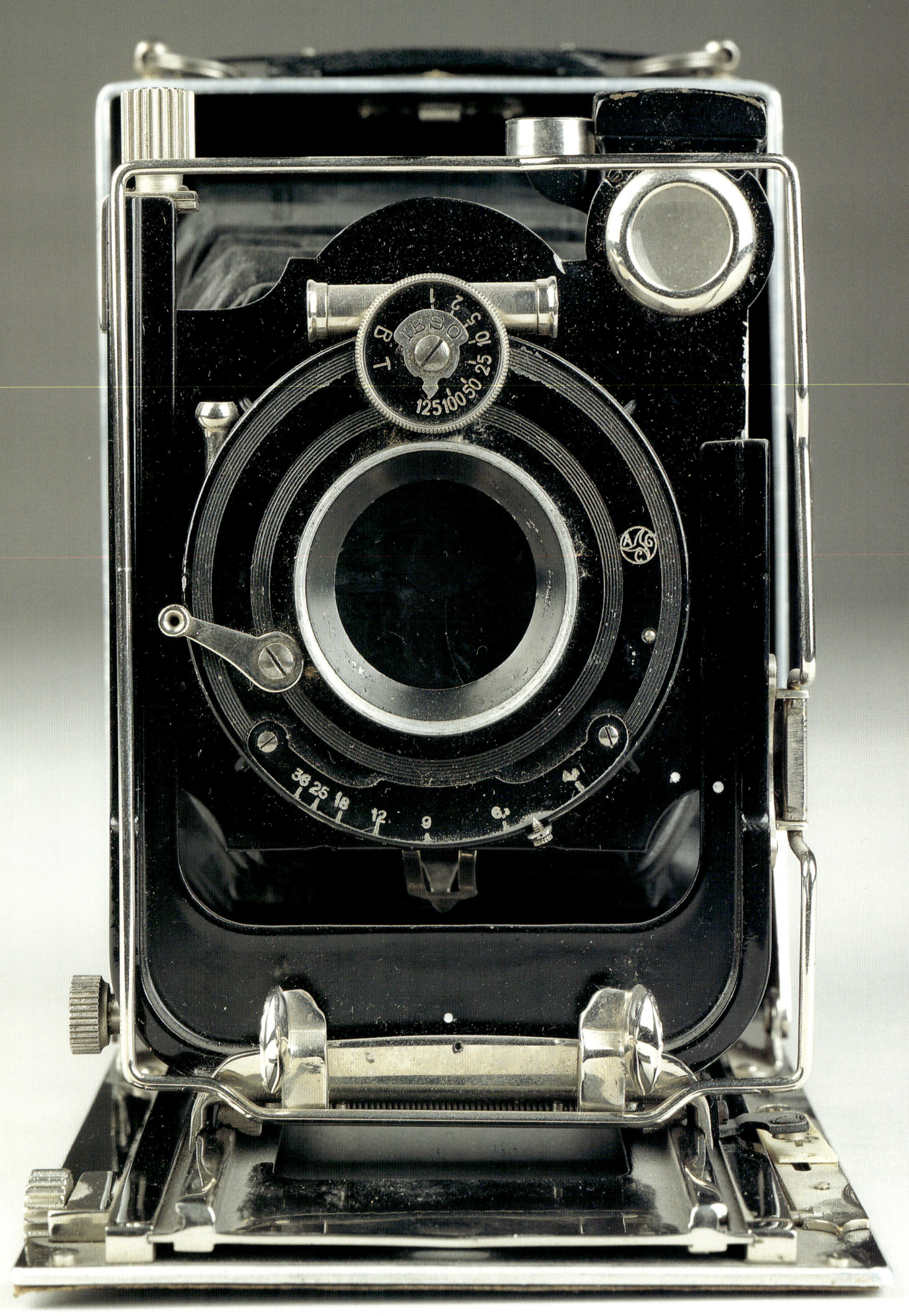
IBSO
B T 1 2 5 10 25 50 100 125
36 25 18 12 9

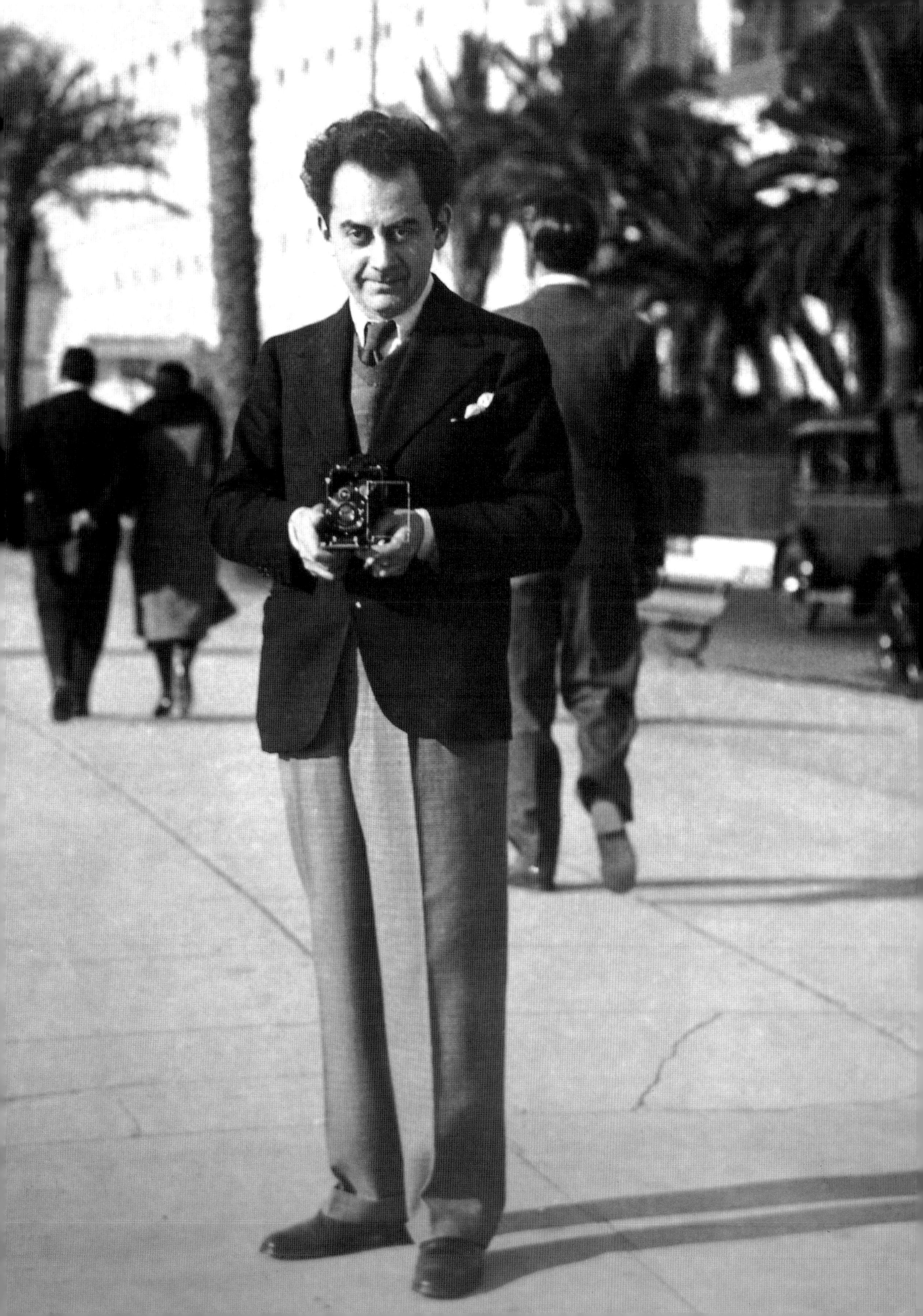

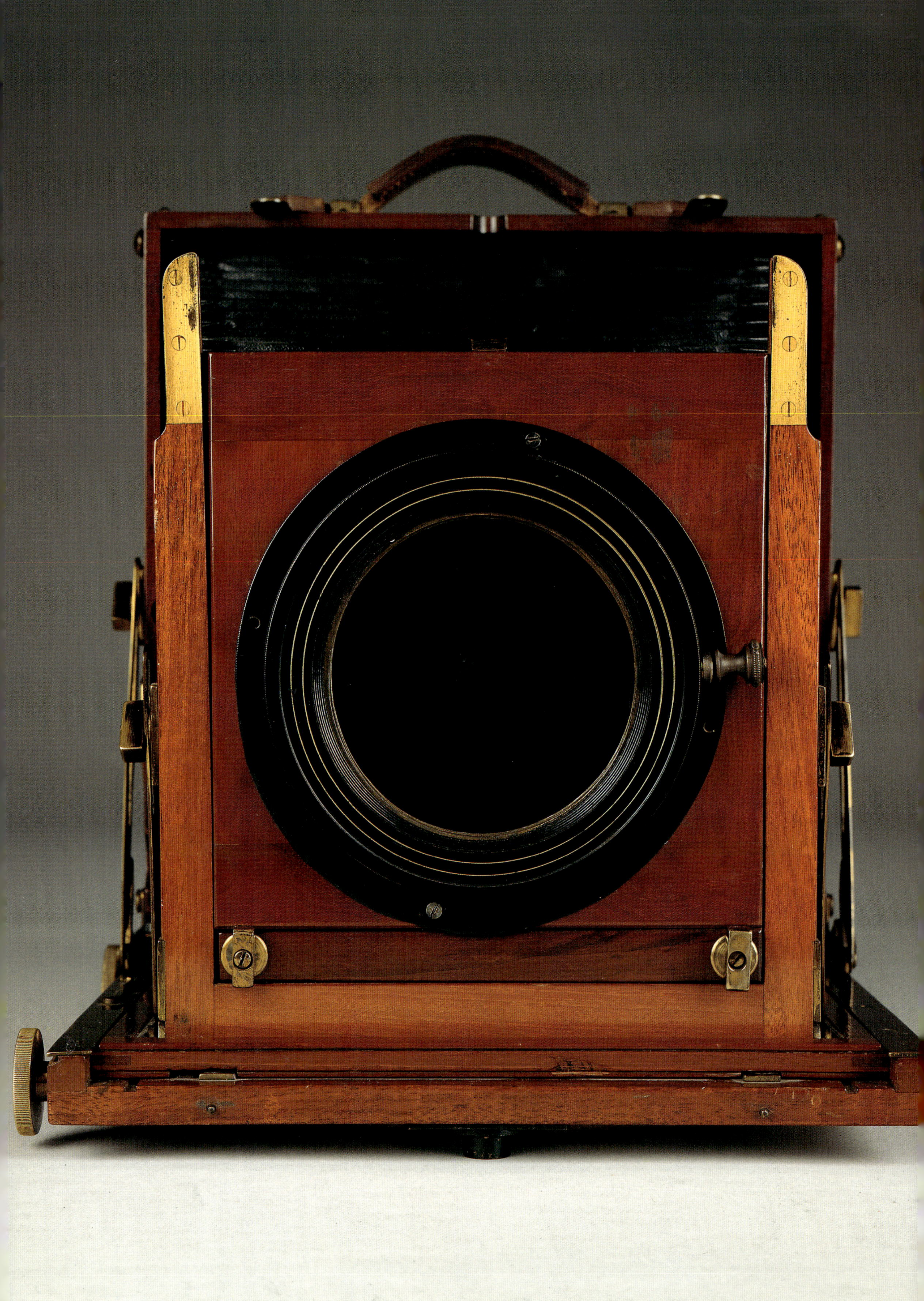

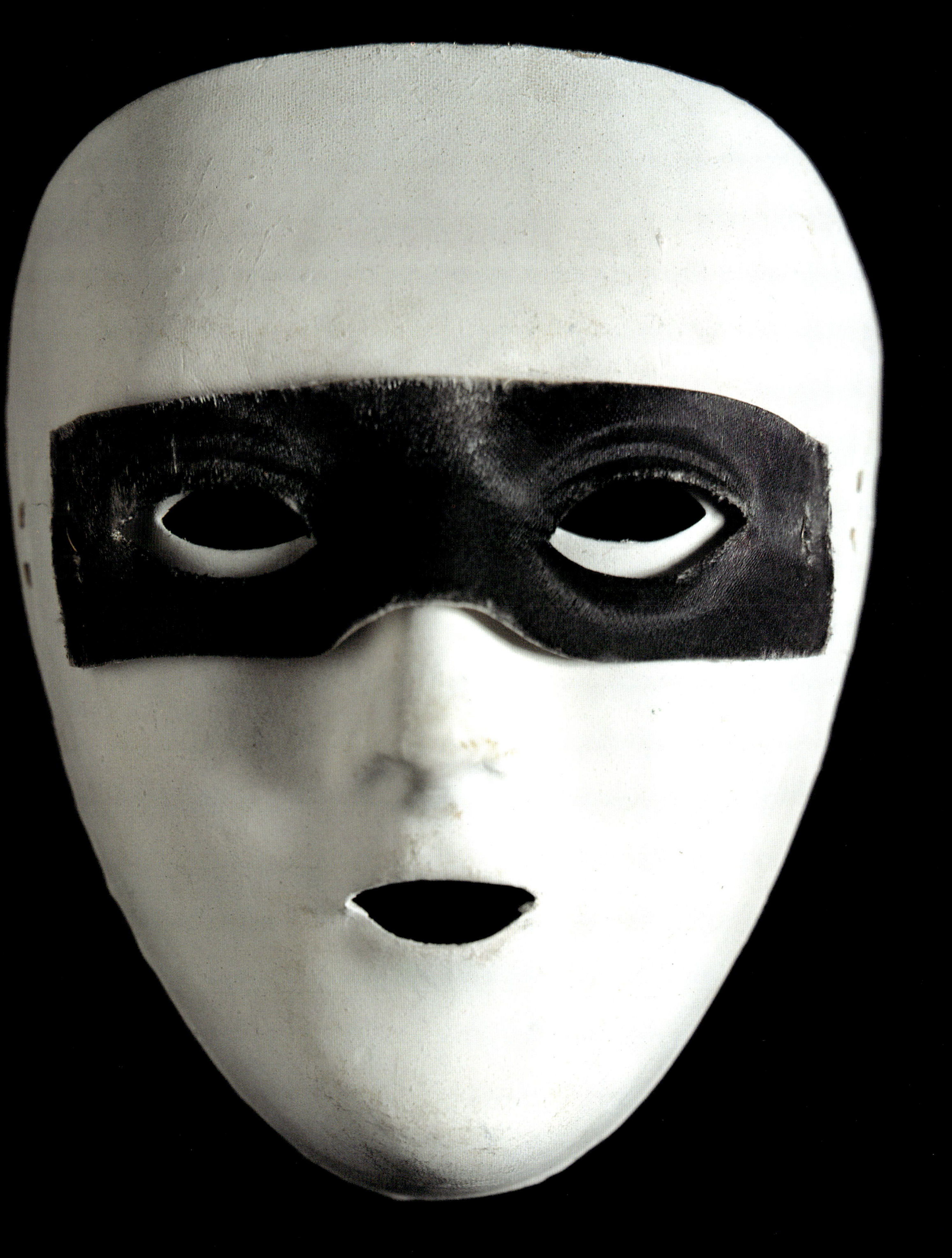

Roses and Revolvers." In Richter's version, the film within the film is explained as a love story, and after the film screening, a cynical Juliet shoots the lovesick protagonist, who has transformed himself into a tree (a hint offered by Man Ray's *View* version).[72] Man Ray apparently vehemently, if not violently, rejected Richter's shooting script.

In a conciliatory letter of December 10, 1945, Richter protested that "it doesn't really help to get excited, rough, tough, unfriendly, for I am really trying to understand what you mean." Interpretation was essential, even though Richter claimed, "I agree completely with you that the best way to realize a script is to drop it into a slot-machine and get a finished product at the bottom." Acceding to Man Ray's demands, Richter abandoned the idea of satirizing Hollywood love stories by scrapping his proposed ending: "No shooting with a revolver? No shooting!"[73]

Later, Richter asked Man Ray to help edit the script by half to maintain a balance with the other segments. He also thought that a "Prie dieu" sequence satirizing a Roman Catholic confession should be excised because it would not get past the censors;[74] nevertheless, the prayer bench and the praying sequence were retained, though an anticlerical protest in "Ruth, Roses and Revolvers" was suppressed. Similarly, the title of the book left beneath the tree was changed from "Sade" to "Ruth, Roses and Revolvers." The back cover, however, was exposed to reveal a self-portrait of a bearded Man Ray, clearly standing in for the dreaded Marquis. The entire segment ends with a montage celebrating liberty.

Despite these minor modifications, Man Ray managed a successful long-distance collaboration, facilitated by Richter's imagination and patience. The filmed version of "Ruth, Roses and Revolvers" has a comic simplicity that belies its complex, self-reflexive structure: a live audience views a fictive audience (filmed in color) viewing a fictive black-and-white film. The fictive audience in turn imitates the absurd behavior of the male actor in the fictive film, seated in front of a rectangular image on the wall—a large photograph of Man Ray's eyes, looking at the fictive audience and beyond *Dreams That Money Can Buy* to the live audience, and ultimately at Man Ray himself. In an unpublished note, he claimed, "Since the movies are a projection, it amused me to carry the idea to a consistent end, and see an interpretation of it realized by others, so that I could get the same surprise out of it that any spectator would have." Enjoying "the combined role of entertainer and entertained," he concluded, "To wear a beard and not wear one at the same time is indeed an achievement." *Dreams That Money Can Buy* opened in Los Angeles at the Esquire Theater on July 16, 1948.[75]

1948 brought the final turning point to Man Ray's stay in Hollywood. William Copley, heir to a Southern California newspaper chain, and his brother-in-law John Ployardt, a Disney animator, decided to open a gallery at 257 North Cañon Drive in Beverly Hills, not far from Romanoff's Restaurant. This project alone would have been unexceptional but for their Surrealist enthusiasms. Calling one morning on a suspicious Man Ray (who turned them away until a civilized hour), they finally convinced him of their sincerity, and subsequently made contact with Duchamp in New York. Exhibitions of the work of Magritte, Cornell, Matta, and Tanguy soon followed. From December 14, 1948, to January 9, 1949, the two partners mounted "Café Man Ray," and the gallery was transformed into a French garden cafe for a gala opening night, with onion soup and other libations served by Vera Stravinsky, the composer's daughter-in-law, who also worked in the gallery.

The most prominent painting repatriated from Paris in the exhibition was *Observatory Time—The Lovers* (1932–1934). Taken out of its frame, the canvas had been rolled up and smuggled out of France by the extraordinarily courageous Mary Reynolds, Duchamp's intimate friend, who had chosen to stay in her apartment on rue Hallé during the occupation until the Gestapo got wind of her activities for Free France. Crossing the Pyrenees on foot, she managed to make it to Lisbon; from there she flew to New York and rejoined Duchamp on January 8, 1943.[76] The result of several incarnations and transformations of past work, *Observatory Time* had in turn been translated from a painting into a photograph, which Copley generously purchased along with the painting.

In addition to a typical array of watercolors, drawings, and objects (including chess sets), Man Ray presented a new series of twenty oil paintings titled "Shakespearean Equations." The starting point had been a group of geometrical objects on display at the Poincaré Institute in Paris whose forms visualized mathematical equations in three dimensions. Fascinated when Max Ernst pointed them out to him, Man Ray photographed them and brought the photographs with him from Paris. As late as April 1948, Juliet jotted on a postcard to Man Ray's niece Naomi that "Man is painting wonderful human equations, that's what he calls the new series of paintings."[77]

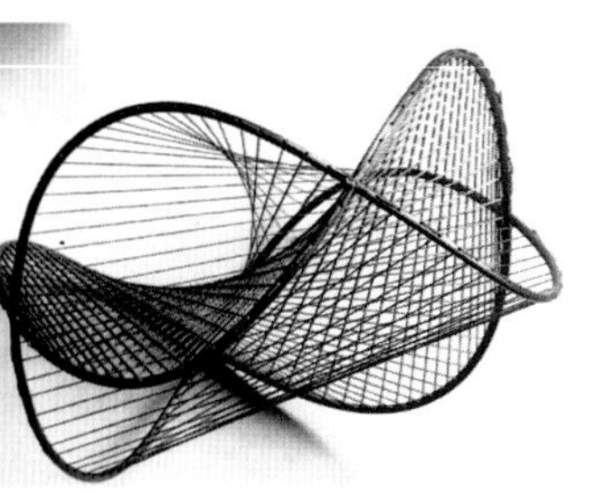

Mathematical Object "Surface a Courbure Constante negative d'enneper, derive de la psuedo-sphere," 1936 *Gelatin-silver print*

The shift to "Shakespearean Equations" became complete with the titles that Man Ray gave to these paintings: *Love's Labors Lost* or *Much Ado About Nothing*, and so forth. James Byrnes, at the time curator of contemporary art at the Los Angeles County Museum, has speculated that Man Ray was slyly alluding to Walter Arensberg and his obsessive quest to prove that Sir Francis Bacon actually wrote the plays and poetry attributed to the Bard. The titles conjoined to the painted forms certainly give rise to a visual puzzle. Yet the viewer's desire to decode these paintings runs up against Man Ray's assertion that he chose his titles freely and automatically, "to take liberties with the legends. . . ."[78]

Human equations, however, get at the heart of the matter. Like his drawing of a human figure against a T-square, like his self-portrait overlaid with a grid, Man Ray tried to integrate the geometric and the mathematical with the human, to avoid false oppositions. In his "Note on the Shakespearean Equations" for the catalogue of the Copley exhibition, he resolved "to seek inspiration as much as possible from man-made objects." The "arbitrary" nature of this project stressed the human creativity involved and in passing invested abstract painting with "inventiveness and imagination."[79]

The catalogue for "Café Man Ray" was a large, elegantly printed portfolio, containing not only illustrations of the "Shakespearean Equations," but also a tipped-in Man Ray photograph along with his commentaries. The show was formally titled "To Be Continued Unnoticed," anagrammatic word play that suggested Man Ray's acceptance of his virtual invisibility in the California art world. The title also echoed his admiration for Knud Merrild, whose unheralded efforts had sustained Man Ray in his early California struggles. Millier's dismissive assessment for *Art Digest* was ironically on the mark. "The colors are nice," he thought, "the craft looks good and they are interesting to those who care."[80]

opposite to
La Chaleur (Love's Labor Los
from the seri
"Shakespearean Equations," 19
Oil on canv

opposite rig
(Maquett
To Be Continued Unnoticed, 19
Ink on pap

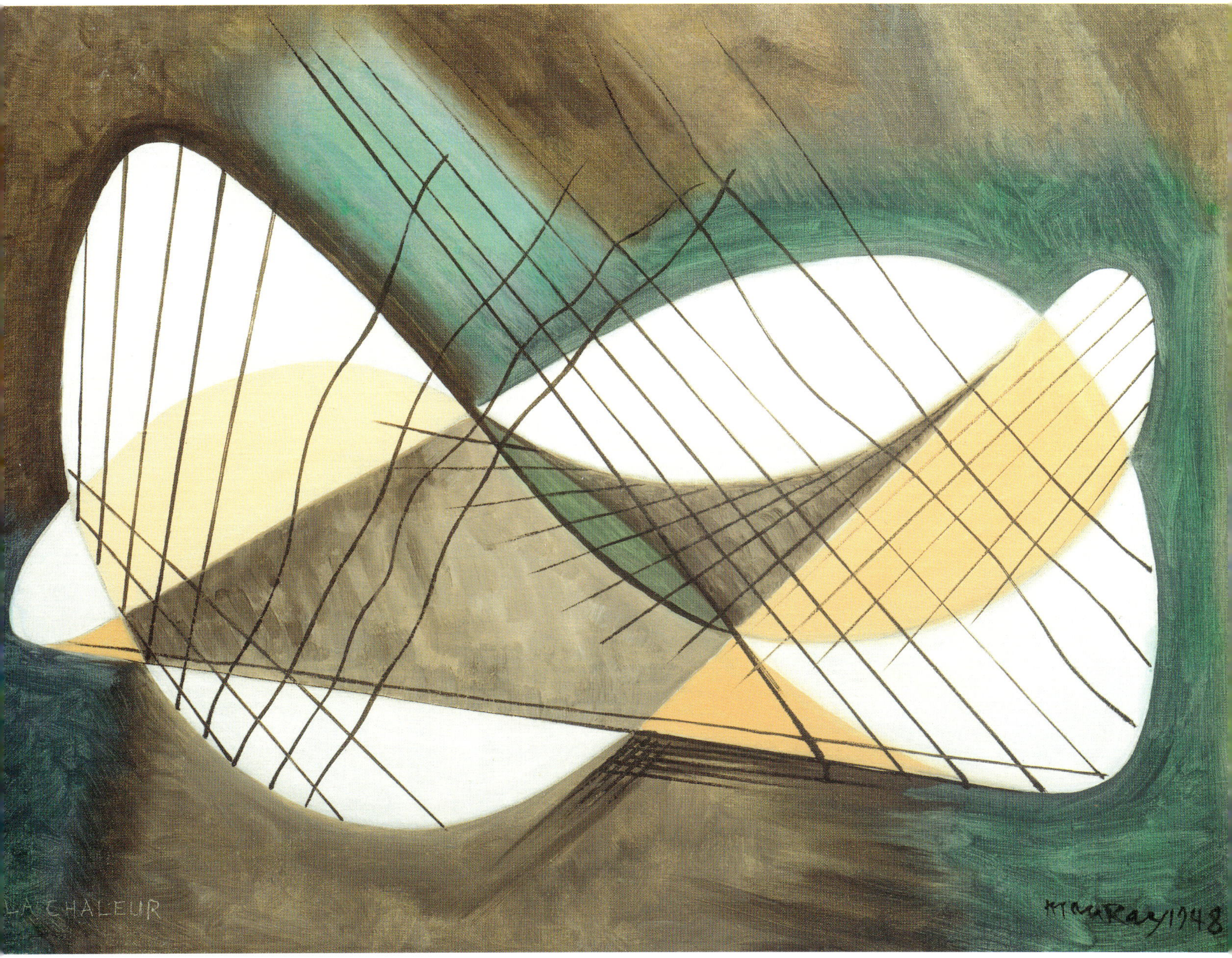

LA CHALEUR

Man Ray 1948

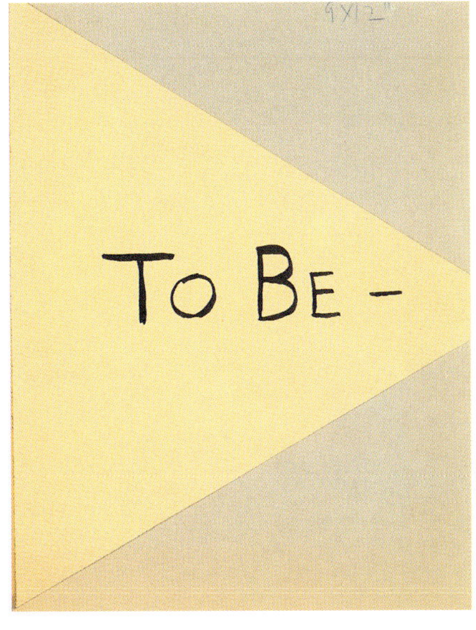

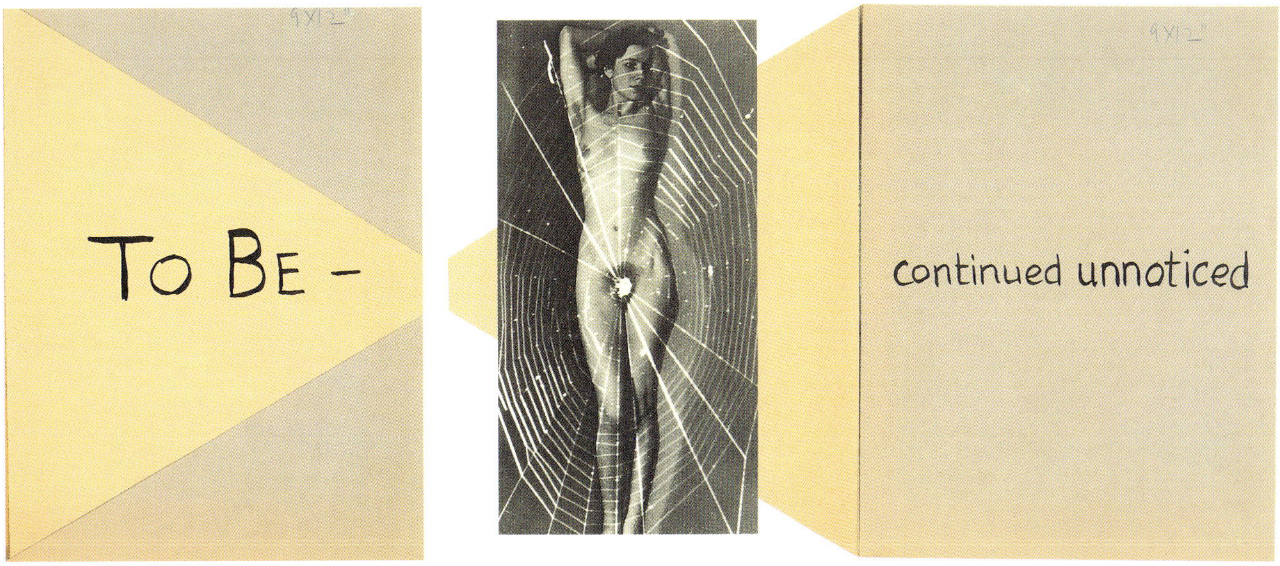

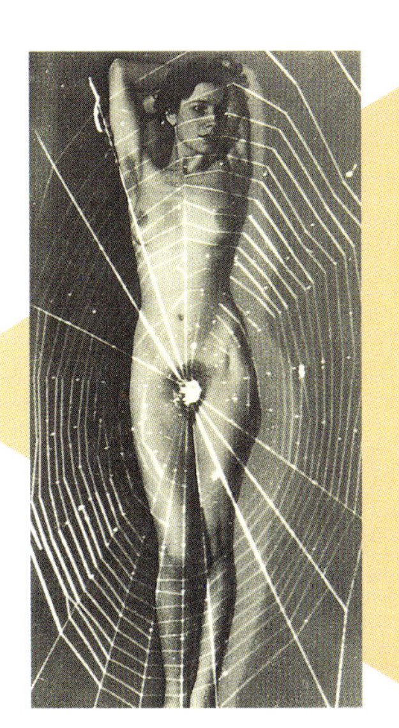

9X12"

continued unnoticed

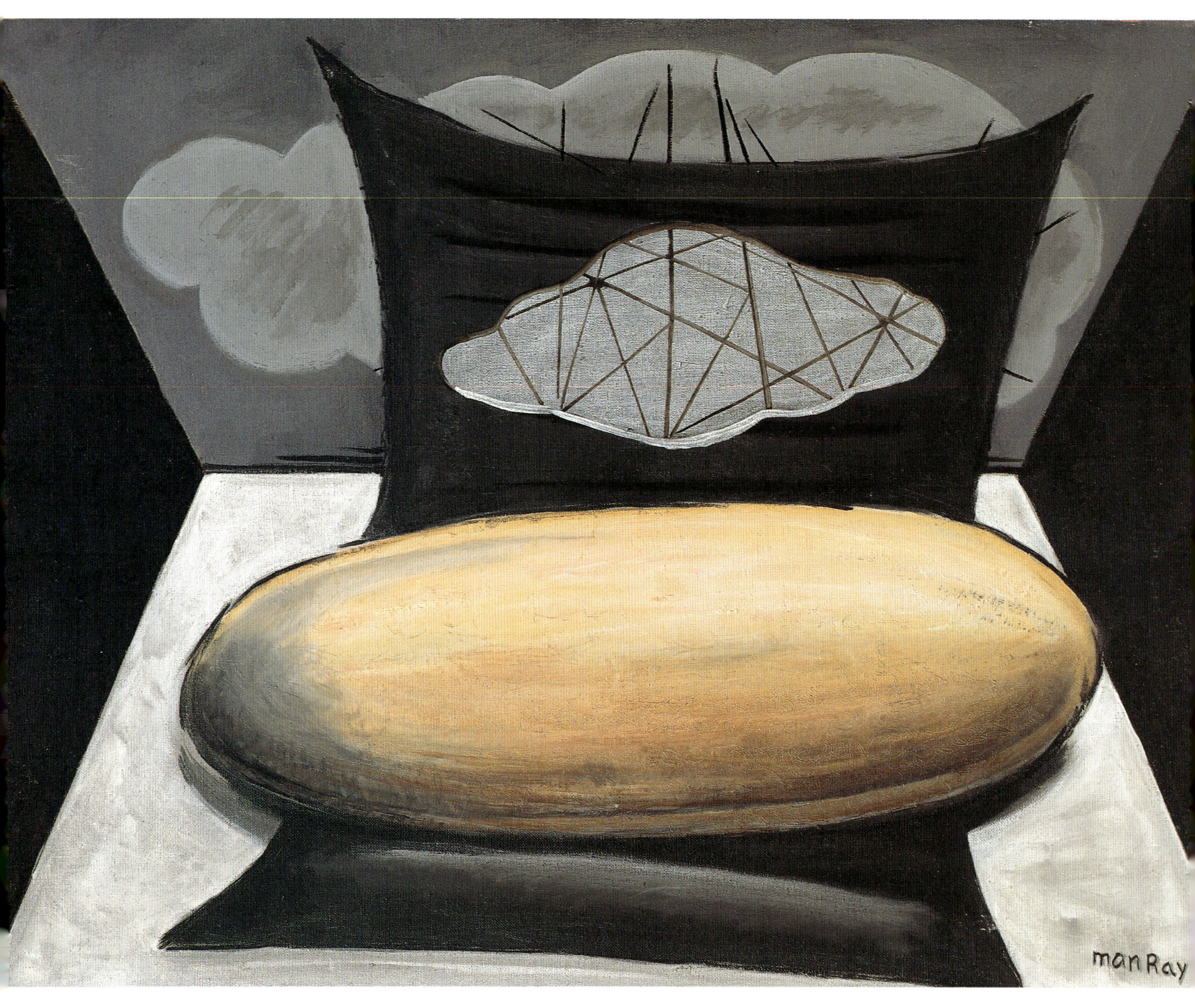

Much Ado About Nothing,
from the series "Shakespearean Equations,"
1948 *Oil on canvas*

At this time Man Ray continued his artistic output in various media. Under the imprimatur of the Copley Galleries, Man Ray published an album of drawings titled *Alphabet for Adults* in December 1948. This was not his first publishing venture during the 1940s. In 1947 a second edition of *Les Mains Libres* appeared in France. This collaboration with Paul Eluard was one of the first things that Man Ray had requested his sister send him in Hollywood. No doubt the book reminded him of better times with the poet. In one of the last self-portraits that Man Ray took before he left Paris, he had posed next to Eluard in uniform, mobilized for the war. They would not be reunited until the painter's brief return to France in 1947 to settle his affairs.

Eluard and his wife Nusch had chosen to remain in Paris, and had joined the underground; Nusch died of malnutrition at the end of the war. Man Ray had eloquently photographed her in conjunction with Eluard's poems in a beautiful volume titled *Facile* in 1935. He had given a copy to Dorothea Tanning, who was extremely moved. "The poems are tragically beautiful," she wrote in 1947, "and your photos of that poor lovely woman are heart breakingly wonderful. What an unforgettable face."[81]

Man Ray made two other photographic albums in California. In 1945 he assembled a series of photographs of watercolors he had done of cacti in Pasadena. On the cover he photographed himself dwarfed by the giant plants. Out of his penchant for manipulation comes a variant self-portrait cut from the corner of the cover original; not content to remain with a single medium, he also rendered in oil a *Desert Plant* in 1946. At this time, too, he assembled an album of photographs titled *Mr. and Mrs. Woodman*, based upon wooden articulated figures in erotic combinations. These figures were also derived from the past: they were posed in his Paris studio, fondled in a self-portrait taken in the 1920s, they climbed over a Duchampian readymade entitled *Bottlerack*.

Alphabet for Adults was Man Ray's most literary visual publication, signalled by the anagram in "To Be Continued Unnoticed" with its own transformational logic. "Concentration" he wrote in the preface, "is the desired end, as in an anagram whose density is the measure of its destiny." (Man Ray may have recalled Charles Henri Ford's poetic *ABC's* from 1941, with an illustrated cover by Joseph Cornell.)

Alphabets are ordinarily for children to learn the written language. An "alphabet for adults" is a reversal. Adults, he claimed, needed to *unlearn* their language—language that has become hackneyed and worn-out. Man Ray wanted instead to "project" these "disinherited symbols . . . into the domain of greater emotional exclamations." He sought nothing less than a "new alphabet" from "the discarded props of convention."[82]

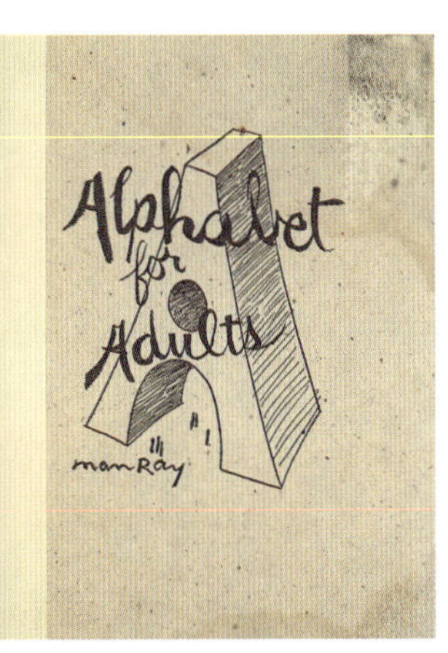

Man Ray made thirty-seven line drawings for twenty-six letters. In each instance he supplied a word whose first letter represents the appropriate letter in the alphabet sequence. The drawing becomes the wild card as Man Ray resorted to the fundamental Surrealist technique of unexpected association. "A," for example, stands for "anchor," with a conventional illustration, but it also stands for "answer," imaged by a padlock with key. To unlock something is to gain an answer, but the closed padlock suggests that answers shut down options. But what answer is there for "Regret," imaged by a cocktail glass?

On February 28, 1948, the Modern Institute of Art opened in Beverly Hills on North Rodeo Drive, with Kenneth Ross as its director. While Duchamp was among those featured in its first exhibition, "Modern Artists in Transition," Man Ray was a strong presence in the subsequent exhibition, "Schools of Twentieth Century Art." He lent four Rayographs, his oil portrait of de Sade, and *Cadeau* (1922), his lethal iron armed with tacks, which was illustrated along with his narrative on Dada in the catalogue.[83]

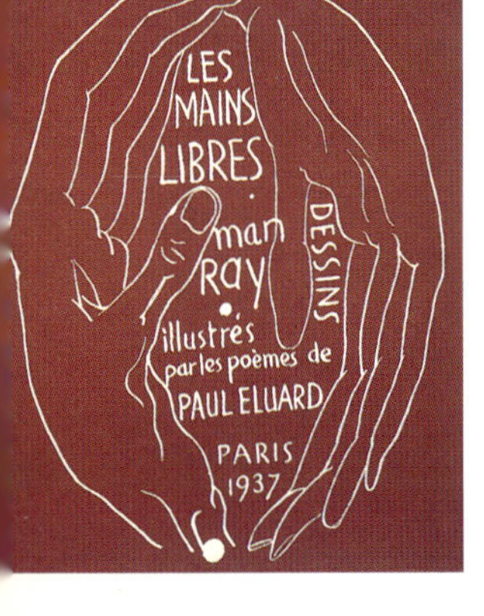

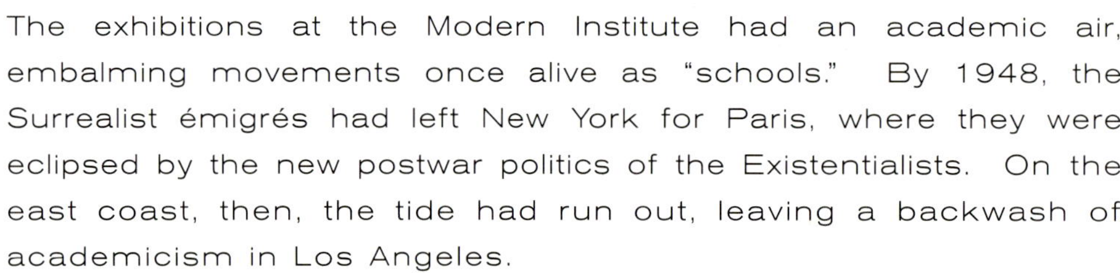

The exhibitions at the Modern Institute had an academic air, embalming movements once alive as "schools." By 1948, the Surrealist émigrés had left New York for Paris, where they were eclipsed by the new postwar politics of the Existentialists. On the east coast, then, the tide had run out, leaving a backwash of academicism in Los Angeles.

top:
***Alphabet for Adults**, published by the Copley Galleries, Beverly Hills,* 1948

above:
Les Main Libres, *Paris,* 1937
Poems by Paul Eluard and illustrations by Man Ray

The Copley Gallery, however, offered a far livelier affair by promoting the work of Surrealist artists still alive and kicking; some were even on the premises. While Man Ray's show was a retrospective of sorts, its informality was indicated by *Café Man Ray*. This absurd doorknocker made out of a child's sand shovel welcomed the viewer to work that was still provocative, with enough energy to insure its notice.

opposite:
***Desert Plant**,* 1946
Oil on canvas

the following pages in order:

p. 106
***Mr. and Mrs. Woodman**,* 1947
Gelatin-silver print

p. 107
***Self-portrait in his studio with lay figure**,* 1927
Gelatin-silver print

p. 108
***La Trou dans la roue**,* c. 1970
Felt-tip pen and pencil on paper

p. 109
***Regret**, from* Alphabet for Adults, 1948 *Ink on paper*

p. 109
Le Sablier–compte-fils
(published in Les Main Libres*),* 1936 *Pen and india ink on paper*

p. 110
***T-Square**,* 1943
Brush and ink on paper

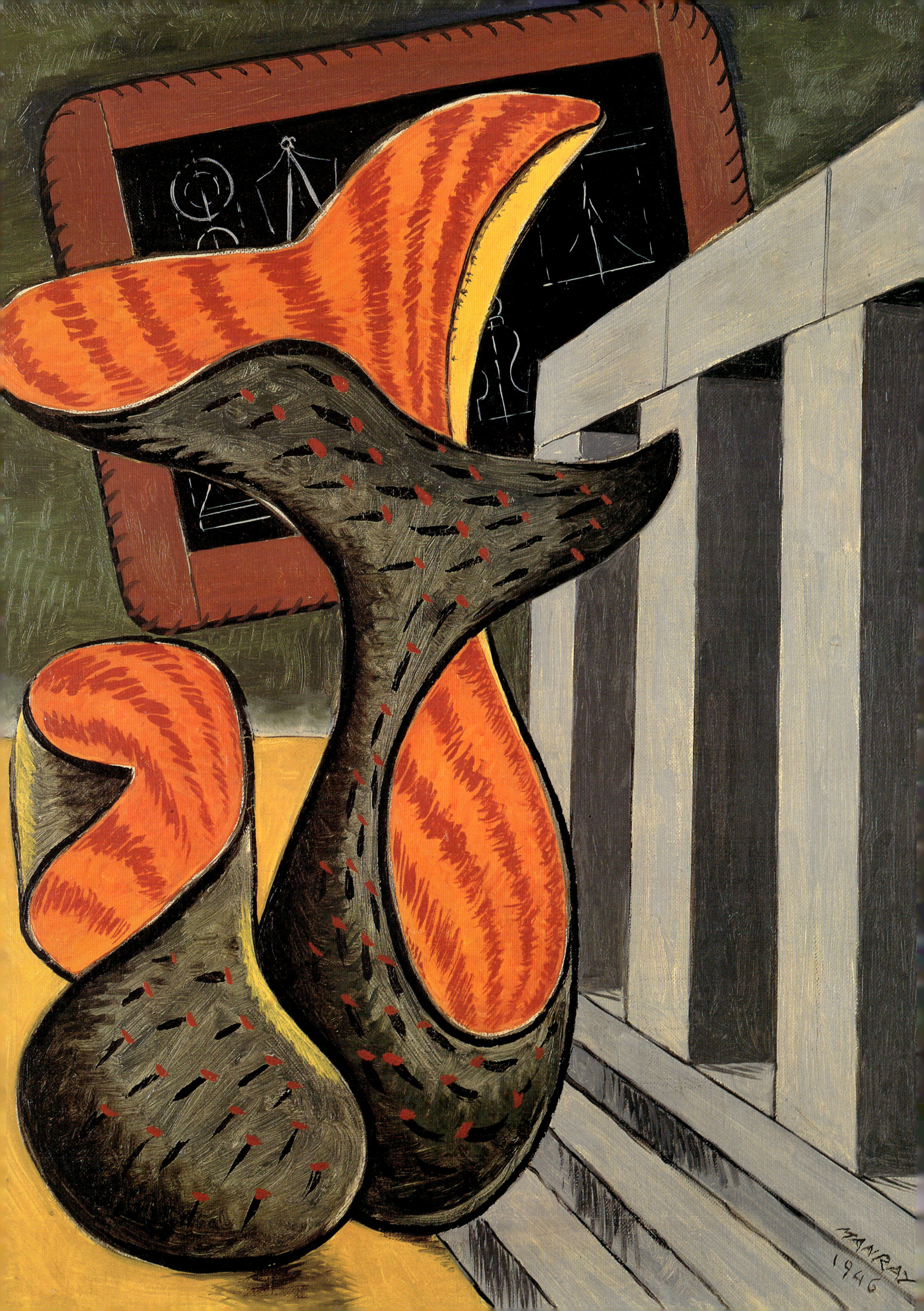
MAN RAY
1946

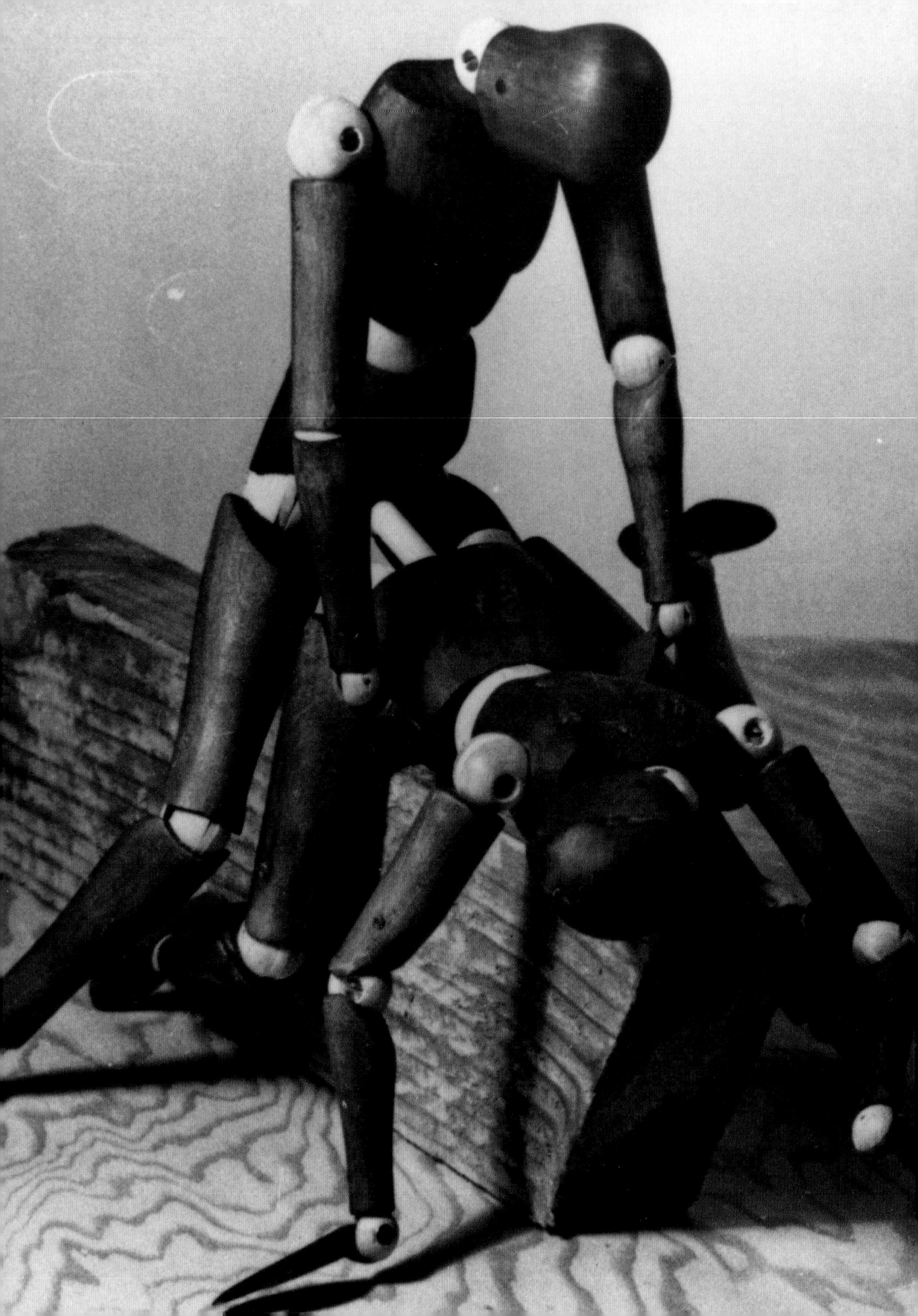

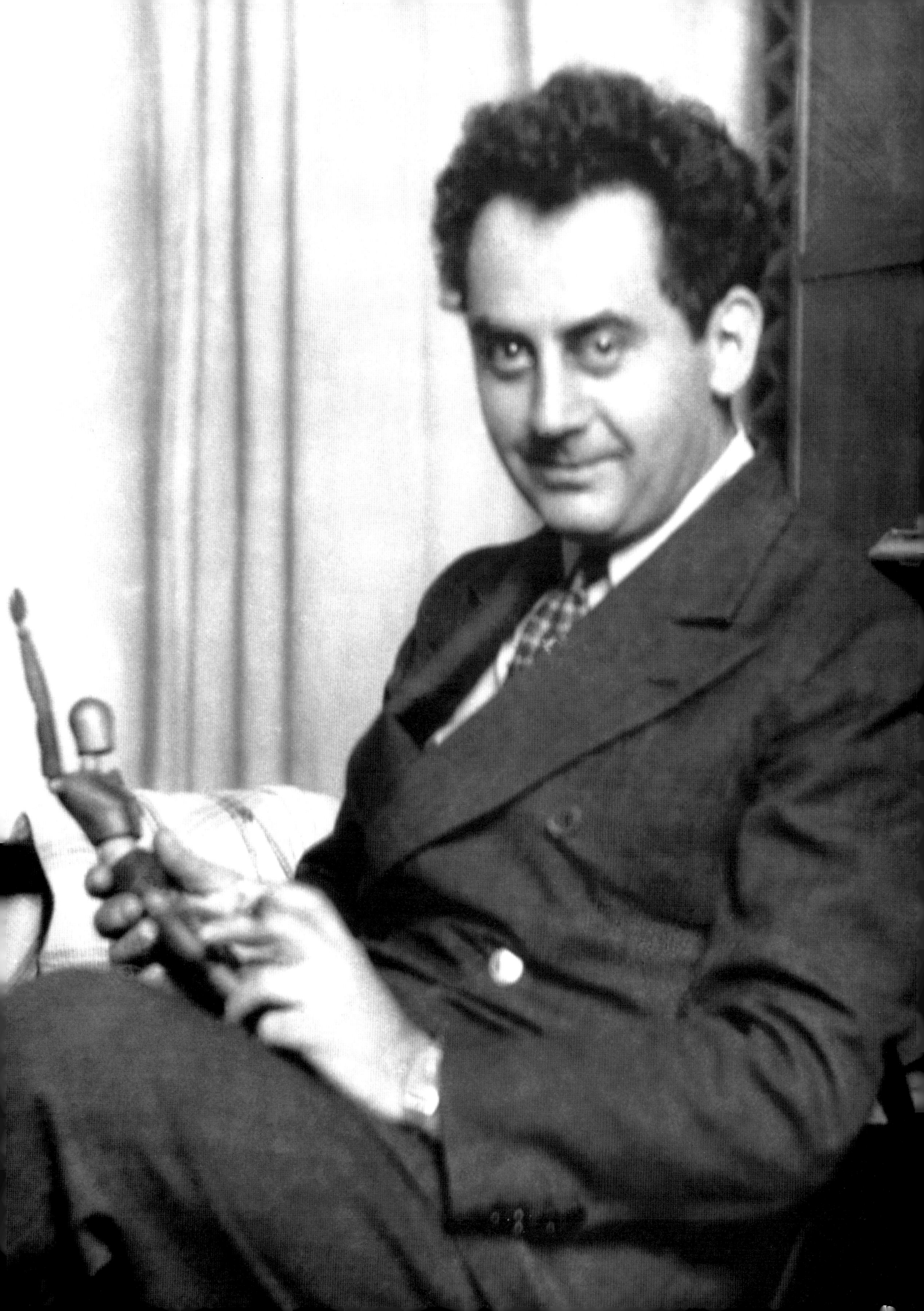

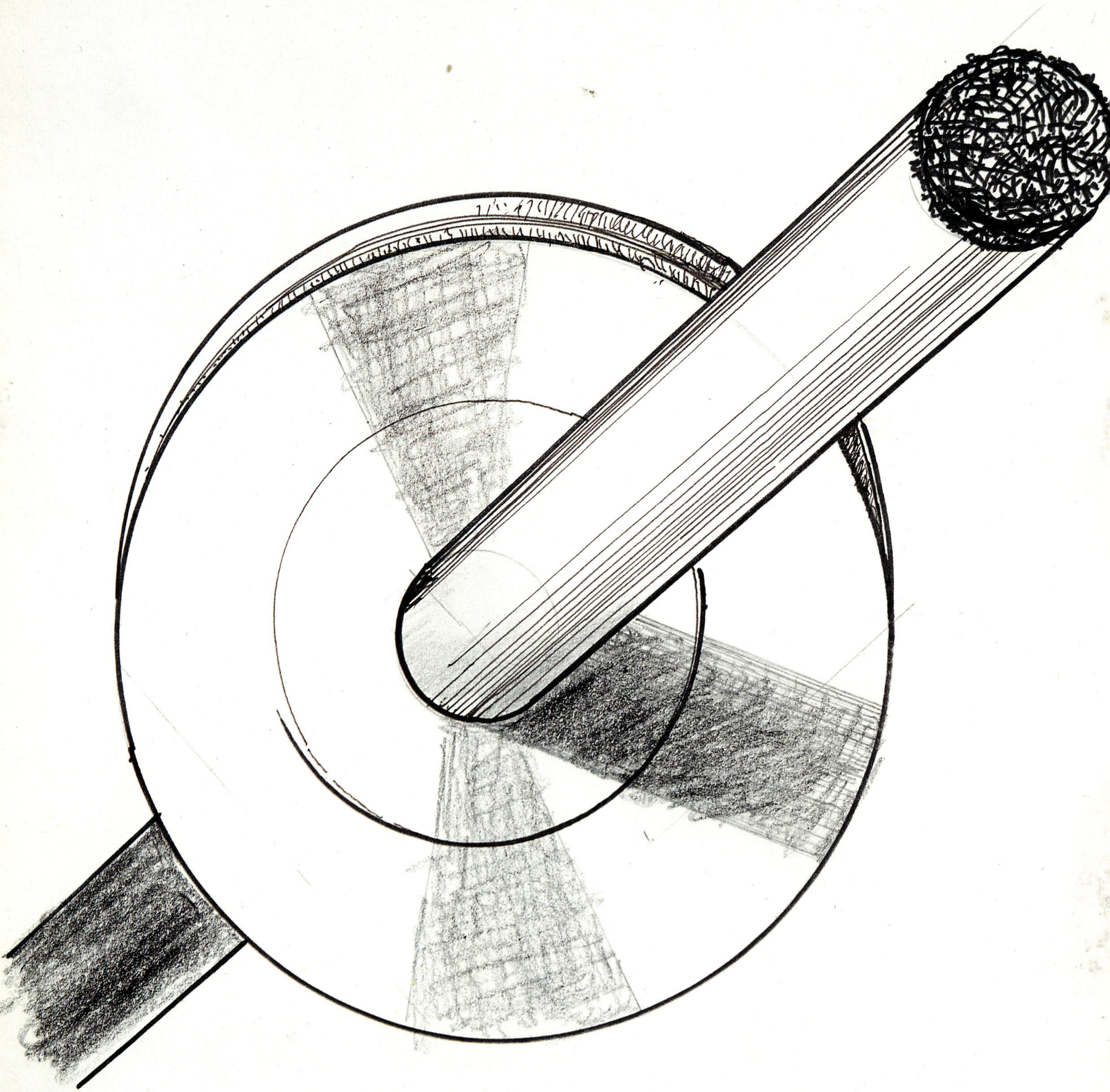

Le trou dans la roue MR

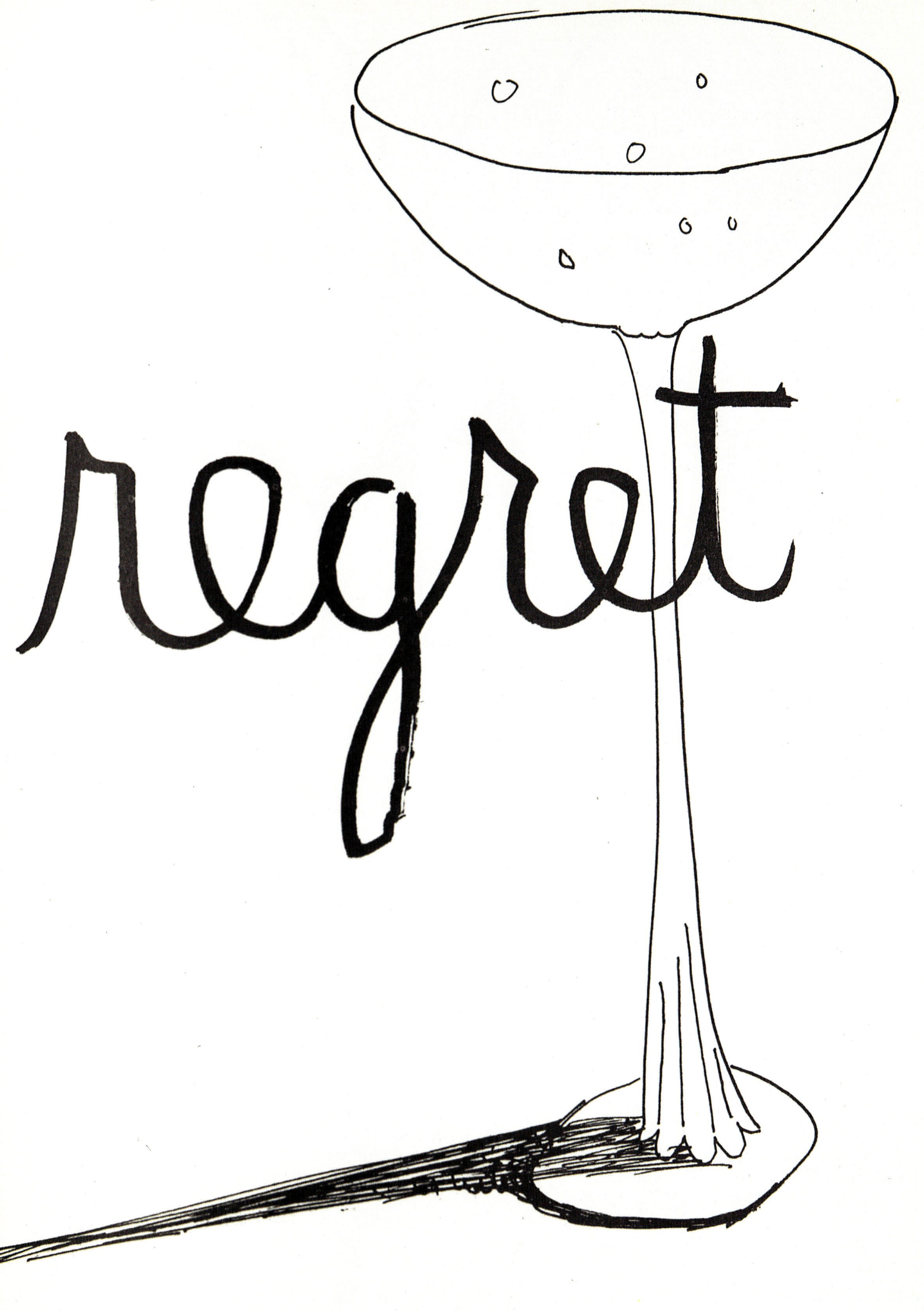
regret

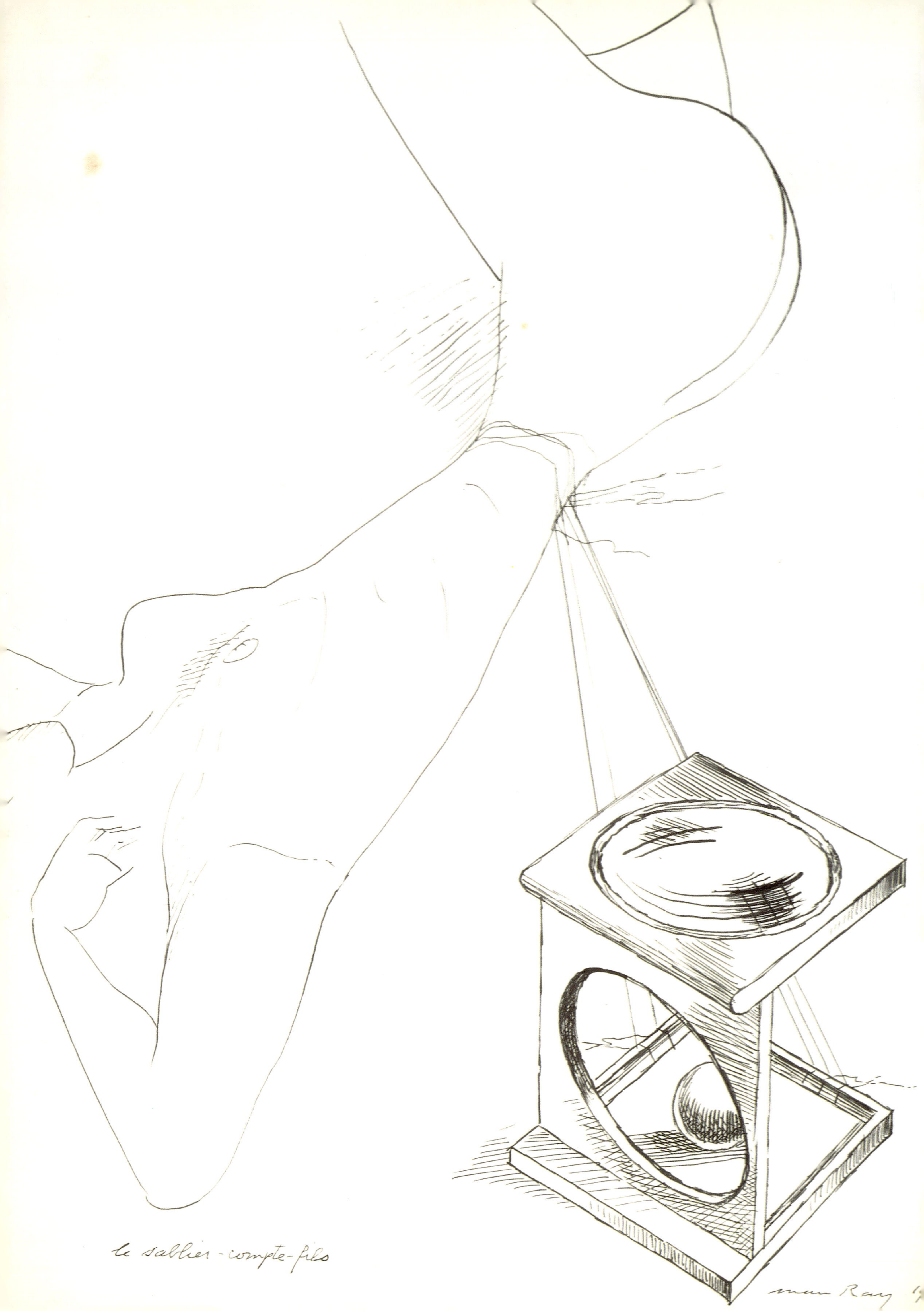
le sablier-compte-fils
man Ray

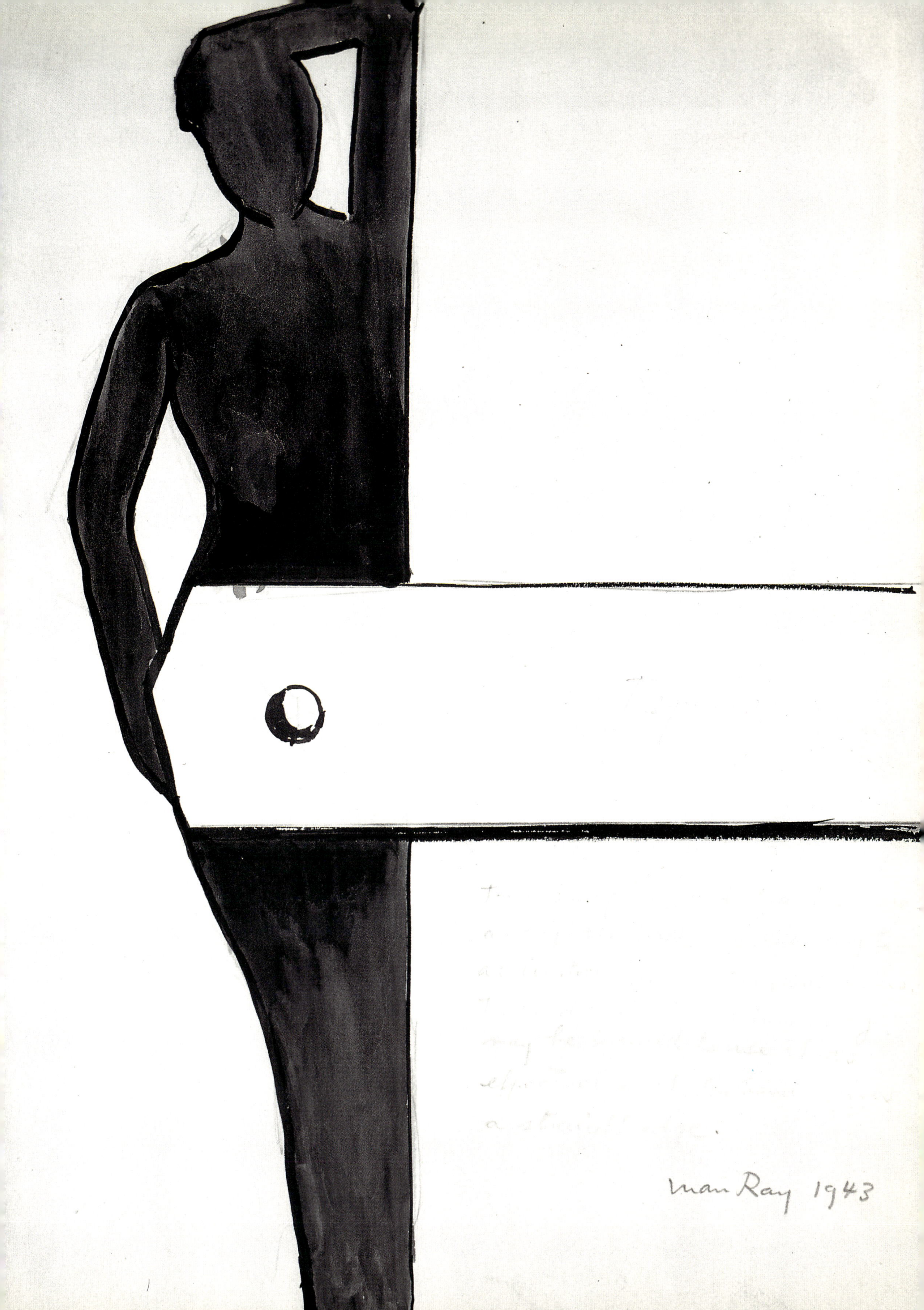
Man Ray 1943

The provocation was immediately at hand. It came from work that appeared casual, almost unfinished, as in the instance of *Life Saver*. It came from objects such as *Emak Bakia*, a cello stripped of function in 1926 by mounting its neck on a base, then given a new function in its conversion to a table lamp in 1947. For Man Ray, the conventional borders between the utilitarian and non-utilitarian, fine art and design, became permeable, signaled by his chess sets, which were meant for play after all. Why not, then, enlarge some pieces and fix them to a board, immovable, as a *Permanent Attraction*?

In his Hollywood decade, Man Ray played back and forth between and among media, especially since it was no longer necessary to concentrate on commercial photography as he had in Paris where, he confessed in Pasadena, he had been "terrified at the prospect" of no income as a foreigner. Decentered in this fashion, his work often appears off-key, moving against the grain of expectation. His *Shakespearean Equations* are precariously balanced on this overlay of shifting media. Beginning with photographs of mathematical objects which, for all Man Ray knew, had been vandalized during the Nazi occupation, the paintings themselves risk misreadings by virtue of their disparate titles. The artist's narrative alone exposes the imaginative process that energizes and completes them.

Man Ray's exhibition at the Copley Galleries was his "last major effort in California," as he wrote to Elsie on the occasion.[84] As the last half of the 1940s wound down, he entertained visitors from out of town—his niece Naomi Siegler from the east coast, Lee Miller and her husband Roland Penrose from London. Duchamp appeared for a week in April 1949 after a symposium in San Francisco on modern art. He stayed with the Arensbergs, whom he had not seen since before the war. Because Man Ray was increasingly disaffected from the Arensbergs (who had never purchased any of his paintings), Duchamp had to slip away from the Arensbergs to meet his friend, waiting in the Graham-Page a block away. It was simply another instance of "continuing unnoticed."

But there were new patrons, such as Mary Stothardt, recently widowed, and new friends, such as Gloria de Herrera, a beautiful young women who worked in James Byrnes's curatorial offices at the Los Angeles County Museum. Speaking engagements ran from San

Francisco to San Diego, where Man Ray was talked about by the members of the Allied Artists' Council as if he were "a very close friend."[85] His work was included in national exhibitions, beginning with "Abstract and Surrealist Art in the United States" in 1944, "Pioneers of Modern Art in America" at the Whitney Museum of American Art in 1946, "Abstract and Surrealist American Art" at the Art Institute of Chicago in 1948, and culminating in "Abstract Painting and Sculpture in America" at The Museum of Modern Art in 1951.

With the close of the decade, Man Ray wrote dramatically to Elsie, "I am organizing things and getting ready for any eventuality–to go back east–or to France. Something is in the air." What he smelled, of course, were the origins of McCarthyism, which infected even the arts during the onset of the cold war. His hand was finally forced by the removal of rent controls in early 1951. With the financial assistance of Copley, he decided to leave Hollywood. "Well, the die is cast," he announced to Elsie. "I am closing my studio and moving everything to New York. We have reservations to sail for Paris on the 12th of March on the *De Grasse*."[86] A yard sale, his landlord's last-minute purchase of the Graham-Page, and then he and Juliet along with William Copley and Gloria de Herrera were off.

On April 1st, Man Ray informed Elsie of "an ideal crossing." A recently wed Naomi and her husband met them at the station in Paris and took them to a hotel. Man Ray's next adventure was beginning: "The great hunt is on for a studio," he wrote. By August "the blanket of tailor's samples" would soon follow him to his new studio on rue Ferou.[87]

To be continued . . .

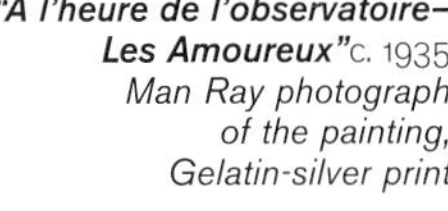

"A l'heure de l'observatoire–Les Amoureux" c. 1935
Man Ray photograph of the painting, Gelatin-silver print

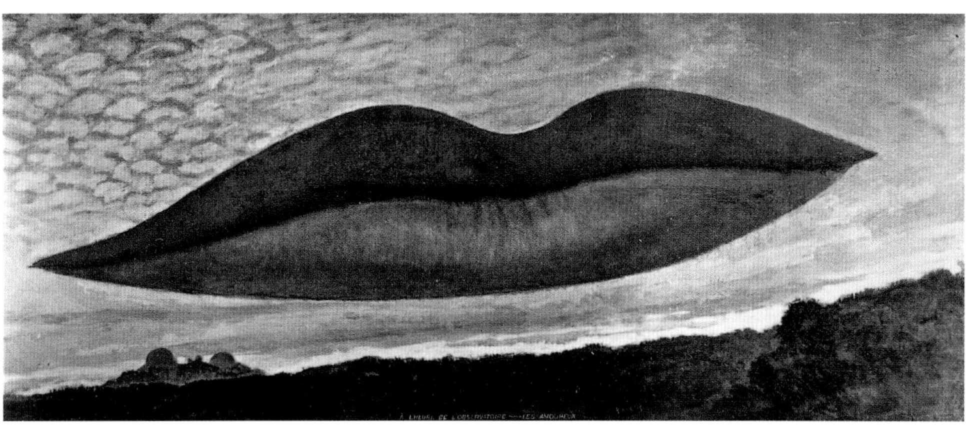

the following pages in order:
p. 114–115
Menu, passenger manifest, baggage tickets, and photographs from the return voyage on the De Grasse, 1951.
(Upper left: Man Ray studio sale invitation; upper right: Man Ray, Gloria de Herrera, Juliet, and Marcel Duchamp; lower right: Juliet, Man Ray, and Gloria de Herrera; lower left: the De Grasse*)*

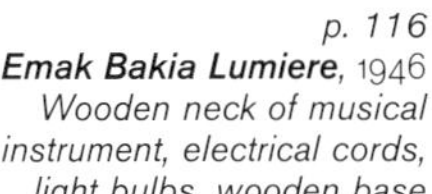

p. 116
Emak Bakia Lumiere, 1946
Wooden neck of musical instrument, electrical cords, light bulbs, wooden base

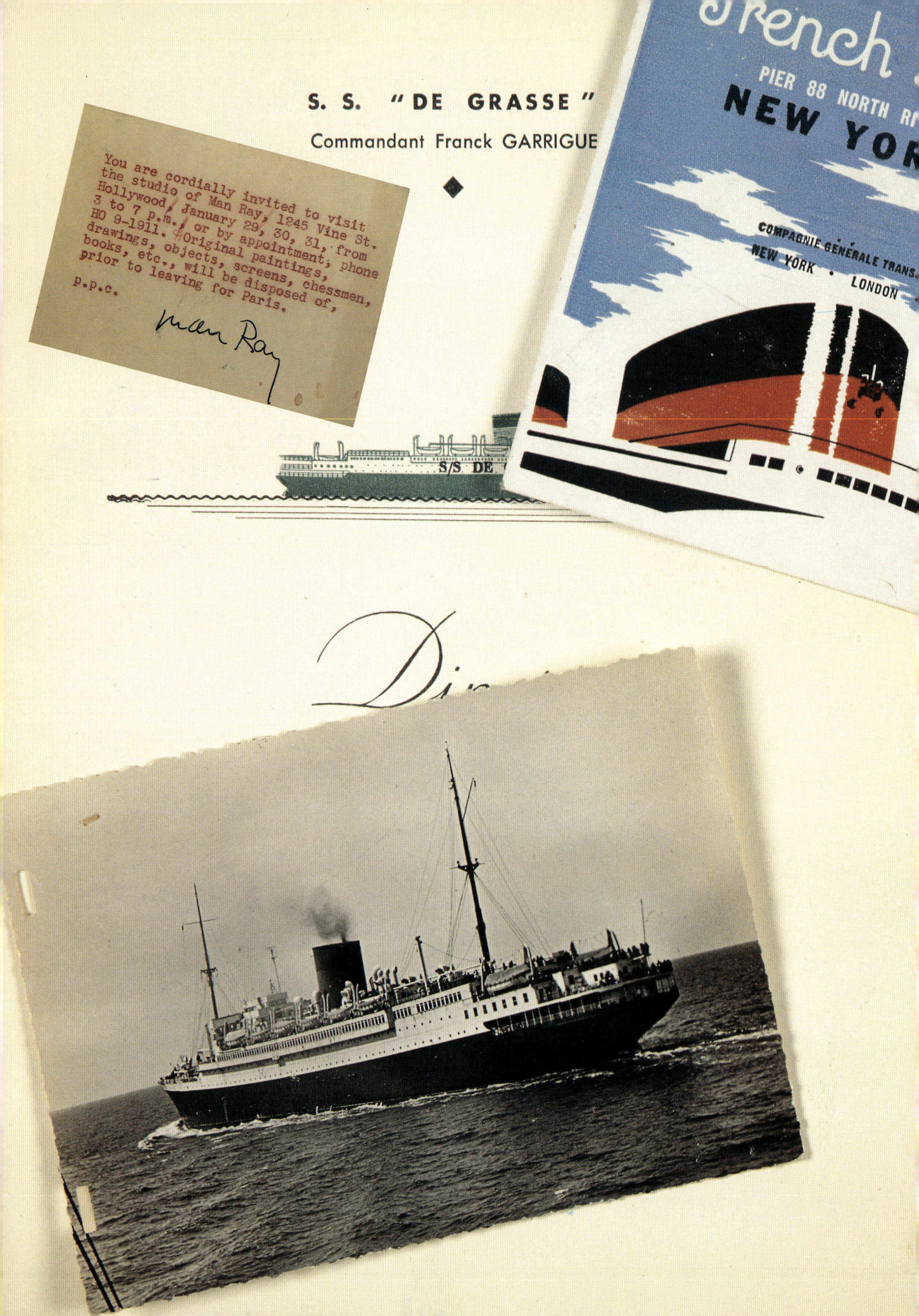
You are cordially invited to visit the studio of Man Ray, 1245 Vine St. Hollywood, January 29, 30, 31, from 3 to 7 p.m., or by appointment; phone HO 9-1911. Original paintings, drawings, objects, screens, chessmen, books, etc., will be disposed of, prior to leaving for Paris.

p.p.c.

Man Ray

ne

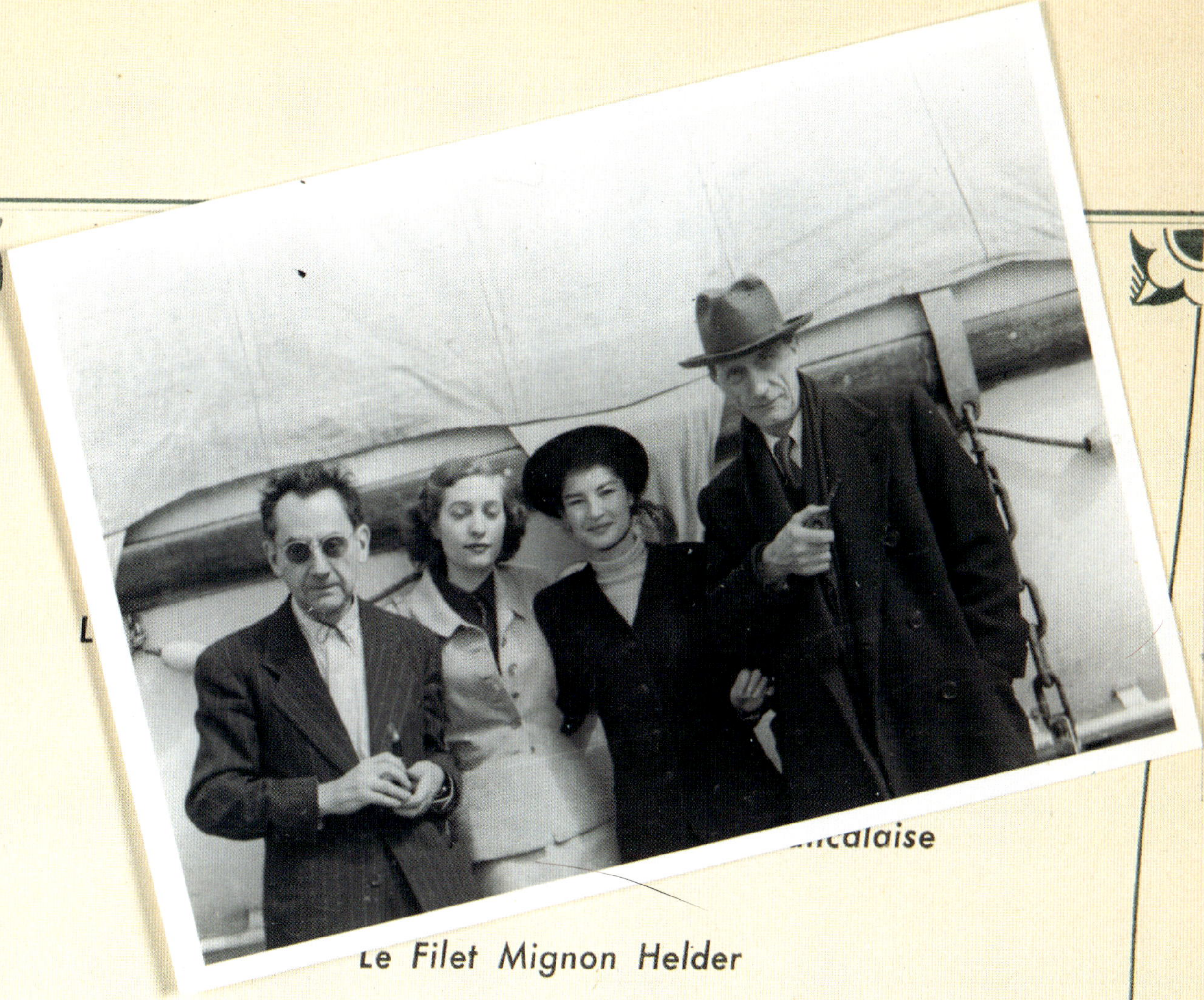

L

…ançaise

Le Filet Mignon Helder

Le Bouquet de Pointes d'Asperges Maltaise

La … udan Rôtie et Flambée au Vieux Marc

…phin

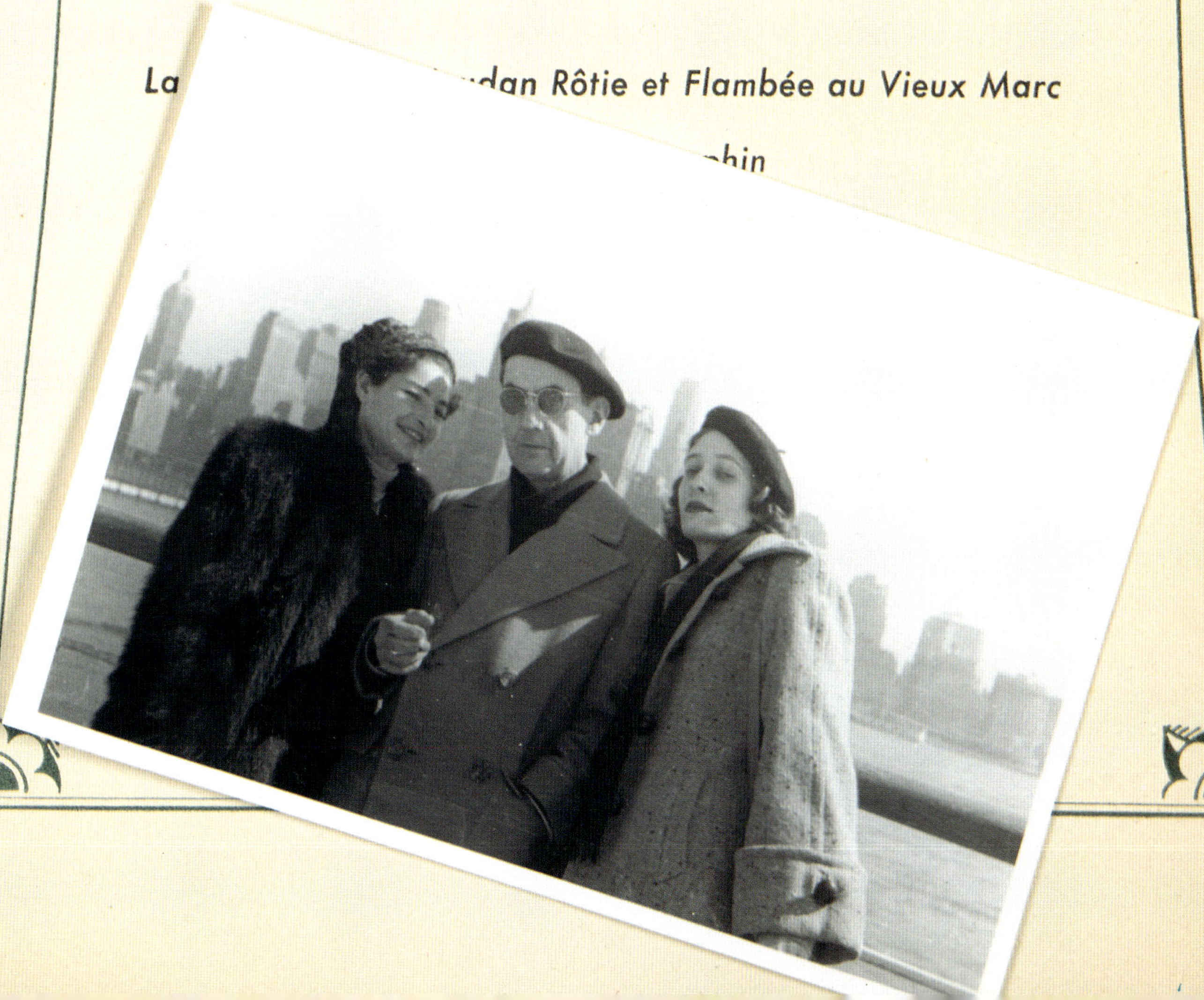

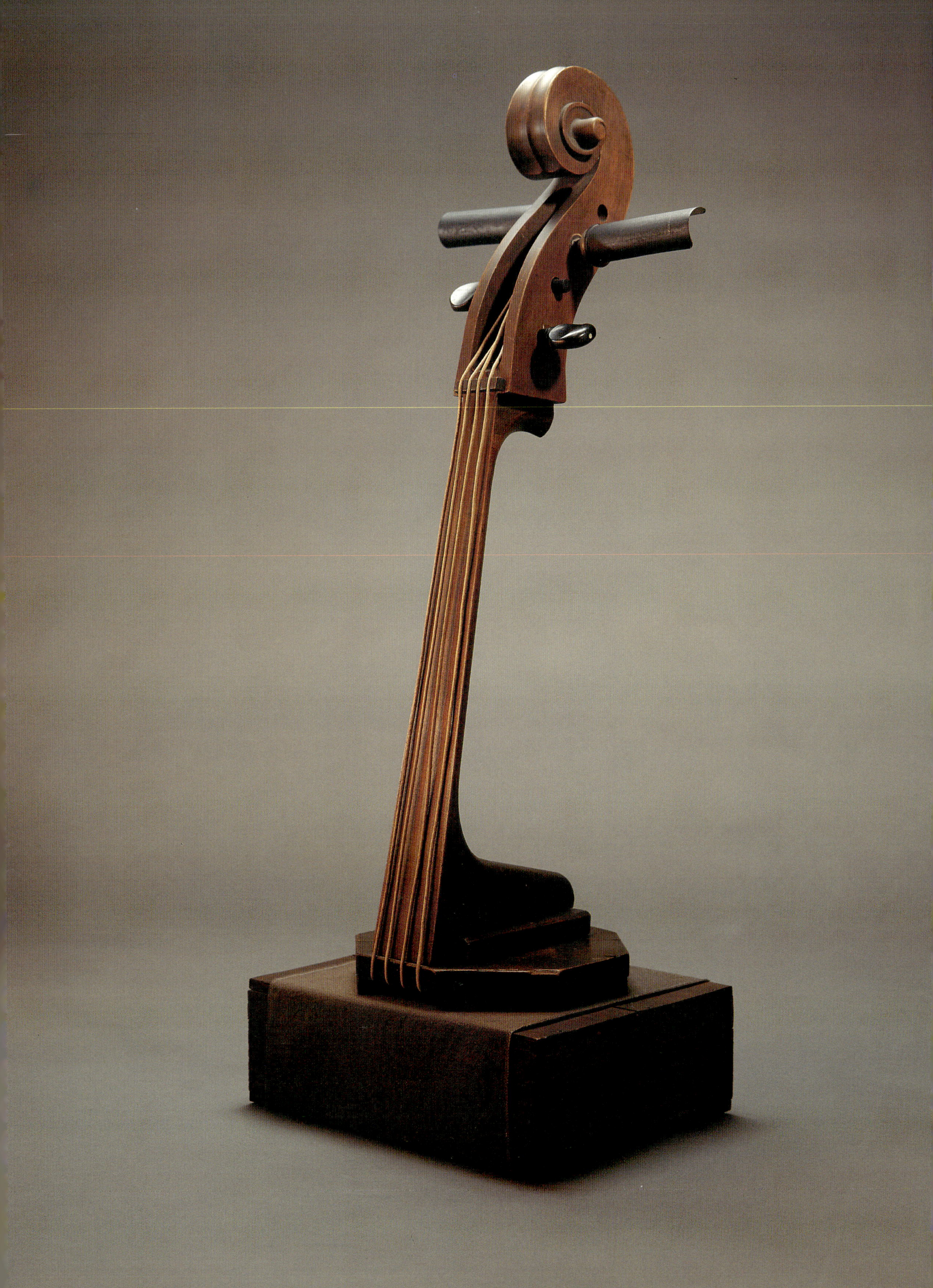

REMEMBERING MAN RAY:

AN INTERVIEW WITH JAMES & BARBARA BYRNES

JANUARY 1996

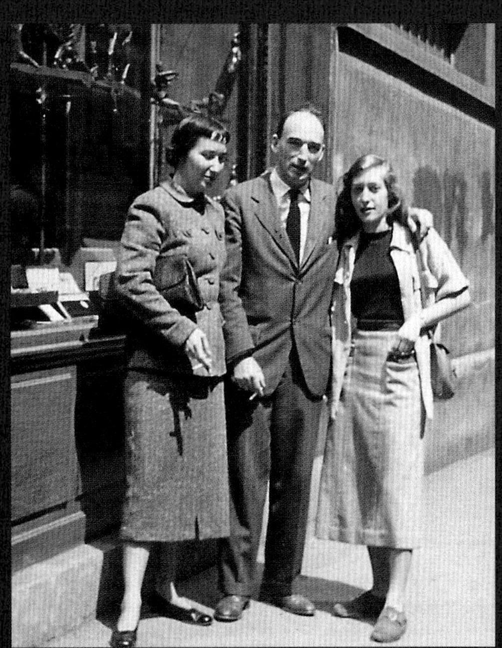

From 1946 to 1953, James Byrnes was Curator of Modern and Contemporary Art at the Los Angeles County Museum of History, Science, and Art. He subsequently became director of the North Carolina Museum of Art in Raleigh, and then of the Isaac Delgado Museum of Art in New Orleans, returning to California to head the Newport Harbor Art Museum from 1973 to 1975. Now a consultant in the fine arts, he lives in Los Angeles with his wife Barbara.

WE'LL GET TO MAN RAY IN A MINUTE, JIM, BUT I'D LIKE TO START WITH YOUR BACKGROUND. WHEN DID YOU COME TO LOS ANGELES? I KNOW THAT YOU WERE IN THE NAVY DURING WORLD WAR II.

That's right, my commanding officer turned out to be Russell Smith, Chief of the Education Department at the Los Angeles County Museum of History, Science, and Art. As the war came to a close, Smith asked me to consider coming to Los Angeles because he was planning an expanded art education program for the museum. In the thirties I had studied art in New York at the National Academy of Design, the Art Students League, and the American Artists School, so he felt I was especially qualified for a post at the County Museum. I eventually became curator of modern and contemporary art after starting as an assistant curator of art education. I was at the museum from April 1946 until December 1953.

AND YOUR WIFE BARBARA BECAME PART OF THE LOS ANGELES ART SCENE AS WELL?

Yes, in October 1946 Barbara bought the key to the American Contemporary Gallery, a well-known art gallery, which was up a long alley next to the Pickwick Bookshop on Hollywood Boulevard. It had been owned by Clara Grossman, and before that, Howard Putzel, who had become Peggy Guggenheim's secretary in New York. Because of its reputation as a vanguard gallery in Los Angeles, the place attracted many studio artists as well as visiting art faculty. But very little sold, and Barbara closed it after briefly relocating to La Cienega Boulevard.

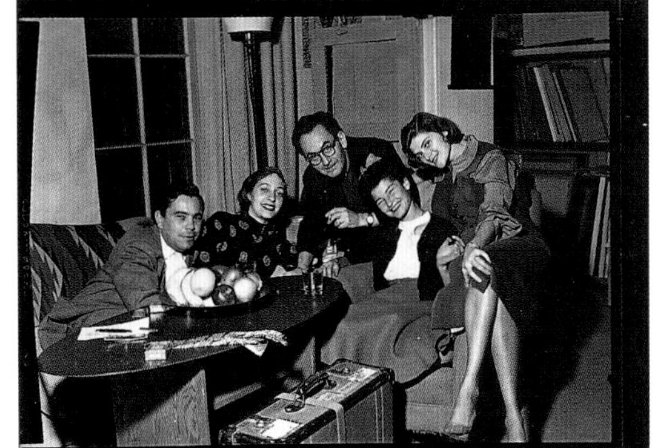

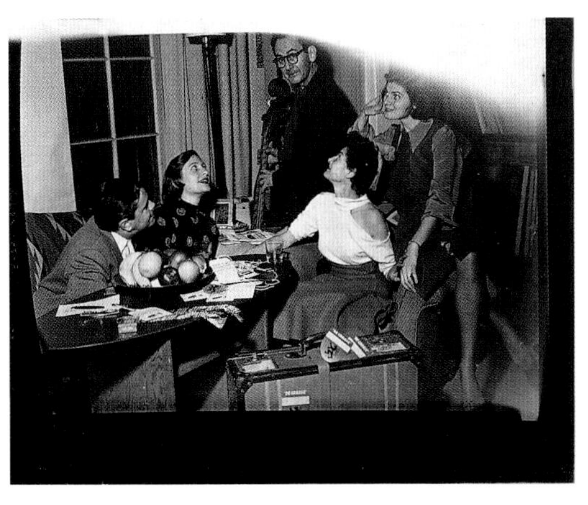

Untitled, 1951 *Gelatin-silver prints*
William Copley, Gloria de Herrera, Man Ray (with Emak Bakia Lumiere*), Juliet, and Selma Browner with suitcases packed on eve of departure for east coast*

WHO WERE YOU WORKING WITH AT THE COUNTY MUSEUM AT THAT TIME?

In the summer of 1946 William Valentiner arrived as director-consultant of the County Museum after reaching the mandatory retirement age as director of the Detroit Institute of Art. Valentiner became my great supporter for modern art. In fact, he was the one who backed me when I bought a Jackson Pollock in 1951, and he helped me get it through the History, Science, and Art Board. They were so opposed to the painting that they decided I could have it only if I agreed to keep it in my office and bring it up for lectures but didn't hang it on the walls of the museum.

NOW TO MAN RAY. AT WHAT POINT DID YOU BECOME AWARE OF HIM?

Barbara and I first met Man Ray socially during the summer of 1949 at a Sunday barbecue at Mary Stothardt's home. We were take-along guests of Paul and Jo Kantor, who later opened their own gallery and gave Man an exhibition. Man and Julie were the guests of honor, and both proved difficult to start a conversation with.

WHY WAS THAT?

Man especially disliked critics and museum people. In 1946 I experienced some of his antipathy when I called him to ask why he didn't submit something to the museum's Annual Artists' Competition. He said, "I don't believe in competition among artists. I don't submit ever. I will respond only to certain invitations to exhibit."

IS IT FAIR TO SAY THAT MAN RAY WAS GENERALLY "DIFFICULT?"

He was darkly serious, always ready to deliver or accept a verbal challenge. I recall that Andrew Ritchie was organizing his exhibition of abstract art in America for The Museum of Modern Art, scheduled for 1951. He wanted to see Man Ray, and so we went over to Vine Street. Inside, along the wall facing the entry was a staircase leading to the bedroom upstairs. We sat on stools to view the paintings Man brought out of the closet. On the wall by the stairwell was that marvelous painting of a billiard table, *La Fortune*. Man kept directing Ritchie's attention to it. Ritchie finally said that the painting he wanted was the *The Rope Dancer Accompanies Herself with Her Shadows* of 1916. Man responded, rather acidly, "Dr. Ritchie, you join the museum curators, critics, and dealers who have me dead as an artist after 1919." Ritchie was noticeably distressed and tried to pass it off by praising Man's unique contributions to art of our time. MoMA eventually got *The Rope Dancer.*

BUT HE DID HAVE SOME SUPPORT IN LOS ANGELES. ALBERT LEWIN, THE FILM DIRECTOR, AND HIS WIFE MILDRED WERE PATRONS OF MAN RAY.

The Lewins were also friends of Mary Stothardt, who had been a child star. She and her sister Constance had been featured in D. W. Griffith's *Way Down East*. Her husband

p. 117
Barbara Byrnes, James Byrnes, Gloria de Herrera in Paris, 1951 (Photograph by William Copley)
Gelatin-silver print

Herbert Stothardt was a noted composer of film scores at MGM; he won an Oscar for *The Wizard of Oz*. When the Lewins moved to New York in 1949, Mary sort of took over and filled the void. When Mary's husband died in 1947, she was receiving (what she considered at that time) enormous ASCAP checks, because everybody was playing Herbert's music. On occasion she gave Man and Julie the whole check. Julie always regarded that as payment for art lessons, which Man interspersed with his views on art history, Dada, and Surrealism. The checks were a windfall for Man and Julie and kept them going. Mary once arranged an exhibition of his paintings and objects at her home on La Mesa Drive in Brentwood. She invited all of the known art collectors and patrons in the Hollywood motion picture colony. When nothing sold, she bought a number of his works for herself, including the original object called *Dumbbells for Lightweights*, and two paintings from the "Shakespearean Equations" series, which were shown at Bill Copley's gallery in 1948. She later gave one to my museum in New Orleans and one to my museum in Raleigh, North Carolina.

BARBARA:

After Mary's husband died, I introduced art historian Paul Wescher to Mary. They were both interested in Man Ray and Surrealism. Paul had seen Man's *Promenade*, the 1916 oil version, in an exhibition as an anonymous loan from Mary, and he knew a collector in Switzerland who was interested in it. I called Man, who delivered a version painted in 1941. Paul was madder than all get out and asked why he had made a substitution. Man replied emphatically, "I have never painted a recent painting!" Of course, after their marriage, Mary shared the 1916 *Promenade* with Paul.

TELL US ABOUT HIRING GLORIA DE HERRERA, AND HER CONNECTION TO MAN RAY.

When the California Centennial came around in 1949, I put in a bid to have an exhibition of contemporary California painting. Since I could not use county employees for this project, I hired Gloria de Herrera, a young girl of eighteen or nineteen. She used to visit Barbara's gallery, where she would sit quietly studying the art and the books.

BARBARA:

It was rather strange because she sort of sniffed at the paintings. She didn't say very much, she'd just say, "Hmm." "Hmm." She came from East L.A. and worked at an insurance company, where she was very unhappy. And she was living with her grandmother, although her mother was alive—she'd had a falling out with her mother, as many young people do. When Gloria was in high school, she would go to the jazz clubs in South Central L.A. and take photographs of the musicians, Duke Ellington and the like, claiming to be a news photographer. She was a very good secretary for Jim, very meticulous.

JIM:

In 1950 I was asked to give a night course on schools of twentieth-century art at USC. Gloria volunteered to be my slide pusher, because she wanted to learn something.

AND YOU INVITED MAN RAY TO SPEAK AT ONE OF THESE CLASSES?

Yes, when the course came to Dada and Surrealism, I called Man and hired him for what I would have been paid for the evening, about fifteen dollars. I knew he could use it. Man Ray was very sharp on art panels, with a genius for disquieting everyone. He had an intellectual radicalism, and an admiration for the Marquis de Sade because of his absolute freedom. That was what guided him.

AND WHAT HAPPENED AT THE LECTURE?

Man arrived with a valise full of his objects, which he displayed on a table. And he challenged the students. They all stayed awake. They were really quite excited about it, and many of them were very upset about some of the things he had to say. "What does it represent?" one student asked. "What do you represent?" he'd retort. Right at the beginning, I recall that Man passed out torn squares of paper with numbers on them and told the students to hold on to these because they would get a fortune at the end of the session. After demonstrating some of his objects, among them his hanging lampshade and the flatiron with tacks, he abruptly interrupted his session and demanded, "Who has number eight?" A hand shot up, and Man asked, "Who doesn't have number eight?" From among the upraised hands, he chose one student and said, "You win." Then he whipped out an old inner tube, damaged and repaired so often that it was

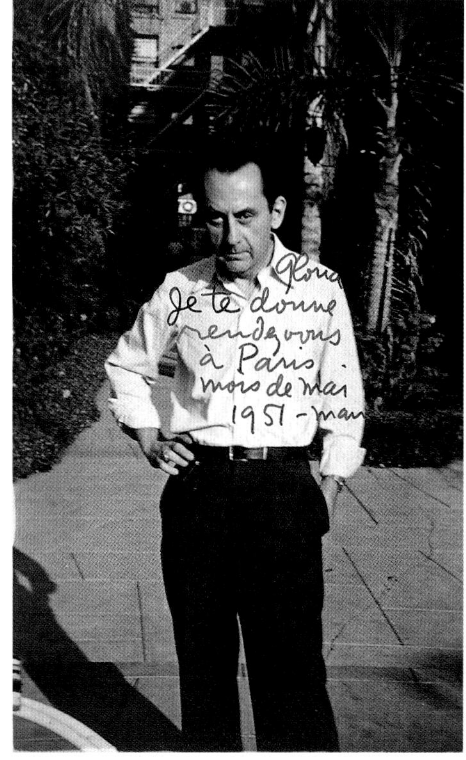

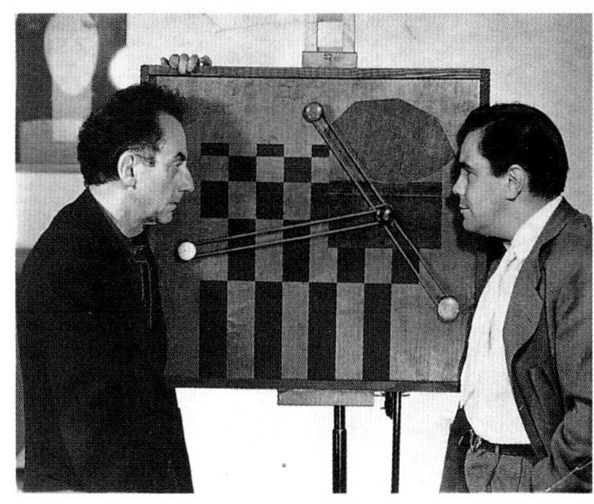

top:
Self-portrait in the Villa Elaine Patio, 1245 Vine Street, 1951
Gelatin-silver print

above:
Man Ray and William Copley, 1948
Gelatin-silver print

all just checkered with red patches. With a huge pair of editing scissors, about twelve inches long, he cut the tube up, gathered it all together and threw it to the kid, who didn't, I'm sure, know what to do with it. I always hoped that he would've kept it.

AND GLORIA ATTENDED THAT LECTURE?

All of the lectures. Gloria had met Man earlier at the Copley Gallery in 1948 and became friendly with him. Eventually she bought and received many paintings, objects, and photographs from Man—*Boardwalk*, for example, with its bullet holes, and the *Emak Bakia* lamp.

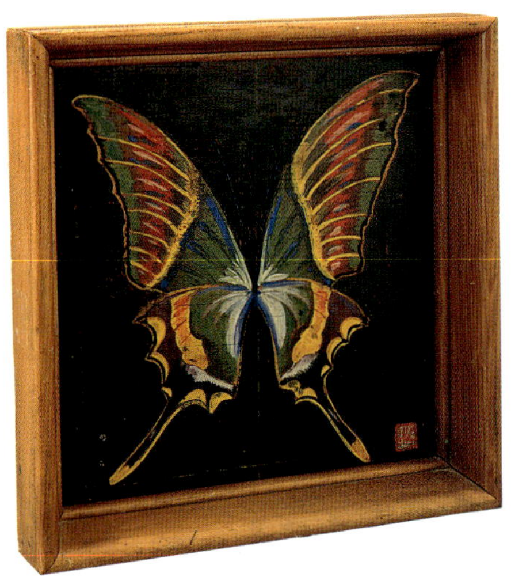

above and below:
Papillion (Lepidoptera Gloria de Herrera), 1948
Opaque media on wood panel set in deep shadowbox wood frame

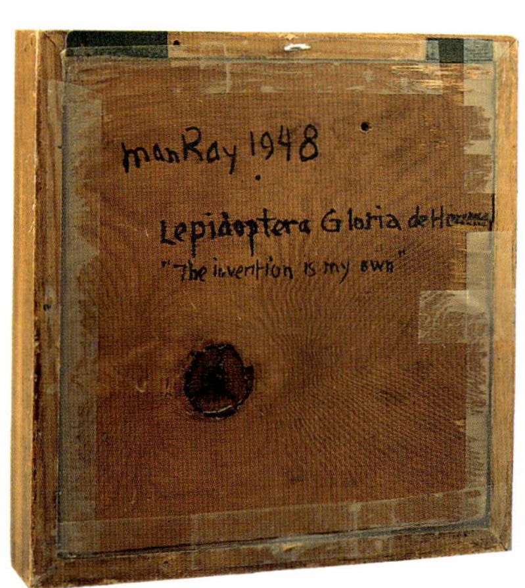

I SEE YOU HAVE GLORIA'S COPY OF *LES MAINS LIBRES.*

Yes, a beautiful copy with a drawing by Man Ray on the title page, featuring morning glories and an inscription that goes with it: "For Gloria (she is like a budding morning glory): her face open like *Les Mains Libres*, just as I would want to be free." It's very touching and warm work.

WHEN WE TALKED BEFORE, YOU HAD SUGGESTED THAT THERE WAS A MARKED RESEMBLANCE BETWEEN GLORIA AND LEE MILLER, MAN RAY'S FORMER LOVER.

I think I see it. I don't know whether anyone else does. But it's rather evident in the photographs that Man Ray did of Gloria. I think that this is a kind of love/object image.

AND THIS BUTTERFLY PAINTING ON A BOARD?

It's *Papillion*.

AND IT BEARS THE INSCRIPTION, "MAN RAY, 1948," ON THE BACK.

Yes, and the tag line "Lepidoptera, Gloria de Herrera, The invention is my own." His little butterfly. You can see how early Gloria came to know Man. It was right around the time of the Copley show.

TELL US ABOUT WILLIAM COPLEY.

Copley was the adopted son of the Copley family of San Diego, who owned a chain of newspapers. His brother was also adopted, very conservative, whereas Copley was the radical artist. We first heard of Copley when he went to the Stendahl Gallery, where Sam Kootz, the New York dealer, was showing a dozen Picassos, his first exhibit in Los Angeles after the war. Kootz had sold out the first dozen in New York, so this was to placate his Hollywood collectors. The prices in those days were very modest by any standard. Copley, who had been mustered out of the army, came with his brother-in-law, John Ployardt, a Disney animator, who also had great interest in Surrealism. Bill spotted a 1943 portrait of Dora Maar wearing a silly hat. He decided to buy it. Stendahl looked at him, and here he was still in his dyed Army uniform, wearing *huaraches*. A strange-looking couple, I must say. Stendahl asked to be excused and got on the phone to Copley's bank: "He wants to buy a painting. He's going to give me a check for twenty-five hundred dollars. That's the price. Will you cover it?" They said, "Anything up to five or six figures is all right." Then shortly after the Picasso show at Stendahl's, Copley started a gallery in Beverly Hills, which was a modest little wooden structure with a porch; it had been a sales agency for MGs. At the Copley Gallery, the Man Ray show, I think, was his last one—I think it was December 1948. I remember the shows, although I don't remember them in particular sequence. Joseph Cornell was early . . . Matta. . . .

MAX ERNST . . .

. . . and Yves Tanguy. I don't remember a Magritte show, although it's possible. Well, at any rate, there were six of them. Dorothea Tanning was scheduled, but when Copley had to close the gallery, her work was exhibited at Barbara's American Contemporary Gallery. The way we heard the story, it sounded as though he was a spendthrift, irresponsible with money; the trustees probably threatened to close him down. But he *had* spent about eighty-seven thousand dollars for those six shows, which was a lot of money in those days. Plus, so few things sold that Copley became a great collector of all those artists.

AND NOW GLORIA AND COPLEY?

Yes, Gloria took up with Bill Copley. He was in bad way with the gallery and had to close it. His marriage had gone on the rocks, so he was at loose ends. Gloria and Copley were living together when Man decided he was going back to Europe. I think he persuaded Bill and Gloria to go along. The Ernsts were also going back. By then the cold war was on. So Bill went, and, apparently, took the Man Rays as his guests. He and Gloria and the Man Rays sailed on the *De Grasse*, I think, on March 15th, 1951.

WHAT HAPPENED TO GLORIA?

Well, she had learned a lot about art conservation and used it to good advantage. Man Ray's friend Maurice LeFebvre, who owned an art supply shop in Paris, first gave Gloria a Mondrian belonging to Nellie van Doesberg to repair, and then a damaged Chagall. The next thing I knew, Matisse had asked Maurice for somebody to do the pasting down of his great cut-outs, and Maurice recommended Gloria. I have her notes on the project. The cut-outs had been either put in place with pins, or they were sketched lightly where they went. Obviously, there had to be some element of choice on her part because they were not affixed before she got hold of them. Then Gloria became involved with the Algerian struggle for independence in the late 1950s; exactly how this came about, I'm not certain. She was arrested with some thirty others in February 1957 for harboring Algerians. The police apparently identified her as an American artist, and they released her every evening to feed her eight cats. With another partisan of that same group, she tried to organize the prostitutes in jail. From what I gather, she was *persona non grata* in France, a carrier of valises. Deprived of her passport, Gloria had to leave Paris daily by train and go to Belgium to stay with friends. In 1983 Gloria developed throat cancer, and she died four years later.

I'M SORRY THAT MAN RAY NEVER MENTIONED HER IN HIS *SELF PORTRAIT*.

Yes, Gloria really was her own invention, not his.

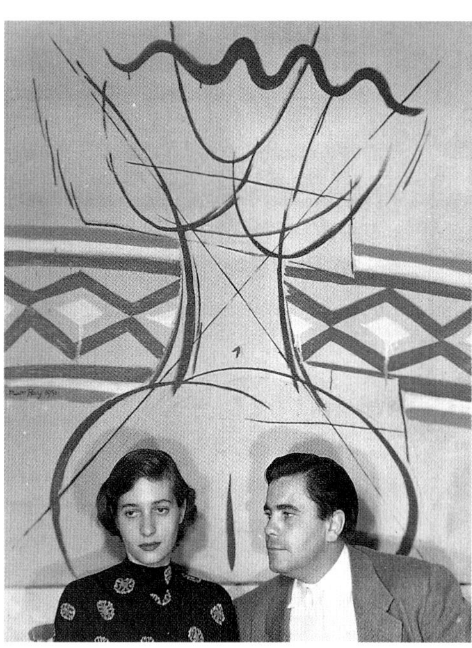

Gloria de Herrera and William Copley, c. 1950 *Gelatin-silver print*

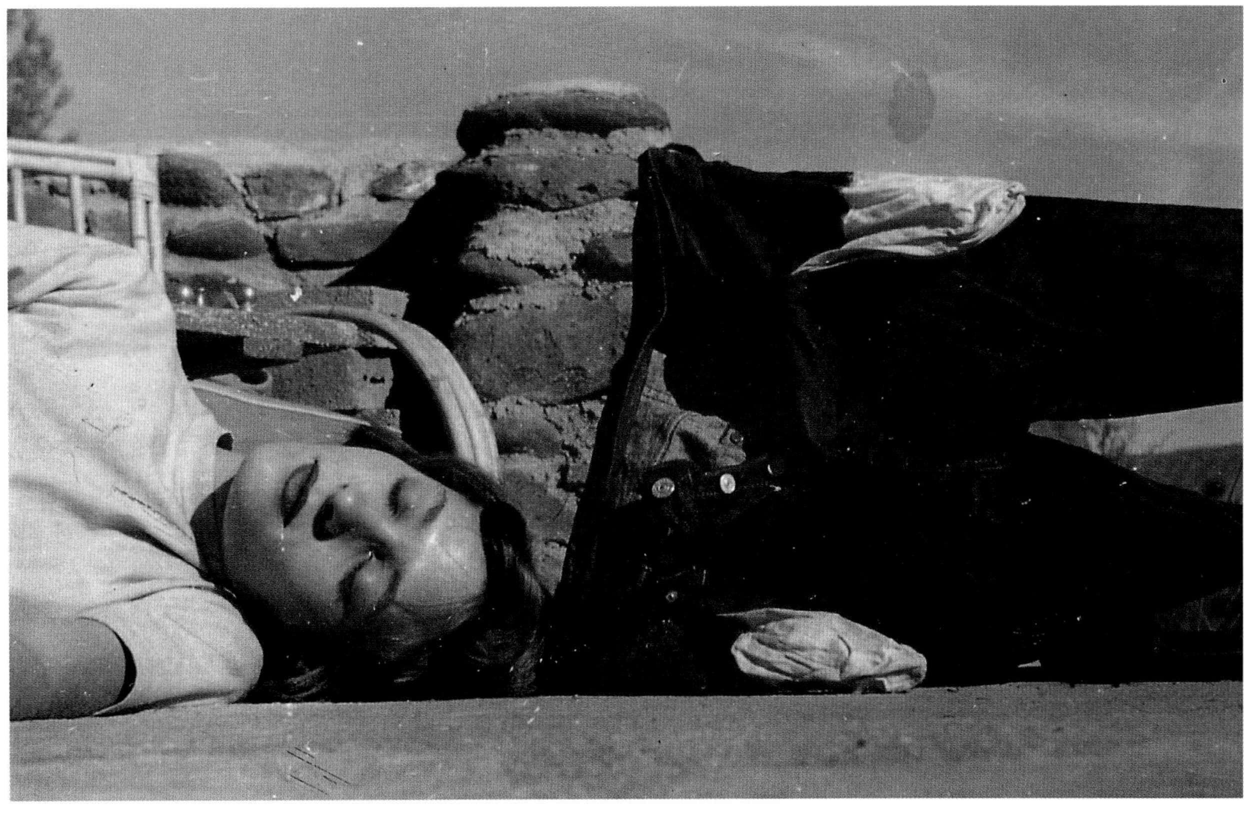

left:
Gloria de Herrera, c. 1950
Gelatin-silver print

overleaf:
p. 122
Gloria de Herrera, 1950
Gelatin-silver print

p. 123
Bottlerack and three articulated wooden lay figures, nd.

Reproductions on pages 117, 118, 119 120, 121 Courtesy of James and Barbara Byrnes

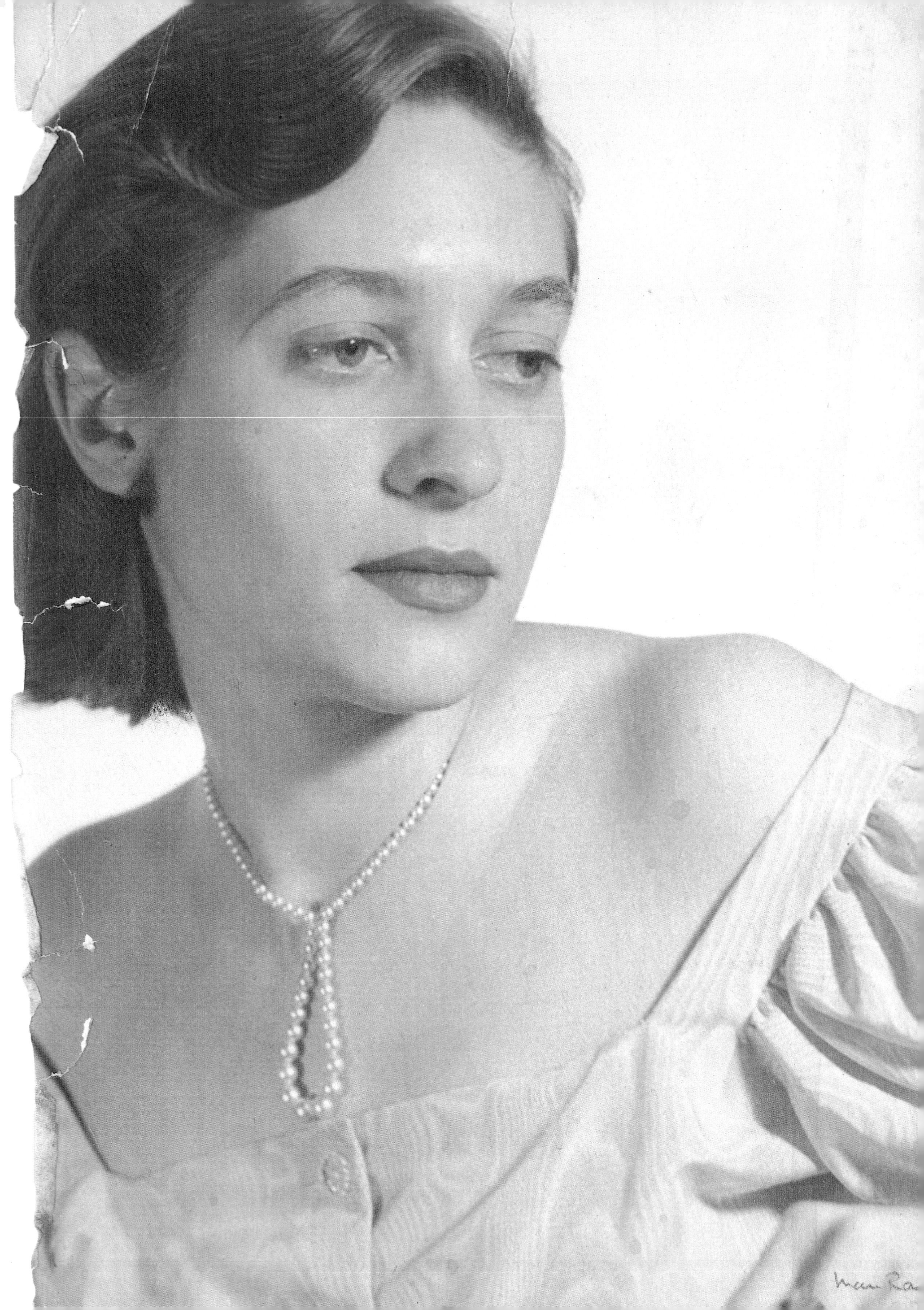

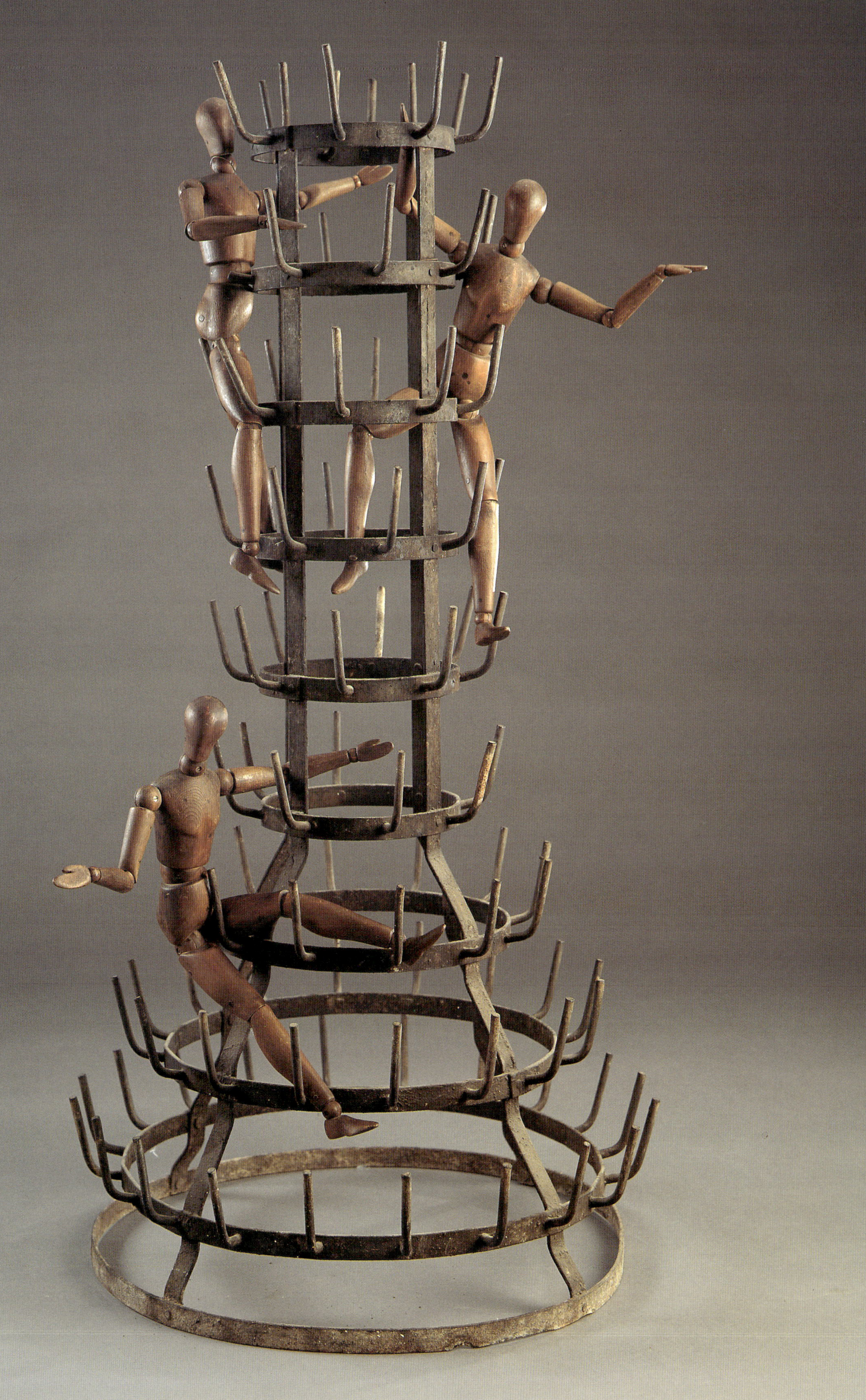

Notes

1. *A Part of Myself*, trans. Richard and Clara Winston (New York: Harcourt Brace Jovanovich, 1966), 329.
2. On August 31, 1934, Man Ray wrote to Elsie Siegler of "a certain feeling of security that there is someone that I can count on for the rest of my life" (Man Ray Family Papers, Inventory 940019: the first box contains letters from Man Ray to Elsie Siegler; the second box, miscellaneous letters to Man Ray; the third box is called "Man Ray, Hollywood Album," and contains unpublished essays and meditations. Special Collections, The Getty Center for the History of Art and the Humanities, Los Angeles, California, henceforth cited as Getty Center.) Elsie's errands for Man Ray increased upon his return from France because she also had to ship his artwork, stored in the vicinity, across the country for exhibitions on the west coast.
3. Author interview with Julien Levy, Bridgewater, Connecticut, October 19, 1980.
4. Henry McBride, for example, identified Man Ray as an expatriate whose Parisian life "automatically" made him French ("Motorized Calder," in Henry McBride, *The Flow of Art* [New York: Atheneum, 1975], 293). In his memoir, Man Ray recounts how during his attempt to escape Paris he felt constrained to speak English "with a strong American accent" in order to avoid trouble and establish his privileged status as an American citizen abroad. (*Self Portrait* [Boston: Little, Brown, 1963], 307).
5. Man Ray wrote to Ady that he had waited two weeks in Lisbon for passage and then slept on a mattress in a common room with thirty others during the weeklong crossing (Man Ray to Adrienne Fidelin, August 19, 1940, Special Collections, Getty Center).
6. Man Ray to Adrienne Fidelin, September 1, 1940, Special Collections, Getty Center.
7. Neil Baldwin, *Man Ray: American Artist* (New York: Clarkson N. Potter, 1988), 233–44. Baldwin has written the standard biography of Man Ray, from which I have derived the basic details of the artist's life.
8. Man Ray to Elsie Siegler, April 11, 1940; September 24, 1942, Special Collections, Getty Center.
9. Man Ray's years in Hollywood have not been fully discussed, and then only infrequently. The prevailing view, erroneous though it is, has been expressed by Gerald Nordland, who claimed that "Man Ray spent eleven unrewarding years in the Southland with little recognition . . ." ("A Succession of Visitors," *Artforum* 2, no. 12 [Summer 1964]: 64). Subsequent writers have commented on a hardworking Man Ray in Southern California from various perspectives. In his biography Baldwin devotes three chapters to California, with an emphasis on surface events (231–77); for accounts that concentrate more fully on the work, see Arturo Schwarz, *Man Ray: The Rigour of Imagination* (New York: Rizzoli, 1977), 74-122; Merry Foresta, "Exile in Paradise: Man Ray in Hollywood," in *Perpetual Motif: The Art of Man Ray* (New York: Abbeville Press, 1988), 273–309; Curtis L. Carter and Francis M. Naumann, *Man Ray in America* (Milwaukee: Haggerty Museum of Art, Marquette University, 1988). Donna Romano tries to balance an historical narrative with art analysis in "Man Ray: A Decade in Hollywood, 1940–1950" (master's thesis, Queens College, City University of New York, 1988).
10. Man Ray, *Self Portrait*, 328, 329.
11. *Self Portrait*, 329; Judith Young-Mallin, "Remembering the Faces of Juliet," *Quest* (Summer 1991): 46.
12. *Self Portrait*, 332–33.
13. Man Ray to Elsie Siegler, January 31, 1941; February 26, 1941, Special Collections, Getty Center; *Self Portrait*, 371.
14. In 1943 at the height of the war, Man Ray wrote to Elsie that "the cars are still running and we do get down to the beach once in a while. As a photographer I get a B card [for gas rationing], and one needs a car out here . . ." (Letter to Elsie Siegler, June 28, 1943, Special Collections, Getty Center).
15. Man Ray to Elsie Siegler, November 14, 1941; January 11, 1950, Special Collections, Getty Center.
16. Man Ray to Elsie Siegler, September 24, 1942; August 30, 1942, Special Collections, Getty Center.
17. Letter from Duchamp to Man Ray, April 27, 1941, Special Collections, Getty Center; Man Ray to Elsie Siegler, July 1, 1947, Special Collections, Getty Center. On May 18, 1941, Man Ray wrote to Elsie that Duchamp had sent word that his property was "O.K. so far in Paris . . . ," but on July 29, 1944, such was his anxiety that he told Elsie he was "not counting any more on what I have lost" and by August 12, 1944, he claimed that he had "lost everything in France" (Special Collections, Getty Center).
18. Early upon his return to the U.S., Man Ray relied on his brother-in-law Sam Siegler, who was an accountant, to straighten out his affairs with the Internal Revenue Service because he had never paid United States income taxes while he was living abroad (Man Ray to Sam Siegler, December 28, 1940, Special Collections, Getty Center). Less than a year later he told Elsie that he had earned some four hundred dollars since his return, "most of which I have spent on [photographic] equipment to replace all I've lost abroad. I am still living on which I had saved in previous years [from his fashion commissions], and on contributions from friends" (Man Ray to Elsie Siegler, November 14, 1941, Special Collections, Getty Center).
19. Man Ray to Elsie Siegler, June 28, 1943; July 22, 1942, Special Collections, Getty Center; Arthur Millier, "L.A. Events," *The Art Digest* 23, no. 20 (September 15, 1949): 29.
20. See, for example, a series of short articles on Hollywood and its collectors: Arthur Millier, "[Charles] Laughton, Art Lover"; Peter Pollack, "Taught by the Ancients"; Millier, "Actors as Collectors"; Pollack, "Between Trains," in *Art Digest* 23, no. 10 (February 15, 1949): 9–11.
21. William Copley, *CPLY: Reflection on a Past Life* (Houston: Institute for the Arts, Rice University, 1979), 6.
22. *Self Portrait*, 346. His "hermit periods" were motivated as much by the necessity to work intensely as they were on occasion by depression and antisocial impulses. For an account of the Arensbergs (and Duchamp) in Los Angeles, see Naomi Sawelson-Gorse, "Hollywood Conversations: Duchamp and the Arensbergs," in Bonnie Clearwater, ed., *West Coast Duchamp* (Miami Beach: Grassfield Press, 1991), 25–45.

Selected Bibliography

Works by Man Ray

"Alphabet for Adults." In *Alphabet for Adults*. Los Angeles: The Copley Galleries, 1948.

"Art in Sanity." *California Arts and Architecture* 58, no. 1 (January 1941): 19, 36-37.

"Cinémage." In *The Shadow and Its Shadow: Surrealist Writings on the Cinema*, edited by Paul Hammond, 142–43. Edinburgh: Polygon, 1978.

"Dadaism." In *Schools of Twentieth Century Art*. Beverly Hills: Modern Institute of Art, 1948.

"First Object/Last Object." *Portfolio* 5 (Plate 9). Washington, D.C.: Black Sun Press, 1947.

"I Have Never Painted a Recent Picture." In Jules Langsner, *Man Ray*. Los Angeles: Los Angeles County Museum of Art, 1966.

"A Letter to the Artist." *California Arts and Architecture* 60, no. 1 (January 1943): 27, 46.

"Man Ray Folio." *Minicam Photography* 8, no. 2 (October 1943): 50–56.

"Man Ray, Hollywood Album." Special Collections, The Getty Center for the History of Art and the Humanities, Los Angeles.

"Man Ray: Photogenic Reflections." *Berkeley*, no. 9 (1950): 1.

"A Note on the Shakespearean Equations." In *To Be Continued Unnoticed*. Beverly Hills: The Copley Galleries, 1948.

[Notes]. In *Man Ray: Retrospective Exhibition*. Pasadena: Pasadena Art Institute, 1944.

Objects de mon affection. Introduction by Jean-Hubert Martin, Paris: Philippe Sers, 1983.

"*Objects of My Affection*." In *Man Ray, Objects*. New York: Julien Levy Gallery, 1945.

"Photogenic Reflections." *Berkeley*, no. 9 (February 1950): 1.

"Ruth, Roses and Revolvers." *View* 4, no. 4 (December 1944): 120–23.

Self Portrait. Boston: Little, Brown, 1963.

"Some Papers by Man Ray." In *To Be Continued Unnoticed*. Beverly Hills: The Copley Galleries, 1948.

[Talk at American Contemporary Gallery, Hollywood, October 15, 1943.] In *Art in Cinema*, edited by Frank Stauffer, 25–26. San Francisco: Art in Cinema Society, San Francisco Museum of Art, 1947.

Secondary Sources

Baldwin, Neil. *Man Ray: American Artist*. New York: Clarkson N. Potter, 1988.

Biddle, George. *The Yes and No of Contemporary Art: An Artist's Evaluation*. Cambridge, Mass.: Harvard University Press, 1957.

23. Man Ray's catalogue comments are quoted in George Biddle, *The Yes and No of Contemporary Art* (Cambridge, Mass.: Harvard University Press, 1957), 124. For a brief account of the exhibition at Perls in 1941, see Romano, "Man Ray: A Decade in Hollywood, 1940–1950," 84–85. The show included twenty-three oil paintings as well as watercolors, drawings, and Rayographs. The catalogue, which I have not seen, apparently had a cover photograph of Man Ray with one of his drawings (presumably a self-portrait).
24. "Man Ray in Hollywood," *Art Digest* 15, no. 11 (March 1, 1941): 14; Millier, "Surrealist Man Ray Puts on Exhibition in Hollywood," *Los Angeles Times*, 9 March, 1941, sec. 3, p. 8.
25. Quoted in "Announcements," *California Arts and Architecture* 59, no. 6 (June 1942): 4.
26. Biddle, *The Yes and No of Contemporary Art*, 124–25.
27. Man Ray to Elsie Siegler, May 18, 1941, Special Collections, Getty Center; *Self Portrait*, 335–37. Though mimeographed notices were sent to the press on the occasion of his 1943 exhibition at the Los Angeles County Museum, there was not even an announcement of the exhibition's schedule in the *Los Angeles Times*, just as there was no announcement for the 1945 exhibition. On November 9, 1943, Man Ray wrote witheringly to Elsie, "You know that aside from the weather, the atmosphere here is stifling" (Special Collections, Getty Center).
28. Caroline Clairborne Kidd, "Art and (?) in Pasadena," *Pasadena Star News*, 16 September, 1944.
29. Jarvis Barlow, in *Man Ray: Retrospective Exhibition* (Pasadena: Pasadena Art Institute,1944), n.p.
30. Kenneth Ross, "Profusion of Confusion," *Pasadena Star News*, 30 September, 1944.
31. *Self Portrait*, 340–43.
32. Peyton Boswell, "Tilting at Windmills," *Art Digest* 15, no. 1 (October 1, 1940): 3; Man Ray, "Art in Sanity," *California Arts and Architecture* 58, no. 1 (January 1941): 19, 36–37. A French translation of this essay, documented as Man Ray's Santa Barbara radio talk in December 1940, has been published as "L'art dans la société" ("Art in Society") in Pierre Bourgeade, *Bonsoir, Man Ray* (Paris: Pierre Belfond, 1972, 1990), 141–49. The discrepancy in titles may have resulted from an error of translation, or Man Ray may have changed the title of his talk when he published it in *California Arts and Architecture*. Merry Foresta convincingly argues the latter in "Exile in Paradise: Man Ray in Hollywood, 1940–1951," in *Perpetual Motif*, 288. Originating in Chicago, the Society for Sanity in Art opened branches in Los Angeles and San Francisco in September 1940, on the eve of Man Ray's arrival.
33. Jacqueline Bograd Weld, *Peggy: The Wayward Guggenheim* (New York: E. P. Dutton, 1986), 63, 248–50.
34. Miller to Man Ray, n.d. [but after they first met in the early 1940s]; November 15, 1945, Special Collections, Getty Center. Always below the poverty line, Miller later checked out of his hotel and lived with the Neimans in a small cabin on Beverly Glen, which he took over when they decamped for Colorado.
35. Henry Miller, "Recollections of Man Ray in Hollywood," in Schwarz, *Man Ray: The Rigour of Imagination*, 32–22; *Self Portrait*, 348.
36. Ibid., 349; Miller to Man Ray and Juliet, January 27, 1946, Special Collections, Getty Center.
37. Man Ray to George Leite (editor of *Circle*), June 7, 1945, private collection. Merrild's photograph appeared in conjunction with Henry Miller, "A Holiday in Paint," *Circle* (Spring 1945): 39–47. This was an appreciation of Merrild's flux paintings.
38. Opening statement by Merrild, in *Knud Merrild: Twenty-Five-Year Retrospective* (Beverly Hills, Calif.: Modern Institute of Art, 1948), n.p. The exhibition ran from June 2 to July 4, 1948, and contained an excerpt from Man Ray's "A Letter to the Artist," previously published in *California Arts and Architecture* 60, no. 1 (January 1943): 27, 46; Merrild to Miller, April 28, 1944, Special Collections, Getty Center.
39. *Self Portrait*, 385.
40. For the catalogue of the retrospective, see Jules Langsner, *Man Ray* (Los Angeles: Los Angeles County Museum of Art, 1966).
41. "A Letter to the Artist," *California Arts and Architecture*, 46.
42. Man Ray to Elsie Siegler, March 18, 1942, Special Collections, Getty Center.
43. For the fullest exposition of this slogan, see *Man Ray*, "I Have Never Painted a Recent Picture," in Langsner, *Man Ray*, 28–31.
44. Man Ray to Elsie Siegler, October 20, 1940, Special Collections, Getty Center.
45. Man Ray, "Black," in "Painting and Photography," [1-2], in "Man Ray, Hollywood Album," folder 1, Special Collections, Getty Center.
46. Man Ray, "Calm Diatribe," 1944; "Straight(laced) Photography," in "Painting and Photography," in "Man Ray, Hollywood Album," Special Collections, Getty Center; Julien Levy, *Memoir of an Art Gallery* (New York: G. P. Putnam's Sons, 1977), 256.
47. Man Ray to Elsie Siegler, January 10, 1941, Special Collections, Getty Center. For a discussion of these albums that served as holiday greetings, see Merry Foresta, "Exile in Paradise: Man Ray in Hollywood, 1940–1951," in *Perpetual Motif*, 298.
48. Charles Henri Ford to Man Ray, July 28, 1943, Special Collections, Getty Center; "Man Ray Folio," *Minicam Photography* 8, no. 2 (October 1943): 52.
49. This occurrence is related in Schwarz, *Man Ray: The Rigour of Imagination*, 157.
50. Duchamp to Man Ray, December 24, 1944, Special Collections, Getty Center; Charles Henri Ford, "Flag of Ecstacy," *View*, Marcel Duchamp Number, Series V, no. 1 (March 1945): 5; "Man Ray: Bilingual Biography," Ibid., 32–51.
51. "Painting and Photography," in "Man Ray, Hollywood Album," Special Collections, Getty Center.
52. Man Ray to Elsie Siegler, March 17, 1930, Special Collections, Getty Center.
53. "Objects of My Affection," in *Man Ray, Objects* (New York: Julien Levy Gallery, 1945). On view were

Buñuel, Luis.
My Last Sigh. Tranlated by Abigail Israel.
New York: Alfred A. Knopf, 1983.

Carter, Curtis L., and Francis M. Naumann,
Man Ray in America. Milwaukee:
Haggerty Museum of Art,
Marquette University, 1988.

Copley, William.
CPLY: Reflection on a Past Life.
Houston: Institute for the Arts,
Rice University, 1979.

Edwards, Hugh.
Surrealism and Its Affinities: The Mary Reynolds Collection.
Chicago: The Art Institute of Chicago, 1973.

Ehrlich, Susan, ed.
Pacific Dreams: Currents of Surrealism and Fantasy in California Art, 1934–1957.
Los Angeles: UCLA at the Armand Hammer Museum of Art and Cultural Center, 1995.

Foresta, Merry.
Perpetual Motif: The Art of Man Ray.
Washington, D.C.: National Museum of American Art; New York: Abbeville Press, 1988.

Friedrich, Otto.
City of Nets: A Portrait of Hollywood in the 1940's.
New York: Harper & Row, 1986.

Goodwin, George M.
Days and Nights of Juliet.
Los Angeles: Oral History Program,
UCLA, 1984.

Heimann, James.
Out with the Stars: Hollywood Nightlife in the Golden Era.
New York: Abbeville Press, 1985.

Langsner, Jules.
Man Ray.
Los Angeles: Los Angeles County
Museum of Art, 1966.

Levy, Julien.
Memoir of an Art Gallery.
New York: G. P. Putnam's Sons, 1977.

Martin, Jay.
Always Merry and Bright: The Life of Henry Miller.
Santa Barbara: Capra Press, 1978.

Knud Merrild: Twenty-Five-Year Retrospective.
Beverly Hills, Calif.: Modern Institute of Art, 1948.

Knud Merrild, 1894–1954.
Los Angeles: Los Angeles County
Museum of Art, 1965.

Miller, Henry.
The Air-Conditioned Nightmare.
New York: New Directions, 1945.

Millier, Arthur.
"Surrealist Man Ray Puts on Exhibition in Hollywood."
Los Angeles Times, 9 March, 1941, sec. 3, p. 8.

ten objects and thirty-five paintings (including the ten oils for *Revolving Doors*) in addition to watercolors, drawings, and photographs. For a brief description of the event, see Levy, *Memoir of an Art Gallery*, 256. A fuller account can be found in Romano, "Man Ray: A Decade in Hollywood, 1940–1950," 91–95.
54. From July 16 to August 3, 1946, the Circle Gallery had included Man Ray in an exhibition of artists called the Open Circle Group. Among the artists were Knud Merrild, Hans Burkhardt, Ray Eames, Grace Clements, and Hilaire Hiler. Man Ray was apparently spokesman for the group. See Arthur Millier, "Abstract Art Enthusiasts Exhibit Work," *Los Angeles Times*, 16 July, 1944, sec. 3, pp. 1, 6. For a full discussion of this exhibition, see Romano, "Man Ray: A Decade in Hollywood, 1940–1950," 96–97.
55. "Objects of My Affection," in *Man Ray, Objects* (New York: Julien Levy Gallery, 1945).
56. Man Ray to Elsie Siegler, October 31, 1946, Special Collections, Getty Center; "Surrealists Get Licenses to Marry," *Los Angeles Times*, 25 October, 1946, sec. 2, p. 1; undated fragment from Dorothea Tanning to Man Ray, Special Collections, Getty Center.
57. *Self Portrait*, 356.
58 Man Ray to Elsie Siegler, August 27, 1947, Special Collections, Getty Center.
59. Man Ray to Elsie Siegler, Special Collections, Getty Center, n.d. ["Friday," sometime in November 1940, from the correspondence sequence]; *Self Portrait*, 344.
60. Man Ray to Naomi Siegler [Savage], postcard [c. 1940]; William Copley, *CPLY: Reflection on a Past Life*, 6.
61. *Self Portrait*, 345. Man Ray's talk at the American Contemporary Gallery on October 15, 1943, was published in *Art in Cinema: A Symposium on the Avantgarde Film*, ed. Frank Stauffacher (San Francisco: Art in Cinema Society, San Francisco Museum of Art, 1947), 25–26. Man Ray's films *Emak Bakia* (1926) and *L'étoile de Mer* (1928) were shown in the third program of the San Francisco series, featuring the "continental avant-garde." The American Contemporary Gallery established a Friday night film series in August 1943, with filmmakers (including René Clair and Jean Renoir) giving talks (notice in *California Arts and Architecture* 60, no. 6 [July 1943]: 7).
62. Man Ray to George Leite, November 16, 1944. Private collection.
63. Man Ray, "Cinema," 2. Unpublished essay in "Man Ray Hollywood Album," folder 1, Special Collections, Getty Center; Man Ray to George Leite, December 16, 1944., private collection.
64. Clair came over on the *Excambion* with Man Ray in 1940.
65. Luis Buñuel, *My Last Sigh*, trans. Abigail Israel (New York: Alfred A. Knopf, 1984), 189. According to John Russell Taylor, their collaboration resulted in a scenario titled "The Sewer of Los Angeles" (*Strangers in Paradise* [London: Faber and Faber, 1983], 214).
66. "Man Ray Folio," *Minicam Photography* 8, no. 2 (October 1943): 55–56.
67. *Self Portrait*, 350–52; Albert Lewin to Man Ray, February 16, 1950; July 8, 1950, Special Collections, Getty Center. Man Ray was absent from Lewin's competition for "The Temptation of St. Anthony" because he refused to participate in any competition.
68. Hans Richter to Man Ray, November 16, 1942, Special Collections, Getty Center.
69. Man Ray, "Ruth, Roses and Revolvers," *View*, Series IV, no. 4 (December 1944): 120–23.
70. Ibid., 121.
71. Talk by Man Ray, *Art in Cinema*, 26; *The Hollywood Reporter*, 15 July, 1948, p. 3.
72. Richter to Man Ray, August 12, 1945, Special Collections, Getty Center.
73. Richter to Man Ray, December 10, 1945, Special Collections, Getty Center.
74. Richter to Man Ray, August 26, 1946, Special Collections, Getty Center.
75. Richter to Man Ray, March 9, 1948, Special Collections, Getty Center. On the back of the letter, Man Ray wrote the short essay that was published in the film catalogue without the final three paragraphs.
76. Duchamp to Man Ray, April 19, 1943, Special Collections, Getty Center. Mary Reynolds had a full complement of Man Ray's publications. Having taken up bookbinding, she bound her own copy presentation copy *Les Mains Libres* from Man Ray in tan morocco: "A kid glove, cut open, has been superimposed on both the front and back covers" (Hugh Edwards, *Surrealism and Its Affinities: The Mary Reynolds Collection* [Chicago: The Art Institute of Chicago, 1973], 102). For Mary Reynolds's narrow escape, see Janet Flanner, "The Escape of Mrs. Jeffries," *The New Yorker* (May 22, 1943): 23–28; (May 29, 1943): 40–47; (June 3, 1943): 50–67.
77. Juliet Man Ray to Naomi Siegler Savage, April 28, 1948, Special Collections, Getty Center.
78. James Byrnes to the author, January 1996; Man Ray, "A Note on the Shakespearean Equations," in *To Be Continued Unnoticed* (Beverly Hills, Calif.: The Copley Galleries, 1948), n.p.
79. Man Ray, "A Note on the Shakespearean Equations," n.p.
80. "Los Angeles Events," *Art Digest* 23, no. 7 (January 1, 1949): 17.
81. Dorothea Tanning to Juliet and Man Ray, October 26, 1947, Special Collections, Getty Center.
82. Man Ray, *Alphabet for Adults* (Los Angeles: The Copley Galleries, 1948), n.p.
83. See *Modern Artists in Transition* (Beverly Hills, Calif.: Modern Institute of Art, 1948); Man Ray, "Dadaism," *Schools of Twentieth Century Art* (Beverly Hills, Calif.: Modern Institute of Art, 1948), n.p.
84. Man Ray to Elsie Siegler, November 1, 1948, Special Collections, Getty Center.
85. Curtis Zahn to Man Ray, n.d., Special Collections, Getty Center.
86. Man Ray to Elsie Siegler, June 7, 1949; February 3, 1951, Special Collections, Getty Center.
87. Man Ray to Elsie Siegler, April 1, 1951; August 5, 1951, Special Collections, Getty Center.

Modern Artists in Transition.
Beverly Hills, Calif.:
Modern Institute of Art, 1948.

Moure, Nancy Dustin Wall.
Painting and Sculpture in Los Angeles, 1900–1945.
Los Angeles: Los Angeles County Museum of Art, 1980.

Naumann, Francis M.
New York Dada, 1915–23.
New York: Abrams, 1994.

Penrose, Antony.
The Lives of Lee Miller.
New York: Holt, Rinehart, and Winston, 1985.

Quinn, Joan.
"Juliet Man Ray."
Interview 14, no. 5 (May 1984): 55–57.

Rohauer, Raymond.
A Tribute to Albert Lewin.
New York: Gallery of Modern Art, 1966.

Romano, Donna.
"Man Ray: A Decade in Hollywood, 1940–1950."
Master's thesis, Queen's College, City University of New York, 1988.

Sawelson-Gorse, Naomi.
"Hollywood Conversations: Duchamp and the Arensbergs." In *West Coast Duchamp.*
Edited by Bonnie Clearwater, Miami Beach: Grassfield Press, 1991.

Schwarz, Arturo.
Man Ray: The Rigour of Imagination.
New York: Rizzoli, 1977.

Starr, Sandra Leonard.
Lost and Found in California: Four Decades of Assemblage Art.
Santa Monica: James Corcoran Gallery, 1988.

Tashjian, Dickran.
Skyscraper Primitives: Dada and the American Avant-Garde, 1910–1925.
Middletown, Conn.: Wesleyan University Press, 1975.
——. *A Boatload of Madmen: Surrealism and the American Avant-Garde, 1920–1950.*
New York: Thames and Hudson, 1995.

Taylor, John Russell.
Strangers in Paradise: The Hollywood Émigrés, 1933–1950.
London: Faber and Faber, 1983.

Weld, Jacqueline Bograd.
Peggy: The Wayward Guggenheim.
New York: E. P. Dutton, 1986.

Young-Mallin, Judith.
"Remembering the Faces of Juliet."
Quest (Summer 1991): 46–51.

Reproductions on pages:
5, 39, 44, 62, 80, 101 courtesy of Timothy Baum, New York
57, 105 courtesy of Marion Meyer, Galerie Meyer Bugel, Paris
47-50, 64, 66-67, 72, 73, 95, 101 (bottom)
courtesy of Claudia Borges da Fonseca, Paris
81, 114, 116, 122, courtesy of James and Barbara Byrnes

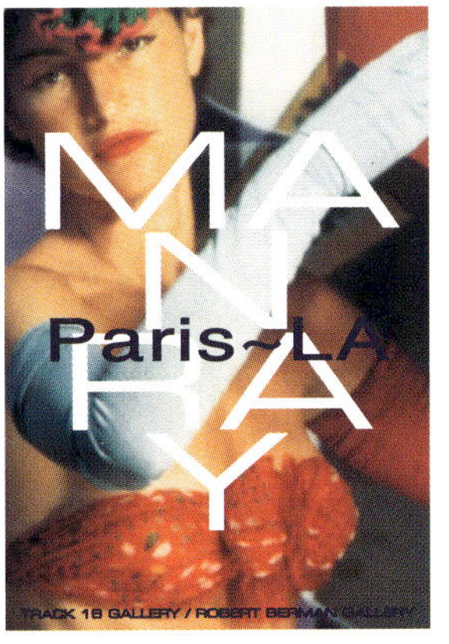

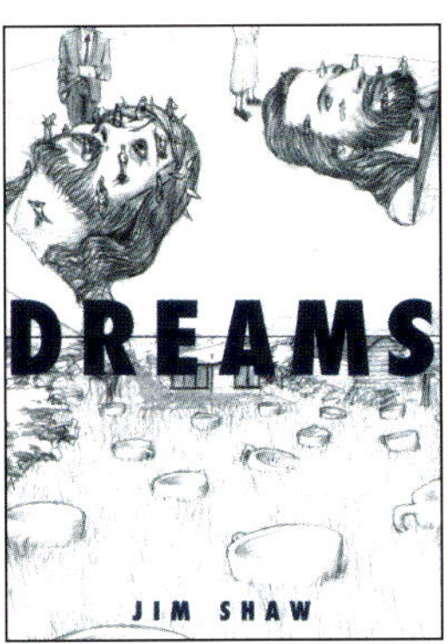

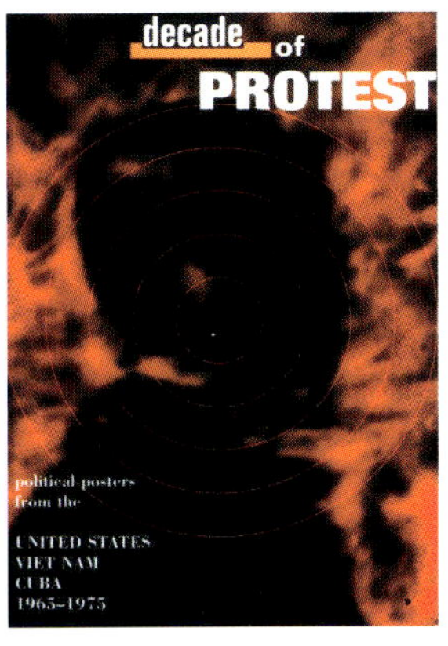

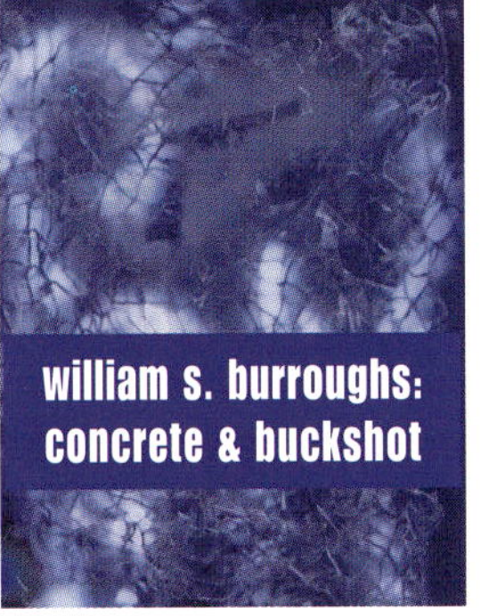

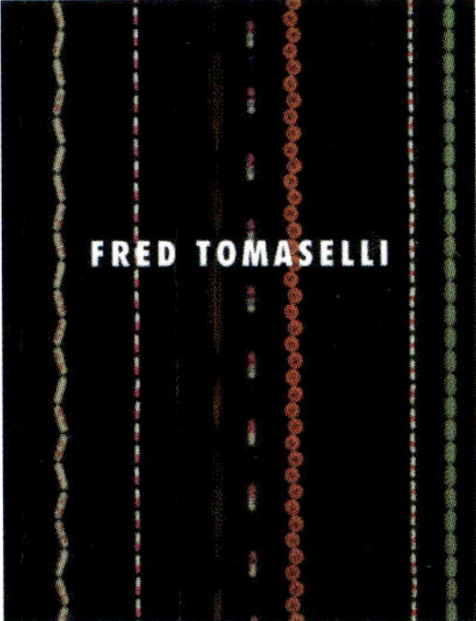

SMART READER:

In this ambitious SAP publication the reader gets the first-ever in depth look at Man Ray's life and work in Los Angeles. As SAP is based in this sunny metropolis of artifice and dreams, we are proud to present the work of this truly groundbreaking artist in the context of the history of art in Southern California. This book, MAN RAY: PARIS~LA is certain to become one of the cornerstones of the Smart Art Press library, a growing collection of more than twenty books and catalogues that mirror the creativity, diversity, and freedom exemplified by Man Ray's work. Pictured here, a few of our other limited edition publications. They're priced individually, but—for the *True Believer*—we invite you to become A SMART READER SUBSCRIBER, which entitles you to the entire library at reduced rates, as well as SAP ephemera such as exhibition announcements, bumper stickers, and other fun stuff.

Tom Patchett

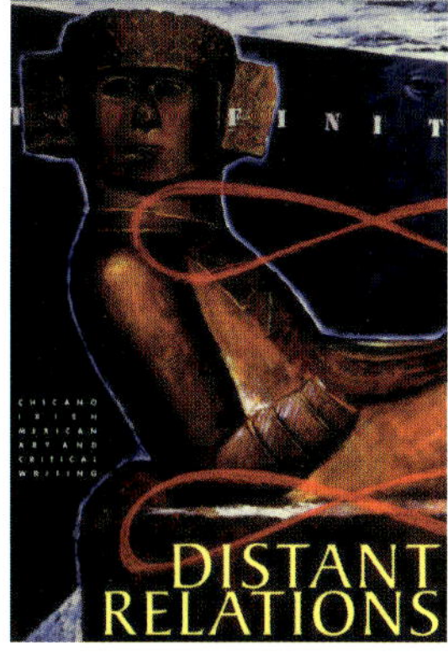

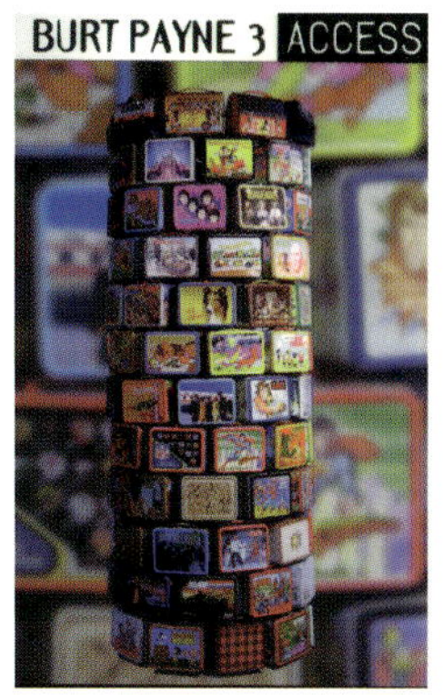

volume one

1 Burt Payne 3: Access ~$15
2 Wheels~$15
3 Jim Butler: Paintings ~$10
4 Murder ~$20
5 The Short Story of the Long History of Bergamot Station ~$10
6 Joe Zucker: A Decade of Paintings ~$10
7 Fool's Paradise ~$10
8 Jim Shaw: Dreams ~$30
9 Alan Rath: Plants, Animals, People, Machines ~$20
10 EATS: An American Obsession ~$15

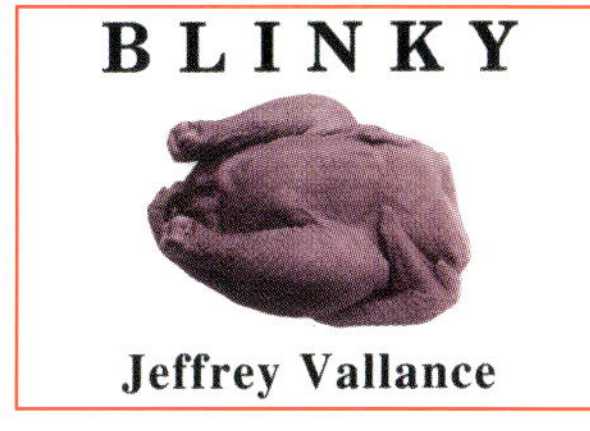

volume two

11 Distant Relations: Chicano, Irish, Mexican Art and Critical Writing ~$25
12 Fred Tomaselli ~$10
13 Decade of Protest: Political Posters from the United States, Viet Nam and Cuba ~$25
14 Lisa Yuskavage ~$10
15 Jeffrey Vallance: Blinky, The Friendly Hen (2nd edition) ~$15
16 Daniel J. Martinez: The Things You See When You Don't Have A Grenade! ~$25
17 Man Ray: Paris>>LA ~$30
18 William S. Burroughs: Concrete & Buckshot ~$20
19 Photographing the L.A. Art Scene, 1955–1975 ~$25
20 Rachel Rosenthal: Tatti Wattles–A Love Story ~$20

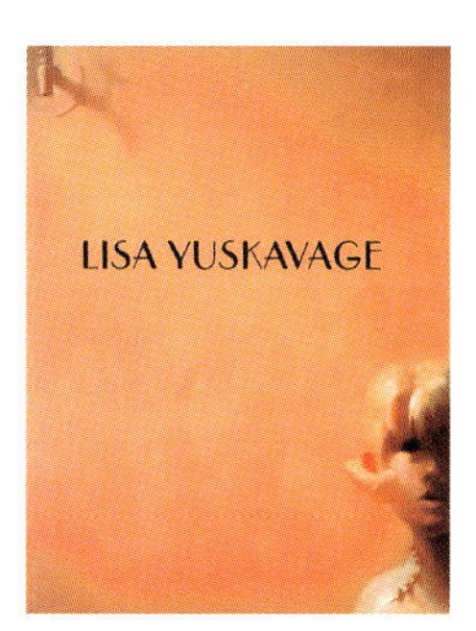

Subscription Information: offer good until January, 1997 while supplies last
Volume 1 (10 catalogues plus accompanying SAP ephemera) $130
Volume 2 (10 catalogues plus similar material) $150

Shipping and handling: Please include $3 for the first item, plus $1 for each additional item. All orders are sent priority mail. Volume 1 and 2 subscription prices include shipping.

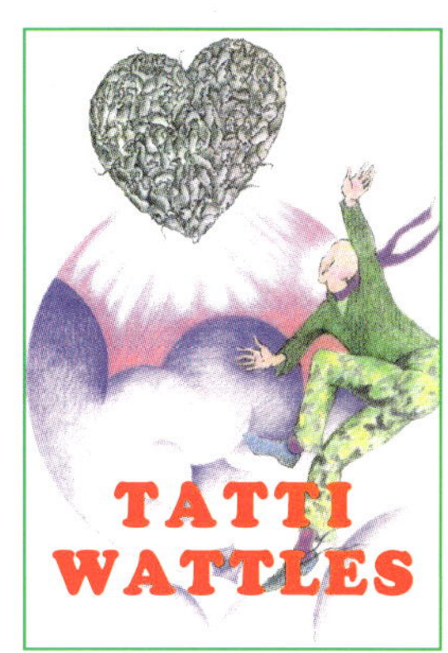

Smart Art Press
2525 Michigan Avenue, Building C1, Santa Monica, California 90404
tel: 310-264-4678 fax: 310-264-4682

overleaf:
***Zeiss Ikonflex III** twin lens reflex camera, 1939 German,*
With Tessar 8-cm f/2.8 lens, Compur-Rapid 1-1/400 shutter,
large folding Albada finder

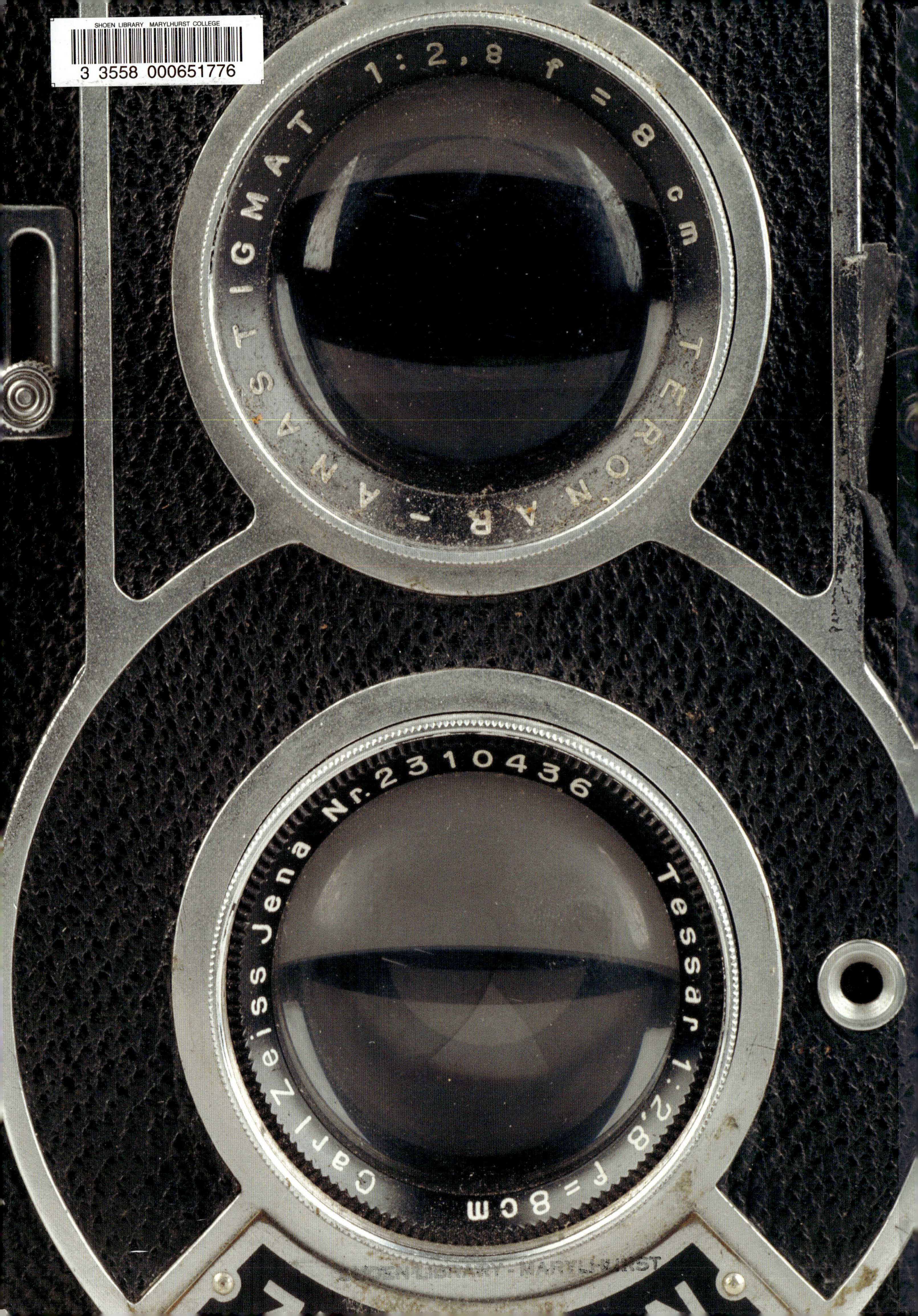
1:2,8 f=8 cm TERONAR-ANASTIGMAT
Carl Zeiss Jena Nr. 2310436 Tessar 1:2,8 f=8cm